THE LAST REFORMATION
THE DAVID CHURCH

THE LAST REFORMATION
THE DAVID CHURCH
By: James W. Kehrli

Copyright 2009 James W. Kehrli

ISBN 978-0-557-16879-8

Contents

Acknowledgements vii

SECTION I. THE SAUL CHURCH
    Chapter 1.   Principles Of The Reformation 1
    Chapter 2.   By God-We'll Be Like The Nations 7
    Chapter 3.   Fishers Of Men 11
    Chapter 4.   The Power Of The People 25
    Chapter 5.   Plumbing The Depths Of Shallowness 35
    Chapter 6.   Religious Deception 45
    Chapter 7.   Religious Activism 51
    Chapter 8.   Religious Correctness 63
    Chapter 9.   Beware The Leaven Of Rationalization 93
    Chapter 10. Rebellion And Worse 107
    Chapter 11. Sweet Smelling Money 117
    Chapter 12. Evil Under The Son 127
    Chapter 13. The King Is Dead; Long Live The King 137

SECTION II. PEARL HARBOR
    Chapter 14. To Judge Or Not To Judge 147
    Chapter 15. If Possible - Even The Elect 159
    Chapter 16. Apostasy: The Key Is Lawlessness 169
    Chapter 17. Second Storm Warning 181
    Chapter 18. Pearl Harbor 195
    Chapter 19. Division, Unity & Revival 201

SECTION III. THE DAVID CHURCH
    Chapter 20. Appointed And Anointed For God Himself 217
    Chapter 21. Just A Sling And Five Smooth Stones 227
    Chapter 22. Revival Is For The Remnant 235
    Chapter 23. Reformation not Renewal: the Great Shaking! 241
    Chapter 24. The Age Of John - Love And Thunder 249

ACKNOWLEDGEMENTS

For the last 25 years my wife, Jackie, has put in many hundreds of hours helping me prepare the manuscript for this book. She has been typist, editor, sounding board and a great companion in both physical and spiritual travail.

Twenty three years ago, both Carl Wilkens and Katherine Avina were especially helpful as proof readers.

I also want to thank Cassandra Johnson for her continual and faithful encouragement over the last 20-25 years in regards to this book.

And finally, I want to thank all those brothers and sisters on the internet who have encouraged me and requested that I get this book published.

SECTION I

THE SAUL CHURCH

CHAPTER 1

PRINCIPLES OF THE REFORMATION

This book, for the most part, comes out of my observations of the Church and experiences with the Holy Spirit, while I was a pastor in Southern California in the 1980's. It was during this time that I wrote the first draft of this book. I unsuccessfully attempted to get the book published in 1987. The title of that book was <u>Reformation Not Renewal,</u> and the three major sections were the same sections that are in this book. In the last several years I have updated some of the material to include events in the Church and revelations about the Church that God has given me since that time. Probably 5-10% of the book comes from this later time. The chapter on "Religious Correctness" was written in 2007. Minor modifications and additions were made to the rest of the book including several visions that God has subsequently given to me.

The first section of this book is essentially teaching and application from I Samuel that is pertinent to the Church of Jesus Christ in America. Because of the tremendous influence that the American church has on the rest of the world, I believe this book would benefit Christians from other countries also. This section is called "The Saul Church." This section refers to the thrust of the Church as it has existed during the last several generations.

The second section is called "Pearl Harbor" and is the bridge between the Saul Church of recent years and the David Church which God is beginning to bring forth now and will bring forth fully in the future. This bridge is the events that will happen and the truth that will be revealed as the Saul Church is set aside by God and the David Church emerges. The Pearl Harbor section will include a number of visions that God has given me regarding how this change will come about.

The third section is called "The David Church" and is a teaching and discussion from I Samuel and church history regarding God's activity in great world changing revivals. This section will also describe the last day's Church that will embody a heart like David's that sought after God for Himself and His glory, and will function in both supernatural power and great supernatural love for Jesus Christ.

In the midst of the teachings from I Samuel, in both the first and third sections, are a number of revelations that God gave me regarding the Saul Church today and the David Church of the future.

The major premise of the book is as follows: the Church as it exists today in the United States in particular and most of the rest of the world is essentially backslidden and only a complete Reformation of God's people by God Himself will enable the Church to defeat the powerful spiritual enemy that we face in these last days. ***If we are to turn the world upside down, we cannot do so without turning the church right side up.*** The Saul Church as it exists today has undone much of the Reformation that occurred in the 16th century through the early part of the 20th century. We must re-do the good that has been done, turn away from that which has been done in the flesh and complete and perfect that which we have missed so far. We MUST go much deeper into the heart of God and the truth of His Word.

What remains of the current Church cannot be renewed because the Church has come to be almost completely out of sync with God's desires. Basically we are a Church that wants to please men. God wants a Church that has a heart to please, first and foremost, Himself. This process of reformation will be, as always, accomplished by God with His people cooperating because He has separated them and empowered them to do so.

When I first wrote this book twenty plus years ago many people, particularly Charismatics, were satisfied that a renewal of the current Church would be both sufficient and pleasing to God. Over the last few years however, this view has begun to shift. Many non-Charismatics have come to understand that the Church needs far more than a renewal; these people believe that only a dramatic and complete Reformation will bring back health, power and a sense of God's pleasure to the Church. At this present time many Charismatics discount the Reformation of the 16th century as being either unnecessary or divisive or both. They yearn to see ALL those who go by the name of Jesus Christ, including Roman Catholics, to unite together regardless of doctrine.

This book also discusses the three principles that will define and unite the Church that is after God's own heart. The first principle is the belief that this Reformation can only be accomplished by a total and exclusive reliance on the truth of Scripture. This can be summed up with the phrase, ***"We must trust the Word, the whole Word and nothing but the Word."*** The second is that those involved must be filled with the Holy Spirit and continue to seek to be filled with the Holy Spirit. They must believe with all their hearts that "it is not by might, not by power, but by My Spirit saith the Lord." The third principle is that we must be correctable in both our doctrine and our conduct. We must listen carefully and respond quickly when we are given plain truth from the Scriptures. We must also be quick to repent when we are shown sin in our lives.

I also believe that it is important to give honor and tolerance for all of God's people that have been used by Him to expound truth and/or have ministered with the supernatural power of the Holy Spirit, regardless of egregious failures in their lives or even in their teachings. John Wesley is one example. For many years, John Wesley taught that Christians could be without sin on this earth. John MacArthur is another example. John still teaches that the manifestly supernatural gifts and ministries of the Holy Spirit mentioned in the New Testament are not for today. These errors do not exclude either man from being great for God.

Many Spirit-filled Charismatics seem to feel that detailed study of the Scripture is unnecessary. They disdainfully refer to seminaries that offer detailed teaching of the Scriptures as being "Cemeteries." They scoff at the learning of these men and have no desire to study the magnificent writings of men such as Martin Luther, John Calvin and Jonathan Edwards. They don't understand that the revelations that these men have received regarding the Scriptures were just as anointed and spiritual as the gifts that they have received. Often they will make jokes about non-Charismatic denominations and they merely criticize and give NO HONOR to the mighty works and mighty doctrinal revelations that so many movements of the past have experienced and given to the Body of Christ.

Another issue that will be discussed throughout the book is that many Charismatics who see the miraculous, believe that if a man or a woman has functioned in the miraculous, they are to be trusted in their doctrines or practices. Also many Charismatics are unable to discern between true prophecies and false prophecies, true healings and false healings, and true miracles and false miracles. Many believe virtually everything they hear or see. They never even attempt to line up these ministries and "miracles" with the Word of God.

Unfortunately many of the non-Charismatic Evangelicals believe the Reformation should only be a restoration of the truths that emerged in the first great Reformation. They completely deny or discount that the supernatural gifts and ministries mentioned in the New Testament, particularly in I Corinthians and Ephesians, are to flow through and amongst God's people.

Unfortunately, even many so-called Charismatics have diluted the ministries of apostles and prophets to mean little more than leaders of local churches and people who prophesy.

The Reformation Remnant that God will raise up is a people, who like David, recognized and honored the anointing that God gave to King Saul, even though the Lord eventually took away that anointing and sent an evil spirit to torment him. This Remnant must recognize and honor historical and current movements and men and women that God has used and is using to restore New Testament doctrines and practices to His people. We must honor and respect the Anabaptists who taught us about believer baptism and immersion. We must recognize and honor men who taught us about the sovereignty of God. We must recognize and honor those who refreshed our minds regarding the scriptural fact that we must be born again. We must recognize and honor those who showed us in the Word and by example the power of the Holy Spirit to heal and work miracles through God's people. We must recognize and honor ALL those that have helped us to see the Scriptures more clearly regardless of their other doctrinal errors and regardless of the sins that they committed.

During the Great Awakening in England in the 18th century, George Whitfield and John Wesley initially were close to one another in the Holy Club at Oxford. But after a few years of ministry, they became divided on the issue of Arminianism vs. Calvinism and their friendship cooled. Later, when George Whitfield was asked by someone whether or not he thought that he would see John Wesley in heaven. He said, "No, I don't believe I will." The man said to him, "Does that mean that you believe that John Wesley was not saved?" Whitfield replied, "Of course not! I will not see him because he will be very close to the throne and I will be a far distance from him." THIS attitude must prevail with God's people!

God WILL raise up a people who desire greatly and are satisfied only with the FULNESS of the Holy Spirit. This same people will desire and be satisfied only with the FULLNESS of His Scriptures. They will wholeheartedly HONOR the anointing and calling of His people throughout history and today. This book will give help in understanding how the Saul Church will make the transition to the David Church and will give glimpses into what we should expect God to do in the coming decades or centuries.

CHAPTER 2

BY GOD-WE'LL BE LIKE THE NATIONS

In 1983 after pastoring a small denominational charismatic church for several years, I was becoming more and more disturbed about the type of ministry that I had encountered in both the Charismatic and Evangelical Movements.

Christian music was populated to a large extent by men and women who were more interested in entertaining people than causing God's people to enter into His presence.

Christian television was often embarrassing; I did not really want unsaved friends and acquaintances to watch the programs. I felt very uncomfortable that people in the world who perhaps casually came upon these Christian programs, would go away believing that the people on television represented the ideas of the Bible and behavior that pleased God. Their looks, style and message often were self-serving. They solicited for donations in a way that seemed to be transparently manipulative.

At the denominational pastoral conferences I attended, it was rare that doctrine was ever discussed or taught. Typically we were told to pray a lot, recognize the value of unity in the Body of Christ and be sure that we did not beat the sheep. For example, when discussing the touchy issue of divorce in the Church, there seemed to be a crusade to make sure everyone knew that divorce was not the unforgivable sin; however Scriptures concerning divorce were rarely mentioned. We NEVER heard the words of Jesus uttered in Matt 5:32, "but I say to you that everyone who divorces his wife except for the reason of unchastely, makes her commit adultery; and whoever marries a divorced woman commits adultery." They never quoted Mark 10:11-

12, where Jesus spoke these words, "Whoever divorces his wife and marries another woman commits adultery against her; and if she herself divorces her husband and marries another man she is committing adultery." Or in Luke 16:18 where Jesus says, "...he who marries one who is divorced from a husband commits adultery." These Scriptures were never referenced nor discussed. Scriptures that were quoted and referenced were basically ones that illustrated His love and forgiveness.

Perhaps the most alarming development was the pulpit popularity of so-called Christian psychology. Even at the Bible College I attended, one teacher taught us that if Paul the Apostle knew as much about the science of psychology as we did, his ministry would have been much more successful.

After observing all of this and watching the ministries that propounded all of these ideas, I began to pray very vigorously for the Lord to show me if these ministries were real, if any of them were anointed and what I should do regarding their presence in the Body of Christ.

He answered by taking me through I Samuel and showing me two men, Saul and David, and one people, His people the Israelites. He revealed much to me about the essential character of this people in I Samuel 8. The Israelites were at a critical time in their history. Samuel was getting old and his sons were not really fit to assume his ministry of judging the twelve tribes. The dreaded enemies of God, particularly the Philistines, were an ever-present threat to God's people. The leaders felt strongly that new and drastic measures must be taken to insure their safety and to ultimately conquer their enemies. Their solution was simple but imitative in a way that God's people had never been imitative before. They wanted to have a king rule over them so that they might be like all the nations (the heathens). Samuel understood that this was not pleasing to God. He knew His people were to be influenced, guided, and ruled by the ways of God rather than the ways of the heathen nations. I Samuel 8:6-8 says, (NASB) ""But the thing was displeasing (evil) in the sight of Samuel when they said, "Give us a king to judge us." And Samuel prayed to the Lord. And the Lord said to Samuel, "Listen to the voice of the people in regard to all that they say to you for they have not rejected you but they have rejected Me from being King over them. Like all the deeds which they have done since the day that I brought them out even to this day - in that they have forsaken Me and served other gods - so they are doing to you also."" God here equates or compares the sin of rejecting His ways and Himself with the sin of idolatry.

The Lord essentially told Samuel that this rejection of God Himself motivated their request for a king. Then the Lord warned the people through Samuel about the many problems that they would suffer under such rulership. But, as I Samuel 8:19-20 says, ""Nevertheless the people refused to listen to the voice of Samuel but they said, "No, but there shall be a king over us that we also may BE LIKE ALL THE NATIONS, that our king may judge us and go out before us and fight our battles."" In these Scriptures, we see the people clearly rebelling against God's method and will. They are rejecting Him and His plan because they desire to BE LIKE ALL THE NATIONS. What follows is a most amazing section of Scripture. Instead of judging His rebellious people immediately with appropriate punishments, verse 22 of chapter 8 says, ""And the Lord said to Samuel: "LISTEN TO THEIR VOICE AND APPOINT THEM A KING."" We see here God granting a request, answering a prayer, apparently against His will. God, knowing that they are asking for a king in part so they could become like the heathen people from whom they are supposed to be separated, still gives them the desires of their heart. Not only does God appoint them a king after their desire but also He ANOINTS this king for them. I Samuel 10:1 says, ""Then Samuel took the flask of oil, poured it on his (Saul's) head, kissed him, and said, "HAS NOT THE LORD ANOINTED YOU a ruler over His inheritance?"" These Scriptures are not unlike Psalm 106:14-15, "but (the Israelites) craved intensely in the wilderness, and tempted God in the desert. So He gave them their request, but sent a wasting disease among them." The King James Version says, (they) "lusted exceedingly in the wilderness, And tempted God in the desert. And He gave them their request but sent leanness into their soul."

We see in these verses a sobering principle established in God's Word. God will actually give His people who are called by His name the desires of their heart, even when they are motivated by a rejection of God Himself and a desire to be like the world (idolatrous concepts to be sure); even when their desire is to fight against the enemies of God using the way and weaponry of the world. We see that God not only grants this desire but He ANOINTS men to lead the people in fulfilling these desires.

Sometime in the twentieth century, probably in the 1920's or 30's or possibly earlier, a cry began to arise from the visible Body of Christ. The cry was, "We are tired of being stodgy, old fashioned and generally unacceptable to the great masses of unsaved people in the world. We desire to be more acceptable to them and even to be more like them. Give us leaders who will speak their language and be like them. Give us leaders who will fulfill our heart's desire. In order to win them for Christ we feel it is necessary that our leaders be like their leaders. Now appoint a king (leaders) for us...like all the nations (people who are not God's people). We want men and women who are polished, educated, great communicators, in touch with the latest philosophies and modern thinking, athletic men and women, entertaining men and women, attractive people who will attract men and women to Jesus. And then O Lord, PLEASE have them encourage us to be just like they are." The cry of the people ascended to the throne of God and, in His infinite wisdom and because of the hardness of their hearts, He answered this prayer and sent them leaders like the heathen. He sent us leaders like the world.

Even as Saul of Benjamin was the answer to the Israelites' prayer to have a king like the nations, we have prayed for and received our Sauls too. Thus in the twentieth century, the Church of Saul emerged. BY GOD, we have indeed become like the nations.

CHAPTER 3

FISHERS OF MEN

When all the elders of Israel came to Samuel at Ramah, they told him to appoint a king for them like all the nations. Satan had already compromised their hearts: they were now no longer interested in being led by God and in fact had rejected Him (1 Sam 8:7). Remember that Saul was a king FOR THE PEOPLE. I Samuel 8:19 says, ""…the people refused to listen to the voice of Samuel. They said, "no, but there SHALL be a king over us that we also may BE LIKE ALL THE NATIONS…"" In 8:22 of I Samuel the Lord said to Samuel, "Listen TO THEIR VOICE and appoint THEM a king." It is no wonder then that God gave them a man who according to I Samuel 9:2 was a "Choice and handsome man and there was not a more handsome person than he among the sons of Israel; from his shoulders and up, he was taller than any of the people." God gave the elders an attractive man of considerable stature who would attract the people and cause them to rally around him and the leadership of Israel. Saul in a sense became the bait the elders dangled before the heretofore lethargic people of God. Saul would give them someone and something to be excited about, and God's people would proudly join in behind their impressive looking king to fight for the Lord. These were shallow qualities to be sure, but they satisfied both the elders and the people. This superficial, fleshly attitude characterized the people of God under Saul.

Even though God appointed and anointed Saul, the people really chose Saul for themselves. Samuel, speaking to the people in I Samuel 12:13 say, "Now therefore here is the king whom YOU HAVE CHOSEN, whom YOU HAVE ASKED FOR." They chose a man who ended up being very much like themselves: shallow and mainly interested in the material realm, one who valued material rewards and blessings, one who, when he wanted to get something difficult done, offered these material rewards as an incentive. He did this because he considered the material to be of great value, something great to strive for.

Even as the elders apparently wanted an attractive man of great stature to lead them as their king against their enemies, so Saul made an attractive offer to anyone in Israel who would kill Goliath. When Saul wanted Goliath killed he did not mention to the people the fact that the honor of God was at stake. He also did not point out to them the spiritual difficulties they would experience if they were under the rule of the Philistines. He did not even arouse their patriotic fervor. The best that he could do was to cover the gigantic hook (the task of slaying Goliath) with attractive bait. I Samuel 17:25 says, "....it will be that the king (Saul) will ENRICH the man who kills him (Goliath) with great riches and will give him his daughter and make his father's house free in Israel."

We Evangelicals and Charismatics make attractive offers to the flesh to get people to be on our side. In fact the attractive allurements that we use have become part of our practical evangelism theology.

In Matthew 4:19 Jesus saw two fishermen, Simon Peter and Andrew, and uttered these words, "follow me Me and I will make you fishers of men." Their predominant occupation from now on, He infers, would not be to gather fish for their own livelihood but to gather souls for the kingdom of God. If these men were construction workers, He probably would have said, "Come follow Me and I will make you builders of My Church."

In the twentieth century we took these words "fishers of men" to imply that we, as men and women of God, were to be involved in the building of His kingdom and were to become good fishers of men in the Spirit. Accompanying this notion of being good fishers of men in the Spirit is that we must choose the appropriate bait for the particular kind of fish we are trying to catch for Jesus. This notion of course is completely unscriptural. The fishermen that Jesus called to be disciples used nets not lines and bait. But no matter, we in the Church still think in terms of bait. If we are dealing with businessmen, or even anyone who wants to get rich, we carefully and abundantly cover the gospel hook with the material rewards that we suppose their hearts would most likely desire. We stress how the Lord will bless their financial situations beyond what they could ask or think. If we are dealing with people who have been lured away from our churches by the entertainment of the world, we will lure them back into our churches by presenting equally enticing entertainment. Large churches often hire men who are entertaining preachers, not necessarily deeply anointed men of God. Some of these men are very good storytellers, some are personable and some are extremely humorous.

In the first Great Awakening in England, George Whitfield was an entertaining preacher who would occasionally act out portions of his sermons. He was naturally gifted in this area. The great difference between his preaching and the preaching of those in the Saul Church is that his preaching convicted men of their sin. His abilities did not cause the people to be drawn away from the Gospel message, but instead helped them to see Jesus much more clearly. Often the Holy Spirit subsequently brought great comfort to those who mourned deeply for their sin. Whitfield's dramatics were not done so more people would come; more people were already there! Whitfield did not preach to please the people, he preached to please God, and believed if he preached the whole counsel of God, that he could trust God to save souls. His mission was to find the lost sheep of Israel and awaken hearts that God had touched. He correctly understood that salvation is completely of the Lord and ultimately for Him, even more than for the people. The will of the Lord was the issue in Whitfield's preaching, even more than the needs or desires of the people. Once again, his trust was completely in God to accomplish His ends and he NEVER shaped his messages to the desires of the people.

However, because the Saul Church believes that people are the issue, it MUST do everything it possibly can to bring them into the church and relationship with Jesus Christ. The Saul Church feels that the ends do justify the means because the issue is so important. The issue is the salvation of souls and they believe that more people will come if you have entertainers and attractions that will bring them to the meeting. Because of this you are more likely to get decisions for Christ. They do not understand that the issue is to preach the whole counsel of God and tell people of their lost and hopeless condition outside of the blood of Jesus Christ. Jesus, Himself, spoke it very clearly when He said, "My sheep hear My voice and they will follow Me wherever I go." The issue is locating His lost sheep. His sheep are identified as such because they want to hear ALL of His truth. They are not afraid of or offended by preaching that exposes the depths of their impure motives or brings to light their corrupt natures. When they hear the Gospel, they eventually will come to know their true motives and their true nature. But, they will also recognize that the blood of Jesus Christ is sufficient for their cleansing of sin and forgiveness. Most importantly, they will be truly born again into His kingdom and have a new nature to cope with the world the flesh and the devil. They also will have new natures to love God with all their hearts, minds, souls and strength. Once again, because we fail to trust God's ways, and honestly believe that we must "get the people in" we frustrate the grace and the power of God even as Israel frustrated God's purposes when they chose a king so they could be like the nations.

To "get the people in" we must use bait that will attract them. We've used magicians as bait, musicians as bait, acting groups as bait, body builders as bait, Miss Americas as bait, pot lucks as bait, and beach parties as bait. We have used everything we could think of to attract the seekers into our churches or meetings.

In the late 1980's the Church coined the phrase "seeker sensitive." Churches strove to be attractive to the people in their area. Churches took polls regarding what made these people happy. They constructed their services and activities and even doctrines to accommodate the spoken or written desires of the seekers. They recognized that in many cases, the people wanted short teaching and preaching. They found that counseling classes based on a mixture of the Bible and secular psychology fit their desires much more than classes that dealt exclusively with the Scriptures. Even when they dealt exclusively with the Scriptures they found out that some portions of Scripture were more attractive than other portions of Scripture. Teachings on end-time events were particularly attractive. They played on the carnal curiosity and the desire of people to have special knowledge. End-time doctrines, that assured or implied to the listener that the Church need not worry about tribulation, judgment or chastening has been particularly popular. In Charismatic circles, many churches major on the gifts and ministries, partly because people are more interested in learning how to be powerful than learning how to be pure and holy. Often, these classes will use psychological profiling so that the students can learn what their gifts and ministries are. In these classes virtually everyone is assured that they have a ministry and a number of supernatural gifts. This information is validated either by the tests they take or the spiritual sensitivity of the teachers overseeing the classes. The problem is that often the anointing of God is COMPLETELY absent, and because of this, virtually NOTHING occurs. However, these classes remain popular and when those who have been told that they have the gift of prophecy speak words that seldom come to pass, nobody notices or comments because they have taught that it is wrong to judge others.

We have done our best to attract every type of individual that we have been able to think of. Our fishing techniques have become quite good. Unfortunately however, we are now involved in a most dangerous game that is offensive to God. We have actually become so bold that we use the Word of God in a deceptive manner. In our teaching and preaching we edit the Word of God in such a way that the sharp barb of the cost of discipleship is virtually unknown to people who come to our gatherings. Discipleship has become an option for those "who want more from God." No longer is discipleship a necessity in the Saul Church even though the requirement is stated in Scripture. One example of this is Luke 9:23-25 where Jesus says, ""If ANY ONE wishes to come after Me, let him deny himself, and take up his cross daily, and follow Me. For whoever wishes to save his life shall lose it, but whoever loses his life for My sake, he is the one who shall save it. For what is a man profited if he gains the whole world, and loses or forfeits himself (KJV uses the phrase "his own soul")." It is ABSOLUTELY NECESSARY, as spoken from the lips of our Savior Himself, that we take up our cross daily and DENY ourselves.

In many churches, we are ALWAYS told to count the blessings that God gives us. However, we are virtually NEVER told to count the cost of being a Christian. Luke 14:28-33 says, "For which one of you, when he wants to build a tower, does not first sit down and calculate the cost to see if he has enough to complete it? Otherwise when he has laid a foundation and is not able to finish, all who observe it begin to ridicule him, saying, 'this man began to build and was not able to finish.' Or what king when he sets out to meet another king in battle, will not first sit down and consider whether he is strong enough with ten thousand men to encounter the one coming against him with twenty thousand? Or else, while the other is still far away, he sends a delegation and asks for terms of peace. So then, none of you can be My disciple who does not give up all his own possessions."

In many cases our editing techniques have either miniaturized, or removed entirely, the ugly hook of the Cross of Jesus Christ. We are not told many of the facts. We are not told that the wrath of God abides on disobedient unbelievers. John 3:36 says, "He who believes in the Son has eternal life; but he who does not obey the Son will not see life, but the wrath of God abides on him."

We are not told that we are to FEAR God. Typically we are told that to fear God means merely to respect, reverence, or worship God. Matt 10:28 makes it very clear. Fear means Fear! This Scripture says, "FEAR Him who is able to destroy both soul and body in hell." In some cases, the word translated fear does mean reverence or worship. However, in most cases the word fear means fear!

The fact that we are miserable, despicable, and entirely hopeless, outside of faith in the blood of Jesus for the forgiveness and remission of our sins, is now largely omitted. Rom 3:10-18 clears up this issue, "THERE IS NONE RIGHTEOUS, NOT EVEN ONE; THERE IS NONE WHO UNDERSTANDS, THERE IS NONE WHO SEEKS FOR GOD; ALL HAVE TURNED ASIDE, TOGETHER THEY HAVE BECOME USELESS; THERE IS NONE WHO DOES GOOD, THERE IS NOT EVEN ONE. THEIR THROAT IS AN OPEN GRAVE, WITH THEIR TONGUES THEY KEEP DECEIVING, THE POISON OF ASPS IS UNDER THEIR LIPS; WHOSE MOUTH IS FULL OF CURSING AND BITTERNESS; THEIR FEET ARE SWIFT TO SHED BLOOD, DESTRUCTION AND MISERY ARE IN THEIR PATHS, AND THE PATH OF PEACE THEY HAVE NOT KNOWN. THERE IS NO FEAR OF GOD BEFORE THEIR EYES."

These facts are virtually buried and sometimes completely missing underneath the attractive bait of the Saul gospel of Blessings. Some churches promise financial prosperity; others promise physical prosperity in healings of the body, and still others promise psychological prosperity through "healing of the memories", "inner healing" or teachings that center on increasing your self-esteem. FEW demands are made on the people except perhaps regarding financial prosperity. In this case the people are often strongly encouraged to give money to the church so they in turn can become wealthy.

While the Saul gospel glamorizes the so-called positive elements of the Gospel, it virtually ignores many other so-called negative aspects of the Gospel. It glamorizes, among others, God's love for man, God's abundant material provision, and God's desire and power to heal broken bodies and broken lives.

Regarding the negative aspects of the Gospel, the Saul Church does acknowledge God's hatred for sin, but one of their favorite non-existent Scriptures is "God hates the sin but loves the sinner." This church does not recognize that God, in some cases, hates the sinner! The psalmist says in Psalm 5:5-6, "The boastful shall not stand before Thine eyes; Thou doest hate all who do iniquity. Thou doest destroy those who speak falsehood; the Lord abhors the man of bloodshed and deceit."

It only gives slight attention to the fact that God has a terrible punishment for sin and the sinner. It is especially unlikely to discuss the fact that God will punish His children who disobey continually. Heb 12:5-6 says, "My son, do not regard lightly the discipline of the Lord, nor faint when you are reproved by Him; for those whom the Lord loves He disciplines, and He SCOURGES every son whom He receives."

The Saul Church also ignores the Scriptures that say that those who reject the true teachings of Scripture will be led astray by false teachers and false prophets (Matt 7:15-20). Very seldom does the Saul Church teach that God will tell some powerful and "successful" ministers who apparently function supernaturally, that they must depart from Him because they were workers of iniquity. He then will declare that HE NEVER KNEW THEM (Matt 7:21-23).

Obviously these are serious mistakes that have misled many concerning who Jesus is and what is the true Gospel of salvation. If we were to use their analogy of Jesus fishing for men, we would have to say that He used a hook with no bait. You would have to say that the hook of the cross was very sharp, very ugly, and very visible. He made sure that people knew the cost and the pain of the cross both to Himself and to all who would be His disciples. But, as people were confronted by the sharp and ugly hook that He so clearly presented, they also saw with equal clarity The Fisherman, Jesus Christ Himself. In fact this hook/cross revealed the greatest manifestation of love the universes have ever known, clearly outlined on and in the cross - Jesus Christ experiencing death and torment in the place of a totally undeserving and otherwise worthless humanity of believers.

To be sure God's love IS attractive and very real. The same could be said for His material provision and His power to heal. But the purpose is not for these things to be used as bait to attract the flesh, but as evidences of His great love and infinite power. When we use these principles to attract the people without telling them the rest of the Gospel we commit a spiritual crime. If they never encounter the true Gospel of Scripture, they will never be born again.

As a result we can make a clear distinction between a positive quality of the Gospel and mere bait. The positive qualities of the Gospel are for the purpose of bringing glory to our Lord Jesus Christ and deliverance to His people. When they are used to attract people to our meetings we are USING the Word of God in a most unscriptural manner. We are speaking half-truths that ultimately can be more dangerous than no truth. Jesus NEVER healed anyone to attract attention to His ministry. He did it to show the power and compassion of God and to relieve suffering. He did it to bring glory to God. When Jesus fed the 5,000, He did not do that to bring the people in. They were already there! In fact, when they made it evident that many were misunderstanding Him by wanting to make Him an earthly political king (probably to lead them against the Romans) He withdrew Himself from them (John 6:15). The next day when they found Him on the other side of the sea, He referred to Himself as the bread of life and He uttered the words that drove the entire multitude away in confusion and disgust. John 6:53 says, ""Jesus said to them, "truly truly I say to you, unless you eat the flesh of the Son of Man and drink His blood, you have no life in yourselves."" John 6:57-58 reads, "As the living Father sent Me and I live because of the Father, so he who eats Me, he also shall live because of Me. This is the bread which came down out of heaven; not as the fathers ate and died, he who eats this bread shall live forever." John 6:63-66 says, ""It is the Spirit who gives life: the flesh profits nothing; the words that I have spoken to you are Spirit and are life. But there are some of you who do not believe." For Jesus knew from the beginning who they were who did not believe, and who it was that would betray Him. And He was saying, "For this reason I have said to you that no one can come to me unless it has been granted him from the Father." As a result of this many of His disciples withdrew, and were not walking with Him anymore. Jesus said therefore to the twelve, "you do not want to go away also do you?""

Jesus and the Church in the Book of Acts did not have any Specials. They did not have any famous personalities. You do not read of one testimony by a famous gladiator or chariot driver in the entire Bible. When they had fellowships it was not to "let the world know that Christians can have fun too!" They did not have the hidden agenda of "if we don't have parties and get-togethers the people will leave." Their fellowships were for the purpose of getting together and loving one another in the Lord and glorifying Him. The Church in the Book of Acts was absolutely BAIT FREE!

How many planning committees have made plans with ulterior motives? The leaders get together and say, "Let's have a fellowship to attract young people." They are not solely concerned to have a fellowship so that FELLOWSHIP can take place; they also are doing this for the purpose of ATTRACTING a crowd. Can you honestly find any place in Scripture where Jesus or the disciples did ANYTHING for the purpose of ATTRACTING people to the Gospel? For some reason, that never occurred. For some reason, these men never used ANY BAIT to attract ANYONE for ANY REASON. The reason is really quite simple. It was not honest. Bait is a trick. It fools the fish into thinking something else is happening. He thinks he is getting only food. But the fisherman knows the fish is getting something else. The fish is getting hooked and will be used to accommodate the desires of the fisherman NOT the needs of the fish! The Father does not stoop to draw anyone to His Son except by the Holy Spirit. The Father would not stoop to any kind of deception, even if it were only momentary. He is not a man that He should misrepresent Himself. He is not a man that He should lie. But we are deceptive individuals from a deceptive race. We are everyday influenced by the attractive bait that television casts out every five minutes or so to those who watch. So we are already conditioned or have been captive to a way of life that not only condones but also promotes deception. We are actually taught by our churches to be afraid to be as simple as Jesus and His disciples. We are taught that we must have Something Else Going to attract people to

Jesus Christ. We MUST have "good" worship. We must have talented musicians or at the very least, talented sound tracks.

New car ads which use sex in their ads to sell cars ALSO sell sex; the man who watches these ads is purposefully tempted to associate the ownership of the new car with the implied fact that he will be more attractive to sexy girls if he owns such a car. Unfortunately, these well thought-out ads have played a great role in changing our values about sex. The ads, whether for autos or diet soda, have really sold us a permissive attitude about sex.

The same thing has happened in the Body of Christ. We have used entertainment, personalities, and material enticements to attract people so we can get them to "accept Jesus." What has really happened is we have attracted and gotten people who have encountered Jesus impurely. They, like the television watchers who purchased both an auto and a change in attitude about sex, have gotten more than Jesus. They have apparently received both Jesus and the bait. And they will perceive Jesus as One who will supply a steady steam of entertainment, personalities and material blessings. Tragically, these manipulative Saul fishermen have played a great role in changing our attitude about Jesus Christ and His Word. The bait, whether it is entertainment or material enticements, has created a sensual, self-pleasing, pleasure loving, deceptive Church.

We must understand fellowships are not bait, if they are held for the purpose of bringing people together to love God and love each other. They become bait when used for ulterior motives. Movies are not bait if they are used solely to teach a principle from the Word of God. A band or music group is not bait if it is at the church solely for the purpose of giving God glory or encouraging people to worship and to love God more. If the dress is not self advertising, if the music has NO INTENTION of pleasing or attracting the people to the musicians, and if the ministers have no desire to fit into any worldly style of behavior, past or present, and if all is done without the hidden agenda of Attracting a Crowd for Jesus, then the band or group or minister can truly present Jesus Christ for who He is.

We must flee from the bait and switch tactics of the world that we have used so "successfully" for so long. We must flee the idea that we can bait them with entertainment and then switch them to Jesus. In the world bait and switch techniques are illegal. In God's economy, it is unlawful, unscriptural and unholy. Deception of any sort has NO PLACE in the kingdom of God. You must understand, in I Samuel it was Satan who tempted the people of God with the attractive notion that they could have an attractive flesh and blood king to be their leader. He lured the Israelites into becoming a carnal powerless people that no longer placed God first.

Baiting the hook can be the first step in developing an attitude of "the ends justify the means." The Saul Church feels that virtually whatever it takes to get people saved or in their churches to hear about Jesus is justifiable. The Scriptural reference point in defending the notion that bait is permissible is I Corinthians 9:22 which states, "....I have become all things to all men that I may by ALL MEANS save some." Obviously Paul did not mean that he would become worldly for the purpose of saving men's souls in the world. Obviously Paul did not mean that he would compromise in any way. He would not sin to save sinners. He would not become effeminate to save the effeminate. He would not become vain to save the vain. He would not become frivolous to save the frivolous. He would not become a man pleaser and use any method that would draw attention to himself or the method he used. He would do nothing that would dishonor or misrepresent the Person of Jesus Christ. With Jesus and Paul the means and the ends were always the same. There was a consistency of holiness and love and separation from the world and its ways and a dependence on God and His ways. The ends would become polluted by anything that would in any way detract from the pure Gospel or bring attention to anyone or anything that was used as a vehicle for the Gospel. John the Baptist made this clear when he said, "He must increase but I must decrease", (John 3:30).

Anything that causes us to shift our attention away from Jesus Christ is wrong. Even the physical presence of Jesus Christ Himself was not something that men would be naturally attracted to. Judas had to identify Him with a kiss when His enemies came to take him away. Isaiah 53:2 CLEARLY settles the issue: "....He has no stately form that we should look upon Him nor appearance that we should be ATTRACTED to Him." God made it CLEAR. Who Jesus Christ IS - is the issue - not what He appears to be.

Humor has become a part of many a preacher's bait bag. We Americans particularly love a funny story. In fact, in a Charismatic seminary homiletics class we were told the value and even the necessity of a humorous story to introduce the message. Unfortunately the use of humor to awaken our congregations, or attract their attention or even to get them to come to our services has in some cases become an end in itself. Often people go away just remembering the jokes and forgetting the point of the sermon. Humor can be used but it must support and be in the context of the point being made. It alone should never be the reason the people come to hear the preacher. Music can be a great backdrop for the Gospel of Jesus Christ. But music in and of itself, regardless of the style, should never be the focal point. The Word of God and Worship of God must always be the focal point. When the people leave, if the Word of God and Worship of God has been the focal point, they will be discussing God Himself and His Word. If humor has been the focal point they will be discussing the jokes. If music has been the focal point they will be discussing the music. If the dress of the preacher or the musicians has been the focal point, they will be discussing the dress. And if the preacher or the musician is sensitive to God's purpose, regardless of what his audience wants, he will get rid of anything that detracts from the Gospel of Jesus Christ. If the Rolex watch is what they discuss, he will get a Timex. If the $800 suit he wears is what they talk about, he will get a $200 suit. If his purple spiked hair is what they are talking about, he will change his hairstyle. Anything that causes the people to shift their attention from Jesus Christ and Him crucified MUST GO! We must decrease, and He must increase. If the means of getting people to hear about Jesus is the focus of attention then the people, if they do come to Jesus, will have double vision or blurred vision. Scripture is clear about the danger of having blurred or double vision. Matthew 6:22-33 says, "The lamp of the body is the eye; if therefore your eye is clear (single, KJV), your whole body is full of light. But if your eye is bad, (does not function properly) your whole body will be full of darkness...." We must be attracted to and depend only upon Jesus. If there is any diversion we will experience visual, mental, and spiritual confusion, which, if not checked, can lead to spiritual blindness ("your whole body will be full of darkness").

Why then do we Charismatics and Evangelicals scrounge out of the earth all manner of bait? Why does the Saul Church of our generation need ATTRACTIONS? Why do we need to edit Scripture so the people will not find it unattractive? The answer is actually quite simple. It is twofold. First of all we LIKE to use bait because it is easier on the flesh than REAL faith, obedience to the Word, prayer, and waiting on God. Secondly we believe that the world is not offended by bait dug from the earth. When we use bait we feel they will treat us with more respect. When we depend solely on preaching the full counsel of God, Jesus Christ and Him crucified, and all its implications; when we depend solely on GOD'S power to save by the preaching of the cross, we become a reproach and fools in the eyes of the world.

Another reason we use bait, and this really is quite tragic, is because the Anointing of God has been gradually disappearing from our churches. In fact the more we use bait the more the Anointing leaves. The more we depend upon our FLESHLY abilities to bring people to Jesus Christ the less evident is the power of the Holy Spirit.

Bait is not merely harmful; it is potentially deadly. If people don't get through the bait to the Cross, they prove themselves not to be His. If their attention continues to be centered on the bait, they prove themselves not to be His. Even if they wander back and forth from Jesus Christ to the bait, they will experience the pain of the double-minded - they will experience spiritual schizophrenia. Eventually they will be forced to choose one or the other. The fishermen/preachers who use this bait to lure people into their churches and the kingdom of God must take another look at their motives and, what is more important; they MUST take another look at Scripture. They must be jolted out of the Saulish mentality, which says we need bigger and better methods to hook them in. The spirit of Scripture is clear - the ends and the means of the Gospel are the same. They highway of holiness (Isaiah 35:8) is the path to the Holy One and His Holy Kingdom. The realm we are leaving is the realm of the world, the flesh (self), and the devil. We renounce and reject this realm as we apprehend by faith the realm of the Kingdom of God, the Holy Spirit, and Jesus Christ Himself. To enter the realm of faith, hope and love we need faith, hope and love. To enter the realm of purity we need to be pure. To enter the realm of the Spirit we need the POWER of the Spirit, repentance, faith in Jesus Christ and Him Crucified, His Word, and the Power of His Resurrection. This is ALL we need for true salvation to take place and true revival to occur.

CHAPTER 4

THE POWER OF THE PEOPLE

Chapter 15 of I Samuel is the recounting of Saul leading the people of Israel in total war against the Amalekites. The Lord, through the prophet Samuel, instructed Saul to "strike Amalek and utterly destroy all that he has, and do not spare him, but put to death both man and woman, child and infant, ox and sheep, camel and donkey." (15:3). Saul achieves a tremendous victory for the Lord but he is only partially obedient to God's directive. Samuel rebukes Saul for his rebellion and tells him that in God's eyes he has lost rulership over God's people. In this chapter we learn a great deal about God's character, Saul's character, the people's character, and their influence on their king. I Samuel 15:9 say, "But Saul and the people spared Agag and the best of the sheep, the oxen, the fatlings, the lands, and ALL THAT WAS GOOD and WERE NOT WILLING TO DESTROY THEM UTTERLY; but everything despised and worthless, that they utterly destroyed." It seems as if there was a conspiracy, either vocalized or understood, between Saul and the people to disobey God and keep the best for themselves. Without question, from the natural way of looking at things, it was the logical thing to do. Perhaps Saul even rationalized that God did not really mean "utterly destroy all." Whatever his thoughts, he and the people functioned with worldly obedience using "practical" wisdom rather than spiritual obedience to the Word of God.

In verse 15 Saul says, "the people spared the best of the sheep and the oxen." He is not merely blaming the people but he is explaining the fact that the people were able to exert pressure on him to do their will. Possibly it was his desire to keep the best, but the people WERE able to influence Saul and validate His disobedience to God. After all, Saul was just being a good "servant leader." It is important to note that before Samuel brought it up, Saul did not reprimand the people for being disobedient.

In the last fifty years, we have seen an unspoken conspiracy between the shepherds and the sheep to spare the best of the world. After all, it makes good sense. The Saul Church, the church that is built predominantly on the desires of the people, understands that it is not necessary to throw out everything that the world has to offer. They openly strive for the best. When they want qualified people to counsel God's people, they strive for a man or woman who is educated in the "best" wisdom of this world. Of course, they recognize that much wisdom is demonic such as evolution, humanistic philosophy, communism, and abortion. But they do keep "the best." They recognize, embrace, and teach many psychological principles that come from the world. We realize that these principles originated in the world thought stream, but we only take the best. We incorporate such ideas as "you've got to love yourself before you can love anybody else" and "without a high sense of self-esteem an individual cannot be a truly whole person."

There are many other such ideas, all of which are completely apart from and opposed to Biblical Christianity that we embrace with equal fervor. Examples include positive confession, healing of memories, name it and claim it, visualization etc. If anyone argues about the legitimacy of these methods they are reminded that "all truth is God's truth." The people who hold this view honestly believe that the world has truth that we must use along with Scripture to present a perfectly balanced message. The problem is that some of these truths are NOT TRUE! They believe that these views are good science; therefore, these views are truth in the same sense that "the shortest distance between two points is a straight line" is a true statement. Their logical error is that the so-called science of psychology changes its views regarding the nature of man and his needs from one decade to another or from one teacher to another. William James, Sigmund Freud, Carl Jung and Carl Rogers all disagree violently but all are recognized as great psychologists by the world, even though their views are totally inconsistent with each other's and outside and contrary to the truth of Scripture.

Concerning our own relationship with the entertainment media we've learned to view only the best they have to offer. We KNOW it is not right to watch X-rated movies, but we are able to redeem some relatively clean R-rated movies on the basis of the fact that they are good art and we are able to handle them because of our Christian maturity. Some Christians have even rationalized watching what amounts to soft porn using this rationale. Others even allow their children to watch such movies. With PG movies we apply this same standard of good sense. We only watch the best. We make sure there is not too much nudity, sexual word plays, and blasphemous or dirty language. We only watch the best semi-filthy movies. Our TV habits are very similar. The Saul Church understands that, to be able to watch The Very Best the world has to offer, you must make slight adjustments to your integrity. But because it's the best, it is usually believed to be worth it.

Unfortunately, like Saul, who ultimately lost the kingdom because he desired and kept the best the world had to offer, so the people of the Saul Church are now losing the Kingdom.

I Samuel 15:24 says, ""Then Saul said to Samuel, "I have sinned. I have indeed transgressed the command of the Lord and your words, because I feared the people and LISTENED TO THEIR VOICE."" Even though Saul had a problem in that he wanted to keep the best, he had what amounted to at least as big a problem in the fact that he was a people pleaser. The people had his ear and knew that if they applied the right pressure they could get him to do what they wanted. In fact, Saul was really more interested in pleasing the people than he was in pleasing God. Perhaps at the time God chose Saul to be king, their desire did not affect him. But later their desire contributed to his rebellion against God. Being a people pleaser was ultimately tragic for Saul.

The Saul Church was called into being by the voice of the people. In the same way today many important ministerial decisions are made based upon what the people want. The pastoral staff knows that the visible Body of Christ is in many ways like a selfish child crying for its own way. They know that many in the Church today cry, "If you won't give us what we want, we will go somewhere else." They know that people demand cool worldly teachers, very little church discipline, tolerance of most secular movies, lots of outings, psychological counseling that does not expose sin, and above all a message that caters to their desire to enhance the outer man with worldly success, money and self-confidence. This cry has been heard and responded to by many of the fastest growing churches in America. Can you imagine what many of the churches would be like in terms of size if they did not give their people entertainment, psychology, doctrines which satisfy their materialistic lusts or doctrines which emphasize their rights and privileges instead of their responsibility? What would happen to their numbers if they decided to exercise Scriptural church discipline and preach convicting messages? The Saul Church in our generation has unfortunately fulfilled II Timothy 4:3. "For the time will come when they will not endure sound doctrine; but wanting to have their ears tickled will accumulate for themselves teachers in accordance to their own desires."

In the Jesus revival of the late 1960's and 1970's, a cry went up from our young people: "We want Christian rock and roll stars just like the world has!" These Christian rockers were merely the spiritual children of earlier entertainment groups that sang everything from country to pop gospel for Middle America. In the 40's and 50's Christian entertainment was a relatively small thing. By the 60's and 70's a generation of young people had grown up who were so addicted to entertainment and television that they veritably demanded to be entertained in the style to which they had become accustomed. Thus we have experienced the influx of Christian movies, Christian rock concerts and Christian comedians, most of which magnified the positive elements of Scripture, such as the love of God and the blessings He had for those who would accept Him as their Savior. The Jesus Movement, in Southern California particularly, was birthed in churches that answered this call with innumerable rock bands and doctrinally suspect movies about the rapture. This movement, with its emphasis on entertainment and escapism from judgment was different than any revival in the past. We had all-day rock festivals instead of all-night prayer meetings. In this revival we did not have thousands of people crowding the altars crying out for hours in repentance and prayer. Instead, we had tens of thousands of people crowding Disneyland on Christian Night to rock out to the sounds of the latest and most popular Christian bands.

The good news is that some Christian singers have lately been changed from being performers into being true ministers of the Gospel and recognize that entertainment is NOT on God's agenda for God's people. These men and women who inspire and lead God's people into true worship are part of the transition from the Saul Church to the David Church.

I Samuel 25:24 mentions one other important characteristic of Saul with regard to the people. He says, "....I have indeed transgressed the command of the Lord and your words because I FEARED THE PEOPLE and listened to their voice." Very likely Saul felt that the support of the people was necessary for his continuing success. Losing the support of the people could mean losing the kingdom. Therefore, Saul feared the people. But, as Saul found out, fearing the people was not the issue. Fear of the Lord was the real issue. Unfortunately Saul didn't really know God well enough to fear Him properly.

Fear of man is probably one of the most common sins among public people. In the entertainment field, if the people do not like you, you will fail, so entertainers must do things and say things in a way that people will like. Most entertainers fear losing the people's support and affection. Many ministers of the Gospel are no different than other public figures that depend upon the support of the people. They are tempted to fear people. However, because many of them have been taught that fear does not mean fear when referring to God but simply means respect or admiration, they have virtually no fear that their loving God would ever discipline them for fearing the people. Many ministers fear that people would reject them if their message was not acceptable or enjoyable. If this occurred, then attendance would drop and they would lose their authority and their reputations as successful ministers. They realize that in this generation most people will not accept the harsh or negative words that are in the Scriptures. Many ministers quickly are brought to a choice regarding their ministry: they must choose whether they will fear displeasing God or fear displeasing people. Once again, they trust that God will always be merciful to them, but that the people are the ones that could really cause them problems. Scripturally they know and are taught to fear God and not man, but experientially they find it much easier to fear man and trust God to see their good intentions and understand their difficult situation.

Saul Church leadership is very much like an insecure mother who gives into her teenage daughter because she is afraid she will run away and become misused by the harsher elements of the world. We are not only afraid of losing the people; we also are afraid of what will happen to them if they leave us. So we give them what they want because of these two fears. Like the aforementioned mother of the rebellious teenage daughter we are so afraid that we cannot even trust God. We keep them close to us by never really confronting them with their sin and "trust God" to change them through prayer and His grace.

Christian leaders have another very practical fear; they are afraid of the people because they pay their salaries. If we anger them they might leave and we would lose a portion of our financial support. Even more important to most ministers, if we lose the people's love, support and/or attendance, we will lose our reputations as Men of God. We really fear and trust man more than we fear and trust God because our perception is that the people are the ones that really hurt or help us. The people are right here and we can readily see the damage or the blessing we receive from them. Because we are shallow in faith, we do not recognize the loss of God's power or presence as we fail to make pleasing Him our single hearted concern. We discount Him and take Him for granted.

The more we depend upon and fear the people the more we prove that we do not depend upon and fear God. We must realize that God is the one who takes care of us and the people are the ones that we are to care for - on God's terms of course. THE PEOPLE ARE NOT OUR SOURCE OF SUPPORT OR APPROVAL. When we do His will, He will provide for us and we will be approved unto Him.

After Samuel told Saul that he was a sinner and had lost the kingdom, Saul said to him in I Samuel 15:30, "....I have sinned but please honor me now before the elders of my people and before Israel, and go back with me that I may worship the Lord your God." In an earlier verse Saul had asked Samuel to go back with him and worship. Samuel refused. This time however when Saul told him the whole truth (which was that he wanted Samuel to go back and worship with him so that he could receive honor from the elders), Samuel went back with him. We see Saul here being more concerned about receiving honor from men than he is about losing the kingdom or disobeying God. Earlier in the chapter we see a telling example of Saul's desire to be honored by the people. He wanted them to remember his great deeds and position. I Samuel 15:12 says, ""...it was told Samuel saying "Saul came to Carmel and behold HE SET UP A MONUMENT FOR HIMSELF...""" Building a monument for yourself is certainly a way to seek honor from men. This desire to receive honor from men had to compromise his desire for God to receive the glory.

The Saul Church is a church that desires to be honored greatly by the people. They love and seek titles and degrees, and many frankly don't care what the title or degree represents. We just like the honor and prestige. In the Charismatic and Evangelical churches of today honorary doctorates are commonplace. The reasons why these degrees are given are many: 1) long involvement with a Bible school, 2) being put in a position where it would look better if you were called Doctor (such as assuming District leadership), 3) pastoring a large church for a reasonably long amount of time and, 4) Fame (because of a successful book or prominent ministry). These honorary degrees sometimes represent love and appreciation but sometimes it is just part of the Saul mutual admiration society.

We saw from the Scripture that one of the ways Saul chose to honor himself was to build himself a monument. This egomaniacal practice is not limited to either the Bible figure Saul or the world. It has become commonplace and perfectly acceptable to build all kinds of monuments for ourselves. The people in the Saul Church, like the people in the world, need to honor their heroes and idols by building them shrines and monuments. The pastor or minister who involves people in a large building program that seems to have little real purpose has rightly, in the past, been accused of building his own kingdom or putting up a monument to himself. However, in most cases, the people actually encouraged him to do so. Building large churches CAN be a legitimate response to the will of God or the real need for more room! However, many larger churches are built on one of the following notions. The first notion is a building program is good for the people because it unites them in a common cause (I actually heard this taught at a minister's retreat). The second notion is that if we build a larger church God will most certainly fill it (even though the small church is not yet filled). The third notion which is the scariest reason for building a larger church is because "God told me to build a larger church because we will need it!" Of course there are men who really do hear from the Lord. The problem is when the pastor or leader did not really hear from the Lord and is just involving his people with great debt when the anticipated increase never comes, the people are either deeply disappointed or feel betrayed.

Every time a church or a people honor a man of God it is not necessarily done as an idolatrous act. We should give honor to whom honor is due. However, we must be careful that we honor men and movements because they deserve that honor and that God wants them to be honored.

The Saul Church is church of Personalities and Stars and Egos. We must be extremely careful not to exalt ourselves. Even more important, we must not allow the people to exalt us unduly. We of all people, the people of the phony gospel of self-love, self-esteem and self-exaltation, will be tempted to build a monument to ourselves. We must be sure not to consciously allow glory or inappropriate attention to fall on us, regardless of the idolatrous desires of the people. We are the generation that must learn to say, "I have been crucified with Christ; and IT IS NO LONGER I WHO LIVE, but Christ lives in me..." (Galatians 2:20). We are the generation that must say and practice what John the Baptist said, "He must increase, BUT I MUST DECREASE." (John 3:30).

The leadership of the household of God must no longer captively listen to the voice of the people. We must no longer be influenced merely by their desires. We must no longer succumb to the fear of losing them. We have spoiled the people of God in the same way that an undisciplined parent spoils their child because that is the way we would have wanted to be treated ourselves! We have given the power of decision to a people who are not mature enough to know the difference between good and evil. We ask them whether they would rather have meat and vegetables or ice cream and candy. Quite naturally they want ice cream and candy three meals a day. Sometimes we are able to slip a LITTLE meat and vegetables into their diet, but not too much lest they become offended. Entertainment and a convictionless Gospel message at church are the equivalent of a steady diet of sweets. Today we know that when a person's diet mainly consists of sweets their chances of getting diabetes are extremely good. A little sugar is good, but too much sugar leads to diabetes. Blindness, loss of limbs, or the inability for men to father children is the inevitable result of diabetes. Because we have given them what they want they are in grave danger of contracting terminal spiritual diabetes and losing the power to see spiritually, to act spiritually, and ultimately even to reproduce spiritually. Spiritual diabetes has already set in, and we have lately seen some of the spiritual parents of the Saul Church begin to go blind and lose their power in the Body of Christ because of self-indulgence. And we see, all around us, followers of the self-indulgent doctrine who are themselves so blind that they will follow their blind leaders into hell itself. We must preach a Gospel that shows the people who is to have the power. We must show them that it is the power of the Holy Spirit that must rule according to the whole counsel of God in Scripture. We must, by good complete Gospel teaching, wrest the power from the people and give it back to God so the people can be healthy. In the world we see the results of letting the people have what they want: unrestrained lusts of all kinds rule both in the streets and in the home. In the Church, because we have given the people what they want, we now see Christians who have the power to shape their churches into the image of their own desire. However, because of the weakened condition of these churches, they have NO power to defeat the enemy. Because of this, many church members are in great danger of losing MUCH of their spiritual inheritance, or worse, discovering at the judgment that they never really were God's children.

CHAPTER 5

PLUMBING THE DEPTHS OF SHALLOWNESS

When Samuel went to find the man whom God had chosen to replace Saul as king of Israel from among Jesse's sons, his criteria for selection were appearance and size. We know this because God had to correct him, as recorded in I Samuel 16:7, ""But the Lord said to Samuel, "do not look at his appearance or at the height of his stature because I have rejected him; for <u>God sees not as man sees, for man looks at the outward appearance, but the Lord looks at the heart.</u>"" Quite likely Samuel was looking for a large, good-looking man because the first king, Saul, was the most handsome and the tallest of all the Israelites. Samuel probably thought that since the Lord gave His people a tall good-looking man to be king the first time that He would do so again. But the Lord wanted Samuel to know that the next king was not going to be a king for the people, to satisfy their desires. This king was going to be, to quote the Lord in chapter 16:1, "....a king FOR MYSELF...." This king did not need to be tall and handsome. The Lord made it clear that when He chose a leader for Himself, He was not concerned with size or beauty; He was ONLY interested in the man's heart. He chose David because David's heart was after (desired) His own heart.

When the first king, Saul, was chosen, there was no mention of his heart or his desire for God. There was no mention of this because Saul was a king *for the people* and the people did not really care if their king had a heart after God. The people were not interested in the inside of a man - all they cared about was the outside. They were interested in what they could see. They likely wanted to see a tall, imposing, good-looking king leading them into battle against the enemy. And what might be even more important was that they possibly wanted the enemy to see and fear them because of the imposing stature of their king. They were a shallow people, and because they did not care about the depth of a man, they were given a shallow king. They never knew nor cared to understand the fear, the love, the character, or the ways of God. They were quite satisfied to look upon God as the one who loved them enough to give them what they wanted; they were quite satisfied that God gave them an impressive but shallow leader. Saul too had no desire to know the fear, the love, the character or the ways of God. As we noted in the previous chapter, Saul was not even concerned about pleasing God; he was basically concerned about pleasing the people. We never see Saul grieving over the possibility of losing the anointing of God, and when he finally loses it, there was no remorse. Unlike David, we never hear Saul truly repent. We hear his confession, but that is merely for the sake of receiving honor from men. We NEVER see in Scripture real repentance from Saul. We never hear Saul cry out to God for holiness, forgiveness or relationship with Him. He inquired of the Lord when the enemy threatened, but this was for protection for himself and his people. In times of peace we never see him strive to communicate with God. He ministered with the anointing of God, but even that was small. I Samuel 10:1 say, ""Then Samuel took the FLASK of oil, poured it on his head, kissed him and said, "Has not the Lord anointed you a ruler over his inheritance?"" Another translation uses the phrase "vial of oil." Regarding David, I Samuel 16:13 says, "then Samuel took THE HORN of oil and anointed him in the midst of his brothers, and the Spirit of the Lord came mightily upon David from that day forward".... David's horn of oil was larger and contained more oil than Saul's flask or vial of oil. We see then, that even Saul's anointing was shallow. It was probably shallow because that was all that was necessary to satisfy both his desire and the desire of the people.

We see evidences in the Saul Church of similar shallow-mindedness. In Charismatic churches, for example, when people are instructed to seek God for the Baptism (or Infilling, or Fullness) of His Holy Spirit, they are usually encouraged to speak in tongues and little else. To be sure, this IS an evidence that an individual has been filled by the Holy Spirit of God. But what a tragedy that leaders would encourage people to merely manifest the *evidence* without concern for them experiencing the *essence* of the Fullness of the Holy Spirit - to know the height, the depth, the length, and the width of God's love and to know the power of God for the purpose of destroying the works of the devil. The people of God have many and varied experiences with God's Holy Spirit. To settle for AN EVIDENCE ONLY is indeed a shallow desire. There is, however, an even greater tragedy concerning the Baptism in the Holy Spirit and speaking in tongues. There are people who teach others to imitate the sounds that they make and then they call this imitation the Baptism in the Holy Spirit. This is worse than shallowness; it is deception. The poor seeker goes away either deluded into thinking he has received something when he hasn't or he goes away very confused. The magnificent Baptism of the Holy Spirit is one of the most awesome experiences one can possibly have. To be inundated and surrounded by God Himself, to have His love coursing through your heart, mind, soul and body; to experience the peace that passes understanding or even to have a sense that God is powerfully infilling you with supernatural abilities to defeat the enemy, is NEVER something to be minimized. The Scriptures are clear: if we seek Him with all our heart we will find Him! And when we find Him we will be forever changed and what is more important, *we will know* that we have encountered God. Some churches teach that we must take the baptism *by faith* and not be concerned if we feel nothing or experience no change in our thoughts or lives regarding God. EVERYWHERE in Scripture where people have encountered God in this way they have been greatly affected. This encounter has caused them to be different people and often they have a different relationship with God after this experience. Some have appeared to be drunk because of the STAGGERING effect of the power and love of God flowing in and over mere human beings. The Old Testament manifestations were often visually profound: Enoch walked and talked with God, Moses encountered God in the burning bush and Jacob physically wrestled with the Angel of the Lord. In the New Testament on the day of Pentecost men and women were so overcome by Him that they had difficulty walking properly and some were anointed at that time to preach, prophesy and do miracles. Paul's entire life was turned around when he was blinded by the appearance of Jesus Christ. In the midst of Peter's preaching, even the Gentiles spoke in tongues without any coaching and it was evident to all that they too had been filled with the Holy Spirit. If a person takes *by faith* their Baptism in the Holy Spirit and has no personal, supernatural encounter with the Holy One of Israel, it is a tragedy. It is important that men and women be taught to expect to encounter God and not give up until they do.

I sought to be filled with the Holy Spirit for eighteen months and while praying in a little chapel I spoke in tongues, and was filled with a supernatural love for God and people (even my enemies)! Because of this phenomenal infilling of love, I was able to <u>completely</u> forgive an individual that I had harbored great bitterness toward. Even more important for me, when I was filled or baptized in the Holy Spirit, I received an UNSHAKEABLE and ABSOLUTE ASSURANCE that I was UNCONDITIONALLY SAVED BY GOD, and that I was His child for eternity and He would never let me go. Previously to this I was often tempted by Satan as to whether or not I was truly His son and often was greatly concerned about falling away from God.

One person's encounter may not be as dramatic as another's, but there is *no doubt* they will KNOW that they have encountered God!

Some Evangelical churches have problems with shallow approaches to God's Holy Spirit. They assure the seeker that he has already experienced the baptism of the Holy Spirit at salvation. Many non-charismatic evangelicals and some Charismatics teach that there should not necessarily be an expectation of a deep emotional, mental or spiritual experience. They recognize that we are to be filled with the Spirit, but they arc highly suspicious of experiences that result in speaking in tongues, prophetic utterance or even profound, personal supernatural experiences. Just as the aforementioned shallow "speaking in tongues" teaching is not universally taught in the Charismatic movement, so every Evangelical church does not discourage people from seeking the supernatural love and power of the supernatural God. However, we have very few churches and ministries that encourage us to hunger and thirst after Jesus Christ and His Holy Spirit in a way that's reflected in the Scriptures. The classic examples are in Psalms and Ephesians. In Psalm 42:1-2 the psalmist says, "As the deer pants for the water brooks, so my soul pants for Thee O God. My soul thirsts for God, for the living God." In the New Testament we hear Paul the Apostle praying, in Ephesians 3:17-19, "....that Christ may dwell in our hearts through faith: and that we, being rooted and grounded in love, may be able to comprehend with all the saints what is the breadth and length and height and depth, and TO KNOW THE LOVE OF CHRIST which surpasses knowledge, that we MAY BE FILLED UP TO ALL THE FULLNESS OF GOD." This is what is available; this is what we must seek for, "to be filled up with all the fullness of God" and experience and know and live all that Paul included in that sublime passage of Scripture and all that David encouraged us to do in the Psalms.

For decades, the Catholic Church and many old-line denominations have been accused of teaching dead ritual with their use of beads, The Book of Common Prayer, chants, and even hymn singing. Very likely at one time the words in The Book of Common Prayer had great meaning to the people who read them. Even the chants, when uttered from the heart of an individual who lived his faith and his love for Jesus Christ, had great meaning. Likewise, the beautiful hymns of Charles Wesley and Robert Newton, when understood and sung in the midst of a faith-filled and obedient life, were true expressions of praise and thanksgiving to our Heavenly Father. But today, in the aforementioned old-line churches, they are for the most part shallow, contrived reminders of an anointing that once was, but has now departed. Because of this shallowness we have rightly called these churches dead churches. But we must understand that the so-called live churches of today are in danger of and in some cases already are seeing the departure of the anointing of God. The reason is the same. We are missing the heart of the issue, and have become satisfied to be proficient in the outward manifestation. In some Charismatic churches today "dancing in the spirit" is actually being choreographed by worship leaders. Spontaneity either cannot be trusted to happen or is feared. Usually the former is the case. To most of us this manipulation of the congregation to "dance in the spirit" is shallow. However, we have been involved in more subtle forms of manipulation. Even as the dance leaders have shown us from Scripture that David danced before the Lord, so the worship leaders give us many examples from Scripture about the raising of hands, the waving of hands, and the clapping of hands. All of these activities, like dancing before the Lord, are valid ways of expressing joy, love, and thanksgiving. The problem is, once again, spontaneity is slipping away. We are not merely encouraged, we are commanded to lift our hands, clap our hands, wave our hands, and in some cases even shout. Just whom we are doing this for is at best questionable. Oftentimes these exercises are for the purpose of developing an "exuberance of worship" that outsiders will notice and church members can be proud of. An evidence of this is the visiting speaker who, if he is familiar with Charismatic etiquette, will compliment the congregation on their ability to "really praise God" or he will say how much he enjoys praising God with this great crowd. He virtually never makes mention of how wonderful God is and how thankful he is to be saved by the blood of Jesus Christ, or how worthy our Lord is. Even though worship is supposed to be a manifestation of love for God, when a congregation is "good at praising the Lord", the remarks about that praise usually always are remarks NOT about God, but how wonderful the people are at praising God. When a congregation truly praises God from their heart, GOD will be glorified, not the people. And with the attention of everyone on God, no one will notice, or care about, the worship style of those nearby.

Another shallow manipulative use of worship is to praise God so we can get something from Him - so we can get a healing, a victory, money, deliverance, or EVEN so we can get the Baptism in the Holy Spirit. This shallow display of "praise" is no more than FLATTERY and will not impress God. Flattery is praising someone so you can get something from him, and the aforementioned type of praise certainly falls into that category. It is like an eight-year-old son telling his father how great he is or how much he loves him so he can get a larger allowance or some new toys.

We see, in the Saul Church, an emphasis on shallow worship rather than deep evidence of heartfelt worship. Worship, as was said before, should be a manifestation of our love for God. Our love for God, according to John 14:21, is evidenced by our obedience from the heart to our Lord Jesus Christ, "He who has My commandments and keeps them, he it is who loves Me; and he who loves Me shall be loved by My Father and I will love him and will disclose Myself to him." Real love from the heart need NEVER be orchestrated. While there are many exhortations to praise God in the Old Testament, it is understood that any religious activity or offering to God, whether it be your tithe, your praise or any sacrifice, if not done on the platform of loving trust or obedience, is not accepted by God. Some forms of worship are in fact hateful to Him. Isaiah 1:11-17 says, "What are your multiplied sacrifices to Me says the Lord... Who requires of you this trampling of My courts? Bring your worthless offering no longer; their incense is an abomination to Me...I cannot endure iniquity in the solemn assemblies...so when you spread out your hands in prayer, I will hide My eyes from you, yes even though you multiply prayers, I will not listen. Your hands are full of bloodshed. Wash yourselves, make yourselves clean; remove the evil of your deeds from My sight. Cease to do evil. Learn to do good."

Today our thanksgiving offering is not a sacrificed animal but is thanksgiving from our lips and heart. The Lord, in this passage of Scripture, is clearly telling us that when offering thanksgiving to Him it must emanate from hearts that love Him enough to trust Him and obey Him. God will not fully accept a sacrifice of praise and thanksgiving from hearts that are casually, willfully, or presumptuously disobedient. To praise God properly we MUST be exhorted to come to Him with a clean heart. We MUST be encouraged to obey Him with a loving, obedient heart and a heart that is quick to recognize and repent of sin. We MUST be warned of the foolishness of coming to Him in a shallow, presumptuous, disobedient manner. During a so-called revival meeting back in the 1980's, the worship leader had just cranked the crowd up into another dimension of volume, when I found I was no longer able to continue. In the midst of the deafening din, I cried out to God, "What is happening Lord, am I so cold that I can't enter into this or is this not of You? PLEASE SHOW ME LORD!" Immediately the Lord showed me a giant playpen with dozens of toddlers in diapers lifting their arms and shouting and jumping and falling and rolling with each other, and getting up and jumping and shouting again. I said to the Lord, "Oh, this is just young, immature worship. Is that it Lord?" And He said to me, "Look closer!" Immediately I was given a close-up of the childish revelers and I saw there was potty (human feces) smeared all over their bodies and oozing from their diapers and the more they "worshipped" the dirtier they got. Then the Lord spoke, "They are like this because they won't let Me CHANGE them." Unrepentant, unchangeable worshippers who will not let God clean them up will not please the Lord with their loud, continuous noise. Proper worship is light years away from mere instruction in technique. The quoting of many Scriptures concerning our obligation to praise God and then accomplish this by raising the emotional tone to the highest level possible is almost always not true praise. Even praising God and thanking Him for what He has done, if done from a hypocritical heart is shallow and probably meaningless worship. It is impossible to live with an unthankful and complaining attitude for the days preceding the worship service, lift your hands and expect God to ignite your offering of worship with His approval if you don't repent of a thankless bitter heart first.

Salvation is the deepest and most beautiful state a human being can possibly experience. Being born again into the Kingdom of God is at once a joyful and serious miracle. The Saul Church has found a way to demean even this. The Bible, through the lips of John the Baptist, Jesus, and Peter exhorts us to repent and believe. Jesus, Peter and Paul tell us what it is to follow Jesus Christ. As was mentioned before, among other things we are told to count the cost. In regards to this, many of our "altar calls" are now so simple that they are misleading. We tell people to accept Jesus, to come to Jesus, and to receive Him as their personal Savior. We neglect, perhaps ignorantly, perhaps purposefully, the rest of the Gospel (see Chapter 2 - Fishers of Men). Preaching conviction of sin is not only unpopular but is completely neglected in many churches. Most churches are content to leave the work of conviction to the Holy Spirit. This may sound spiritual but that would be like saying maybe we should let the Holy Spirit tell them "you must be born again", or "the just are saved by faith." Often we "trust" the Holy Spirit to deliver the "negative" parts of Scripture. This is both unscriptural and displeasing to God. We are exhorted to preach the Word, the whole Word and nothing but the Word.

Many churches today substitute the concept that "Jesus wants to heal your hurts" for the concept of "you need to repent of your sins." The seeker in many churches today is portrayed not as a sinner but as a victim who has been wounded, either in childhood or bad marriages. Today we have a therapeutic Gospel where Jesus will heal your hurts, but He does not necessarily need to forgive your sins. Often moral failures are classified as mistakes rather than sins. Rarely are the seekers encouraged to repent of their sins. The spiritual Gospel includes a need to repent. Jesus can never forgive a hurt; He only forgives SIN. This shallow people-pleasing approach keeps people away from true salvation. If people are never brought to an understanding of their great need for Jesus Christ to forgive their sin, they do not and cannot know Him as the forgiver of their sin. The therapeutic approach can build huge churches but it will never enlarge the kingdom of God. People who raise their hand and accept Jesus as their personal Savior and the great Physician who heals their hurts, may become members of their local church, but may never become a member in particular of the Body of Christ.

Much of what we discussed: worship, altar calls, a desire to get people to speak in tongues, and even our orchestrated acts of love and our verbal and visual ways of expressing allegiance to our Lord can be done from a sincere motive with a heart that loves Jesus completely and absolutely. The point of this chapter is not to put down sincere people who practice any or all of the things mentioned. The purpose is to expose an attitude that prevails in our current Church age. We are seeing shallowness in the Church in America like never before. We must avoid with all our heart the temptation to be mechanical, and to do things without real understanding. We must resist all manipulation. We must resist anything that would have us perform either for each other, for visitors, for the satisfaction of the preacher, or even to perform for God. We live in an age where Image is the issue. I have even heard, at pastors' conferences, the phrase "You don't sell the steak, you sell the sizzle." Leaders in the Church of Jesus Christ are being taught to be image conscious and indirectly, as we learn to create the right appearance, we are losing our hold on what is essential. Image and sizzle work with the shallow people who are the victims of uncaring advertising men; but we are not looking for dumb sheep to respond to an image and ultimately be led to a slaughter. As men and women of God we must be ABSOLUTELY SURE there is a commensurate, honest substance behind what people see or hear. There must be a perfectly prepared prime steak from the Master Himself behind every sizzle they hear and smell.

CHAPTER 6

RELIGIOUS DECEPTION

In the last chapter we looked at the concept of shallowness. Shallowness is a superficial attitude of the heart and mind. It is more interested in image than in essence. Because the Lord tells us that He looks on the heart of the man and not on his appearance, it is evident that God does not want us to be superficial shallow people. To do so would be disobedience to Him.

Closely connected with shallowness is "religious" disobedience. Religious disobedience is different from standard disobedience in that the latter always has an apparently spiritual rationale. To many people the word "religion" today has a negative connotation. When some witness to unsaved people, they often say, "I don't want to speak to you about religion; I want to tell you about relationship." We recognize that there is something negative, generally speaking, about the term religion, particularly when compared to the term spirituality. If we heard that an individual was spiritual, we would feel comfortable with him; but if we heard that he was religious, we would be suspicious. It is in this sense that the term religious disobedience is used in this chapter. Of course, we are familiar with the King James use of the word and also with other translations, which do not use the word in a negative sense, but in a favorable sense. To quote James 1:27 "This is pure and undefiled religion in the sight of God and the Father, to visit orphans and widows in their distress, and to keep oneself unstained by the world." Saul however is a man to whom the first reference to religion applies. In looking at Scripture we can see that Saul was religiously disobedient. He wanted to appear holy and acceptable unto God. He used religion or the outward trappings of spirituality, as a way of covering up his shallow people-pleasing and self-pleasing heart.

A common manifestation of religious disobedience is the use of religious language for purposes other than glorifying God. I Samuel 15:13 is a classic example of a man who is in utter rebellion but wants to sound very spiritual. "And Samuel came to Saul, and Saul said to him, "blessed are you of the Lord! I have carried out the command of the Lord!" Saul was actually trying to deceive Samuel with his opening religious barrage because earlier Samuel had given Saul precise instructions on what to do with the Amalekites and their livestock and possessions: he was to destroy everything and everyone. Saul, at the prompting of his own self-willed heart and the prompting of the people, only obeyed part of the command that he was given. Saul willfully spared all of the best in direct violation of God's command. But Saul, apparently being familiar with the psychological effectiveness of sounding religious in a questionable situation, greets the prophet with a complimentary and high sounding "blessed are you of the Lord!" Saul tosses around the Holy Name of God as it fits his need. He immediately follows up with a not-so-humble declaration of his obedience; apparently realizing that sometimes the best defense is a good offense. He goes on the offensive with Samuel and says, "I have carried out the command of the Lord!" He no doubt expected Samuel to overlook the trifling fact that he spared a small percentage of the possessions of the Amalekites and the fact that he did not kill Agag the king. Samuel, however, was not at all impressed with Saul's glib religious talk. In a matter of minutes he proclaimed God's judgment against Saul.

The Saul Church of our generation also tosses the Holy Name of God around in a frivolous religious manner. We cover up our disobedience with such impressive phrases as: 1) "The Lord told me it was alright to marry Ken, even though he is an unbeliever", 2) "I prayed about buying that expensive car and the Lord gave me a peace about it", and 3) "We need to pray about Fred because he is drinking again and they caught his son cheating in a math exam and his wife says he is abusive."

In the first case, when people say that the Lord told them to do something, they often are merely proclaiming their own desire and validating it by invoking the Name of the Lord. In Charismatic circles particularly, we are guilty of invoking the Name of Jesus when we are in the midst of justifying some personal desire. A famous example is when a former healing evangelist was supposedly told by a very tall Jesus (I believe He was 900 feet tall) to write letters to innumerable people soliciting donations ranging from $25.00 to $1,000.00. When many of the recipients of this letter heard the Name of Jesus they then believed that this message had to be from God. Unfortunately, thousands of church building programs in both Charismatic and Evangelical churches have been financed by the same invocation of the Name of Jesus Christ or the apparent peace that the leader says that he received from the Lord regarding the building program. The sheep have also learned well from their shepherds, so that whenever they want to purchase a new car or a new house they religiously invoke the Name of Jesus Christ. They will say, "Jesus told me that I deserve a new car and I should get a $20,000 loan to pay for it. Jesus said that I would be stepping out in faith, and that He would take care of me." People have even been able to use this ploy for the purpose of disposing of an unwanted spouse. They will say, "Jesus told me I should leave my husband. I sense in my spirit that my time of trial is now over. It is just too much for me to live with a man who treats me so poorly, and gives me so little attention. I know that my next husband will be much more spiritual. In fact, I believe the Lord has even shown me who he will be."

The "I prayed about it" game is even easier to play. You do not even need to refer to Jesus. The situation generally is as follows: You pray about a certain thing, perhaps it is a new car. You don't sense horrible conviction, no great calamity seems imminent, and what's more important, after you've prayed about it and presented your offer to the automobile salesman, he accepts! You prayed about it, God did not stop it, and the door was Open. True, you really could not afford it, but once again you feel it is a step of faith because you "prayed about it." The beautiful thing about this religious delusion is you do not even need to get a vision or a dream or a strong sense of God's approval. All you need to do is pray about it and if "the door is open" you can religiously assume it is God's will. Of course, you NEVER stop to think that the automobile salesman's job is to sell you a car. For some unbelievable reason if he offers you the car at a price that you both know is more than you can really afford, you assume that God has put His stamp of approval on the deal BECAUSE YOU PRAYED ABOUT IT! The typical Saul Christian quits jobs oftentimes without even giving proper notice, dissolves marriages, changes churches, buys things he cannot afford, and dates unsaved people, all on the religious pretext that he PRAYED ABOUT IT and God "opened the door." For many in the Saul Church this religious exercise is the ultimate in God's guidance.

One of the best ways to sound spiritual, but really disguise a treacherous heart is, in the midst of several of the brothers and sisters in church, to request prayer for someone not in attendance who has sinned. This presents a perfect opportunity to share (translate gossip) about the brother or sister. It usually goes something like this, "I really have a burden for Brother Fred. I love that brother. He is really growing. But, do you know what he did to Ralph? He borrowed $10.00 last week and hasn't paid it back! And what's more, I think he used the money to buy a carton of cigarettes! And I think he was drinking beer last Thursday. At least his breath smelled weird." Prayer is one of the most devastating weapons we have against Satan. However, in the name of prayer, we can be used by the enemy to either damage or assassinate a brother's or sister's character. We can religiously use the prayer circle as a gossip circle.

I Samuel 15:14, "Then Saul said to Samuel, I have sinned. I have indeed transgressed the command of the Lord and your words because I feared the people and listened to their voice." This sounds like a very complete repentance on the part of Saul. It sounds spiritual, but Samuel, representing the Lord, rejects it because Saul is not repenting for sinning against the Lord. He is merely confessing or acknowledging what he has done so that Samuel will honor him before the elders and Israel. I Samuel 15:30 says, "....I have sinned but please honor me now before the elders of my people and before Israel, and go back with me that I may worship the Lord your God." His repentance was an act of religious deception. It was calculated to bring about a certain response that had nothing to do with real sorrow for sin, a desire to be clean and pure before God, or a longing to be re-established in relationship with the Lord. It was merely a game that Saul was playing to get Samuel to honor him before the elders and the people. It was religious deception calculated to save face and Samuel saw right through it, and would not go back with Saul until Saul acknowledged what was really on his heart: the desire to be honored by the elders and the people.

In the Saul Church of today we see public confessions of wrongdoing but some of them are calculated to please man and not to please God. Even as Saul did not repent or even confess his self-willed rebellion against God, neither do we acknowledge our real sins of lukewarmness, materialism, and rebellion. In fact, we are likely to hear confessions from our leaders as, "Please forgive me, I failed you my people, because I was afraid to ask you for money. I have not been faithful to the Word in asking you for tithes and offerings. I confess it was the fear of man that kept me from doing this. God has dealt with me. I have repented so...I'm just going to share my heart with you: we are $330,000 short in our gymnasium fund and $10,000 short for the youth department's trip to Israel. Church...God is building His kingdom and only you can supply the money we need here at California Community Church! Please forgive me; I can assure you I will be obedient in this area in the future." This is a very deceptive way to take an offering. It SOUNDS like the pastor is humbling himself before his people because of his sin, but REALLY all he is doing is exercising yet another way to fleece the sheep.

As Saul used religious phrases to cover his divided and disobedient heart, so the Saul Church in our generation has hypocritically used religious language to justify selfishness, rebellion, slander, and the attainment of its own financial well being.

CHAPTER 7

RELIGIOUS ACTIVISM

Another characteristic of a religious man is that he feels it necessary when confronted with a difficult situation to DO something - ANYthing! This is religious activity as opposed to spiritual activity and often takes the form of religious activism or Christian activism. Religious activism is doing something that is in the opinion of most moral people a GOOD thing to do. Often, to the natural mind, this activity seems logical and appropriate. There IS a place for doing good and moral things. There are people who are called by God to enter in to many of these activities. However, it is important to note that this is not the ESSENTIAL call of the Church of Jesus Christ. Christians are called to preach the Gospel and change the hearts of men from being hardened against God to being obedient to God. We are called to make disciples and to teach them to obey all that He has commanded to do!

A good example of aberrant religious activity is I Samuel 13:8-10.

""Now he (Saul) waited seven days according to the appointed time set by Samuel, but Samuel did not come to Gilgal; and the people were scattering from him. So Saul said, "bring to me the burnt offering and the peace offerings." And he offered the burnt offering. And it came about as soon as he finished offering the burnt offering that behold, Samuel came; and Saul went out to meet him and to greet him. But Samuel said, "What have you done?" And Saul said, "because I saw that the people were scattering from me, and that you did not come within the appointed days, and that the Philistines were assembling at Michmash, therefore I said, 'Now the Philistines will come down against me at Gilgal, and I have not asked the favor of the Lord.' So I forced myself and offered the burnt offering.""

In this portion of Scripture we see the perfect example of a spirit of religious activism. Saul, motivated by fear of the Philistines and fear that the people would leave him, FORCED HIMSELF to do something that, in light of the events, seemed to be the best thing to do, but was in fact, totally disobedient to God. He was told to wait for Samuel to offer the sacrifice. But because of his fears, his impatience and his need to see fulfilled immediately the religious act of offering sacrifices, he disobeyed God. He presumptuously volunteered to act apart from God's direction. Perhaps he did it for religious luck much as a boxer will cross himself before each round of a fight. It really does not matter; Saul did things mainly to please himself or others. He did things in his way and in his time. In Proverbs we are warned to "lean not unto our own understanding", but Saul never really understood this principle and God viewed his volunteerism as flagrant, gross disobedience, for which He punished Saul in the most severe and final manner.

I Samuel 13:13-14 says, ""And Samuel said to Saul, "you have acted foolishly; you have not kept the commandment of the Lord your God which he commanded you, for now the Lord would have established your kingdom over Israel forever. But now your kingdom shall not endure. The Lord has sought out for Himself a man after His own heart, and the Lord has appointed him as ruler over His people, BECAUSE YOU HAVE NOT KEPT WHAT THE LORD COMMANDED YOU..""

This passage of Scripture is of utmost importance for the people of our generation. Matthew 28:18-20, ""And Jesus came up and spoke to them, saying, "All authority has been given to Me in heaven and on earth. Go therefore and MAKE DISCIPLES OF ALL THE NATIONS, baptizing them in the name of the Father, and the Son and the Holy Spirit, TEACHING THEM TO OBSERVE (obey) ALL THAT I COMMANDED YOU; and lo, I am with you always, even to the end of the age.""

Even as Saul did not keep the commandment of the Lord, so the Saul Church has not kept the commandment of the Lord. The Great Commission in Matthew 28 tells His Church to MAKE DISCIPLES and to teach them to observe ALL THAT HE COMMANDS US TO DO! He does not tell the Church to teach men to accept Jesus as their personal Savior. He says to us that if we want to come after Him we must deny ourselves, take up our cross daily and follow Him. Many Saul Christians would refer to the command that we teach His disciples to obey all that He commands us to do as legalistic. They would say we are "under grace and not under law." Some Saul Christians would even suggest that it is not important to initially come to Jesus as Lord, but merely "accept Him as your Savior", and if you decide at a later time, you can recognize Him as Lord. The Scripture; however, says that we are to believe in the LORD Jesus Christ. Acts 14 makes it clear that all Christians are disciples. It says, "And it was at Antioch that the disciples were first called Christians."

When an anointed man or woman of God functions presumptuously in ministry it is disobedience. God has no room for volunteers in His army who do things in their own time or their own way. In the Saul Church of our generation we see religious volunteerism running rampant. We have taken upon ourselves duties that God does not call us to perform. What is worse but also very consistent with a religious works-oriented spirit, is that many of these religious zealots INSIST that others also do what they are doing. The more people that join with them, the more secure and justified they feel. Most religious zealots feel very righteous in what they are doing and are critical of those who do not join them. Many ministers of the Gospel have wrongly taken upon themselves the mantle of political and moral leadership. Many shepherds in the flock of the Lord have become activists in the political and social arena. They have sensed, correctly, that terrible wrongs and sins are being committed in our country. They have seen the abortion mills murder millions of babies in recent years. They have seen Communism spread from Russia to China to Eastern Europe to Cuba to Africa and to Central and South America. They are aware of the tremendous threat it poses to our own country and our own moral and spiritual values. They have seen the in-roads that liberal and radical thinking has made in education, the media, and in our judicial and political systems. Many have watched the Democrat Party become an anti-Christian political party that has more love for Mao Tze Dung than Jesus Christ. They have seen the terrible influx of pornography in magazines, movies and television. They have watched appalled as humanism has become the prevailing religion that rules our courts and our schools. They have watched, with apparent helplessness, the greatest country in the world, sink morally and spiritually, lower than anyone would have ever imagined. They have observed Mohammedism and other Eastern Religions fill the spiritual void that we have left both in the United States and all over the world. They have watched with fear as the Philistine presence of Organized Evil goes deeper and deeper into our culture.

The Church's solution has been a Saul solution. Do something! Do Anything! Get involved in the cultural and political war! To fight abortion - demonstrate! Join forces with anyone else no matter their spiritual condition or viewpoint. True, the anti-abortion activists do evangelize, but in most cases it is merely an after-thought to religiously validate their hatred for the murder of unborn babies. Were this not the case, they would not platform men who have no relationship with Jesus Christ whatsoever. They would not platform women who openly practice idolatry by worshipping Mary. What they have really done is conveniently (and religiously) fit Jesus Christ into their anti-abortion political activism. Their spirit is a Zealot spirit and they are so zealous that they have compromised their spiritual values in order to see the slaughter stopped. II Cor. 6:14 says, "Do not be bound together with unbelievers; for what partnership have righteousness and lawlessness, or what fellowship has light with darkness?"

We have Christian Activists today who truly believe that the answer to the very real threat of Communism taking control of our nation and the Muslim onslaught is to spend millions of dollars and millions of man-hours in the political arena for the purpose of getting True Conservatives or even Moderates elected to Congress and thc White House. Some Christians become active in the Republican Party and we are all urged to vote. Strange as it is, we are NOT all urged to be disciples and obey all His commandments! Christians now are a recognizable, organized political force in America—the Religious Right. We Christians now have our Steering Committees, our men of political influence, our candidates, and our own very special brand of political propaganda. Of course, in order to play the political game we have had to make political compromises and join forces with men who act very contrary to the precepts of Christianity and sometimes even contrary to the precepts of common decency. Often we are asked to join forces to overhaul the political and cultural structure of our nation, but we are NOT asked to overhaul the people pleasing Saul Church in America.

We have rightfully been concerned about pornography but we have wrongfully attempted to solve the problem by involving ourselves with congressional committees, demonstrations, signing petitions, organizing boycotts, and other political-religious activities. We have missed the point that Jesus wants to purify the heart from the inside with the Gospel. The essential job of the Church has never been to effect superficial changes by applying political pressure. Jesus never let the people make Him the political leader of the Jews. He said it very clearly to Pilot, "My kingdom is not of this world." Our kingdom is not of this world. We need to focus on the task and privilege of seeing men and women born into the kingdom of God and growing by grace in the teaching of the Word, the whole Word and nothing but the Word. In the kingdom of God, there are the ministries of apostle, prophet, evangelist, pastor and teacher. There is no room for political operatives. Please understand, it is not wrong for Christians to be involved in the political process, but it is wrong for the Church to shift the emphasis from the spiritual to the political.

All of the aforementioned problems indicate quite graphically the terrible plummet of morality and spirituality in America. We look back to the seventeenth, eighteenth, and nineteenth centuries, and we see written on many pages of history the influence of Jesus Christ and His people. We desire so much to gain back for Him what has been lost. We desire to see the Re-Christianization of our nation. But we haven't really asked God if this is in His plan. We have missed the point of Scripture.

The Moral Majority was an alliance of people coming from various backgrounds; particularly from the Judeo-Christian heritage in America. The group was to be, at least in part, a political power base to affect change with regard to the influence of Communism and Humanism and to abolish abortion and pornography. The Moral Majority as a titled group no longer exists, but the moral majority as a mentality does exist. This way of thinking is an affront to the Blood of Jesus Christ. God has NEVER LOOKED FOR nor DESIRED a merely *moral majority*. He has ALWAYS sought out a *HOLY REMNANT* FOR HIMSELF! Morality is something that can be experienced in a culture without any Christian influence whatsoever. In heathen Asian cultures there is much more respect for parents and the elderly than there is in our culture. Thievery and violence when compared to America are much less evident. These cultures are hard working, diligent, comparatively honest, and by American standards, relatively chaste; but they are not Christians. Morality can easily be experienced without Jesus Christ. It is essentially a quality that is for the benefit of the people; it is for man and the society in which he lives, and it is accomplished by man. It is essentially a self-justifying concept that succeeds with group pressure. Moral people feel good or righteous merely on the basis of their adherence to a code. Morality is personal, cultural, or religious law. Holiness is something completely different. Holiness is not based on what you do to satisfy yourself, your culture, your nation or your religion. Holiness can only be experienced and manifested by people who are born again by the HOLY Spirit of God. Holiness is accomplished by the indwelling presence of Jesus Christ. Holiness is never meant to satisfy nor please a person, culture, nation or religion. Holiness is to satisfy God Himself. Holiness then is for God alone, and accomplished by God alone. Morality is BY man and FOR man; Holiness is BY God and FOR God. The Saul Church wants to change society through legislation and to create a good moral atmosphere. They don't understand that they have missed the point. God is creating a Spiritual kingdom for Himself. The great tragedy of Christian activism is that we have taken away time, thought and energy from building this Holy Spiritual Kingdom. We are involved in this moral battle because we don't seem to realize that we wrestle not against flesh and blood, but against powers and principalities in high places. If we are to win the spiritual battle, it is because we have decided to live and die for the Word of God by the power of His Spirit. England was changed because the hearts of her people were changed. They had NEW natures that loved holiness and hated sin. The spirit of love, holiness, forgiveness and conviction of sin swept through England and America in the First Great Awakening through the preaching, praying and supernatural obedience of George Whitfield, Jonathan Edwards, the Wesleys and others.

We cannot Christianize the Congress, the Supreme Court, the Presidency, or the laws and decisions that come from these powerful institutions. True Christianity is not the imposition of power on ANY body of influence. The Religious Right, functioning as a political force supposedly ordained by God to fight against the evil of the corrupt majority, is no more spiritual than the Zealots who fought against the tyranny of Rome. These men would not recognize that their bondage came from their sin and their misunderstanding of Scripture. They

HAD TO DO SOMETHING. They truly felt that if they took the initiative to fight the Romans that God would join them in their battle and they would win because God was on their side. They did not understand that the reason they were oppressed was because they, as a nation, had for years and years selfishly chosen to go their own religious way regardless of what the Lord had commanded them and ultimately they chose to REJECT their Messiah, Jesus. Their political involvement was not a natural outgrowth of the culture that had been permeated by an understanding of God's ways and an anticipation and reception of Messiah. Their political involvement was an attempt to overthrow the rule of their oppressors. Many centuries later, we see that the Gospel of Jesus Christ so permeated the American culture that America eventually became the most powerful national progenitor of the Gospel of Jesus Christ in the history of mankind. Even her political system was permeated by many Christians, and Christians in a naturally supernatural way assumed office because many of the people in the nation were God fearing Christians. It was accomplished by the pure Gospel of Jesus Christ changing MANY hearts for God.

When we do our job of making men spiritual, our city or our state or our country will, because the people have new hearts, also have new values. We will have leavened our nation, state or city with the righteousness of Christ in the hearts of born again people. Because they are truly born again, they will have a desire to obey God and see His justice reign in our nation. Then the culture will change radically. The problem with the Christian activist is that he is more concerned with the manifestation of immorality or morality than he is with the hearts of the men and women in his culture. The abuses of slavery and slavery itself eventually disappeared in 19th century England because the hearts of men had been changed by the Gospel call "You must be born again." The first Great Awakening occurred in the 18th century under the ministry of Whitfield, the Wesleys and others. George Whitfield, however, was NOT against slavery and never preached against slavery. In America today, we desire to see the fruits of revival without revival happening in the Church. It is always the Church that becomes strong and then because so many hearts have been touched and changed, the nation becomes strong. We Christians are the only Spiritual leaven that exists in ANY nation. If we are trusting in, living and preaching the Word, the whole Word and nothing but the Word, by the power of Almighty God's Holy Spirit the nation WILL be leavened for righteousness and good, and many will be birthed into the kingdom of God. Justice, mercy, love and obedience to God will be reestablished, not by which party is in the White House but by the fact that God, through Jesus Christ and the power of His Holy Spirit, rules in the hearts of many people and the people will settle for nothing less than honest righteous political parties.

When the true Gospel reigns in the hearts of the people, ANY nation will be strengthen by God. It is no coincidence that when the nations of Spain, Italy and France rejected Reformation truth in the 16th century, they were weakened politically, militarily and morally and were soon no longer super powers in the world as they once had been. After England had been immersed in the Great Awakening of the 18th century, she became the most powerful nation on the planet in the 19th century. The Church of Jesus Christ in America preached the uncompromising Gospel, from the time of the Puritans through the time of the holiness preachers in the 19th century. After this great time of the Word and the Spirit, America reaped the benefits and became the most powerful country in the world in the 20th century. Because the Church has neglected the true Gospel and made up a message that pleases the carnal hearts of the people, our country has been weakened tremendously. Eventually, we will lose our leadership in the world and be judged SEVERELY by God. It will not be enough for us to support moral men for public office. Christians have entered the political arena and have attempted to legislate morality in a country that has come to hate the morality of the Scriptures. Religious activism in the current moral, cultural and political arenas will not accomplish the strengthening of a nation. We must first strengthen the message, the messengers, the people of God and the Church that represent Jesus Christ in America.

It is not enough to pray for revival! We must first pray that God would cleanse OUR hearts and OUR doctrines from all the idolatry that we have embraced. We must pray that God will give us, His own people, a spirit of REPENTANCE! Only then will we see the move of God that we so desperately need in America. The Saul Church in America will continue to see our nation given over to godless liberals and eventually to godless conservatives because we have not humbled ourselves, repented of OUR sins and asked God to change His Holy Nation. We Christians ARE His Holy Nation, NOT America! The people of God,

God's Holy Nation, is the land that needs to be healed because it has a divided heart.

"But you are a chosen race, a royal priesthood, A HOLY NATION, a people for God's own possession…for you once were not a people but now you are THE PEOPLE OF GOD…" (I Peter 2:9-10). "If MY PEOPLE which are called by my name, shall HUMBLE THEMSELVES, and pray, and seek my face, and TURN FROM THEIR WICKED WAYS; then will I hear from heaven, and will forgive their sin, and will HEAL THEIR LAND" (II Chron 7:14 KJV).

The *LAND* spoken of here is the holy nation of God's people. It is not the place or country where God's people happen to live. This prayer was not meant that when the Jews lived in Babylon they were to pray that the Babylonians would turn from their wicked ways and repent of their sins. It was the Jewish people that needed to pray, humble themselves, seek His face and turn away from *THEIR* wicked ways! Then and only then would God forgive their sin and make them a strong spiritual people and heal their land/nation!

The Holy Nation of God's people need to change before the secular nation of America will change! When we change, then and only then will we leaven the nation with the righteousness of Christ and then and only then will the people of America have new hearts that are able to obey the call of God and the commands of God. Our prayers must be directed at changing the people of God, not the godless sinners that have so much influence in the United States. Religious activists do not recognize that the Church has monumental influence and responsibility regarding the condition of the country in which it dwells. Religious activists want to change the worldly system without changing the hearts of its people.

The Evangelicals and the Charismatics, the people who believe that you must be born-again, have failed in their responsibility. We are quick to rally Christians to vote, either for leaders or for laws. We are slow to gather Christians to repent of our accommodation to the world, our shallowness and our wholesale editing of the Word of God. We are slow to repent of our lukewarmness. We have hearts more like Saul than David. Saul was successful for a season but ultimately all who followed him and supported him were defeated in their final battle against the Philistine gentiles.

The religious right and the Saul Church activists are trying to impose spiritual and moral values on a culture that no longer is permeated by the Gospel of Jesus Christ (such as the United States of America was in the eighteenth and nineteenth centuries); their political involvement has been merely an imposition of religious values on a culture that for the most part has no heart for Jesus.

There is a way to attack terrible social evils as a Christian. The Salvation Army under General Booth reclaimed many wasted lives for Jesus Christ. Teen Challenge has been able to free tens of thousands of people from drugs, alcoholism, sexual perversion, gangs and ghetto poverty. Both have been shining examples of Gospel activism. Each organization's burden was to preach Jesus Christ and Him crucified. This was their message. This was their method. They were not political or social activists. They were obedient to the Lord and were not for the most part pushed into a lot of useless and disobedient religious activity by the very real and pressing needs they observed; and they did not join with the State and become compromised. As these organizations have lived and burned with the Gospel message, they have given birth to preachers of the Gospel of Jesus Christ, not religious social workers.

The Saul Church desperately desires political influence. The Saul Church desperately desires to rule and reign in the social, economic, and political sphere. If they were alive during the time of the disciples, they might well have had the same mentality that the disciples had BEFORE they were filled with the Holy Spirit of Jesus Christ. They would have asked Jesus, with a certain amount of personal interest, when He was going to establish His Kingdom. They would have been looking to make Jesus King of the Jews, then Emperor of Rome. John 6:15 says, "Jesus therefore perceiving that they were intending to come and take Him by force, to make Him a king, withdrew again to the mountain by Himself alone." And John 18:36 says, ""Jesus answered, "My kingdom is not of this world. If My kingdom were of this world, then My servants would be fighting, that I might not be delivered up to the Jews; but as it is, My kingdom is not of this world..""

They would have been looking forward to the power that they themselves personally could wield in the Roman Senate or perhaps even the ecclesiastical realm as leaders of the Sanhedrin. They would have been coveting control over the courts of Rome so that justice and mercy could prevail and the terrible crimes of infanticide, pornography and idolatry could be wiped out. But REMEMBER! This was the mentality of God's people BEFORE they received the out-pouring of the Holy Spirit. After they were filled with God's presence and power and baptized in His Holy Spirit, they understood what Jesus had been saying all along. They understood that HE is the Kingdom of God and that HE dwells in them. They understood that it does not matter who rules on the outside, it only matters who rules on the inside. The zealot spirit that so desperately wanted social change and political influence was burned out of their minds by the Tongues of Fire that rested upon their heads and changed their hearts and filled their beings with a new revelation of the Kingdom of God. They understood that the Gospel could be preached both in a country that chose to give them limited freedom or a country that chose to persecute them to the death. They understood the most important issue was not whether or not babies were allowed to be born, but whether or not people became truly born again. It is not that their hearts did not go out to the slaughtered children or the people who were bound by lust because of the impurity of their generation; it is not that their hearts did not go out to the terrible victims of a demonically unjust and ruthless government, it is just that they understood the real issue that was to dominate their entire attention: loving the Lord Jesus Christ so much that they were compelled to preach the unadorned Gospel of Jesus Christ and Him Crucified. They would not be side-tracked into comparatively useless religious activity. We must learn again the lessons of those who were thus filled with the love of God and had the mind of Christ. They knew that nothing permanent would be accomplished by imposing their good and holy desires on a recalcitrant majority. If society was going to change, it was going to be because their hearts were different. If laws were going to correspond to the law of God, it would be because the law of God was written on the hearts of the people.

EVEN NOW God is clearly revealing to us, in no uncertain terms, that we CANNOT trust in the Democrat or Republican Party to fix the ills of this country. One party is unabashedly evil and the other is pathetically weak and afraid of offending both our perceived friends and at times even our enemies. NEITHER will EVER be able to restore true goodness to our country. That responsibility can only be accomplished by the people of God as they once again realize that their kingdom is not of this world. They must also know that their fight is against powers and principalities in high places, and their weapon is the Word of God. Their power to destroy the enemy, whether it is the ACLU or the demons that back similar anti-Christ organizations, is the power of the Holy Spirit.

CHAPTER 8

RELIGIOUS CORRECTNESS

1. The definition, examples and agenda of Political Correctness
2. The definition and agenda of Religious Correctness
3. Examples & Dangers of Religious Correctness
4. Defeating Religious Correctness

DEFINITION, Examples & Agenda of Political Correctness:

In order to understand Religious Correctness, as I am using the term, we must also understand Political Correctness. Political Correctness is a group of both written and unwritten ideas, definitions of words and redefinitions of words that are used to establish a code of conduct and a way of thinking that all people in the culture must adhere to or suffer painful penalties. However, if one does adhere to Political Correctness, the culture is quick to grant liberal rewards and great opportunity for advancement either politically or practically. In politics and culture Political Correctness came to replace the term "party line" that was popular in radical American politics up to the 1980's. The party referred to was the Communist Party. An important aspect of the "party line" was the proper use of words. Even then it was important to vilify "capitalists and the rich." Even today the liberals encourage us to use appropriate left wing terminology and discourage us from using "inappropriate" outdated and offensive language.

When I became a Christian in the Berkeley, California area in 1969 I was quite surprised that the views that I had previously held were almost totally against the Scriptures. This was because the left wing organizations that I was involved with taught us unscriptural and anti-scriptural principles.

The party line taught hatred for the law of God. Two principles that I heard many times were: 1) the ultimate goal of communism was anarchy or lawlessness and 2) religion was the opiate of the people. Their cultural and political views were almost COMPLETELY against God's Word and Christianity. The party line that I had learned seemed to support EVERYTHING that was against Scripture and HATE everything that was in Scripture.

Later in the 1980's or 90's the term "party line" began to go out of fashion. The term "Politically Correct" supplanted the older term. Over the decades following I came to learn that what was true of the term party line was also true of the term Political Correctness. At its heart both concepts are essentially Anti-Christ. Both phrases come from Marxism/Communism which is essentially Anti-Christ. As most of us know, Communism is dead set against Christianity and the Scriptures.

Most of us have a fairly good idea of what is Politically Correct and politically incorrect. For example, it is Politically Correct to call people of the Negroid race African Americans or People of Color. It is now incorrect to call them Negroes. It is politically incorrect to name your sports team anything to do with Native American people. For example names such as the Cleveland Indians, the Atlanta Braves or Florida State Seminoles are now politically incorrect. It is Politically Correct to look at criminals as victims of society or even more Politically Correct to recognize criminals as victims of capitalism or the rich. There is a Politically Correct way to respond to Christians. There is a Politically Correct way to treat or to view women. Because of the influence of feminism in the media and on the college campus, we no longer refer to the head of a committee as "chairman" rather the head is to be called "chairperson." Political Correctness even has a handicap system to level the playing field. From an employer's standpoint, it is economically advantageous to hire women and people of color. However, it must be noted that if a woman of any color exhibits a Christian, conservative, or capitalist view, she is essentially disqualified from receiving preferential treatment.

Another aspect of Political Correctness, as was earlier alluded to is the twisting and redefinition of terms and the removal of words that represented the "old" order. It is also important if one is to be Politically Correct to use new words or use different words, which speak of different concepts to replace the words of the old order. The impact of certain terms has been changed significantly by Political Correctness. As was earlier mentioned, we cringe when someone is referred to as a Negro. Terms such as the "rich" and "capitalist" have come to have a negative connotation in America. Both the rich and capitalists are people that we cannot trust. Much of Political Correctness has as its goal the over sensitization of people, and the creation of dissatisfaction with the present old fashioned male dominated puritanical capitalistic rulership that needs to be overthrown. Women in general and many racial and national groups have become extremely sensitive about what they are called by other people and how they are to be treated.

Women are particularly sensitive regarding their role as abused servants in the marriage relationship and how motherhood has become just another shackle so they can be kept down. To be fair, in the last few years, many left wing Hollywood movie actresses have made it clear that Motherhood is good. For a while in America the term Ms. had supplanted the terms "Miss or Mrs." by some in our culture. At that same time many women chose to either cast off the last names they had been given by their husbands and use their maiden names or use a hyphenated name that included both their last name and their husband's last name. Some women expected their husbands to also use the hyphenated name.

The reason feminism is such an important issue in Political Correctness is because the Scriptures, especially the New Testament, have such a unique view regarding the place of women in the marriage relationship. Heathen religions typically have not protected women in the marriage relationship. Often they are just slaves of their husbands. In some heathen religions, however, women are inordinately elevated as objects of reverence. In the Bible we see Baal worship which denigrates women and Ashtorah worship which both elevates and perverts women. The Christian view of women in the marriage relationship is that they are to be subject to their husbands, but the husband is commanded by God to love his wife as Christ loves the Church.

Satan's perversion of the Christian view of the roles of men and women in the marriage relationship has greatly harmed the American family and especially the Church of Jesus Christ in America. The politically correct among us have called for the wife to reject the Scriptures which say that she is submit herself to her husband as her head. The Scriptures teach that the husband is to be the head of the wife has been mocked and vilified by them because these notions were said to be old fashioned and the products of a male dominated culture. Satan has successfully used these views to pervert the Scriptural view of marriage and family.

Political Correctness also has popularized terms to describe perverse sexual behavior in a positive light. Homosexuals are called "Gay." Criminals are not sinners but victims. Drunkenness is not a sin; it is relabeled "alcoholism" and is referred to as a disease. Homosexuality is not a sin; it is an alternative lifestyle. This twisting and redefinition of terms has done great damage to our culture. Much of what I have mentioned here tends towards a lawless attitude. The dictum and teachings of God's law in the Scriptures are essentially politically incorrect. Much of Political Correctness is also against the Person of Jesus Christ.

Satan has used Political Correctness to partially eliminate the Name of Jesus Christ from our buildings, our language and our thinking. Political correctness dictates that we give more than equal attention to all other religions. Multiculturalism has been used as a platform to sympathetically introduce children to religions such as Hinduism, Mohammedism, Animism and Wicca. Multiculturalism is really ultimately about giving attention to all religions except Christianity. Multiculturalism says that it is unfair to only worship Jesus Christ. We must respect and honor all other religions and their gods. This, of course, completely ignores the fact that the overwhelmingly predominant religion of the United States for hundreds of years has been the Christianity of the Protestant Reformation. These other religions have been used in the government schools supposedly to help explain culture. However, these same government schools will not even allow the majority religion (Christianity) to be represented. Even terms like "Merry Christmas" are deemed unacceptable. As we all know, "Happy Holidays" is the appropriate Politically Correct term to use. This term too may eventually be discarded when they discover that the original meaning of HOLIDAYS was Holy-Days.

If the Person of Jesus Christ is to be discussed on most television programs, He is discussed in terms that challenge the Scriptures and greatly weaken or destroy His divinity. Satan has used the government schools, the educational system, the culture and the media to pervert the Person and the ministry of Jesus Christ as it is revealed and expounded in the New Testament. By doing so, he has even created doubt in the minds of church attendees as to who He is and what He has called us to do. If looked at closely, it is very evident that Satan is the innovator and initiator of Political Correctness in the culture of America.

Satan's ultimate agenda of Political Correctness is not merely to weaken the culture. His true goal is the weakening of the Church of Jesus Christ. When the Church becomes weak and worldly, it is powerless to fight off the will of the enemy and the establishment of his kingdom in America and on this earth. First he must break down the culture and its Christian foundation through the courts, the political process, the educational systems and the media. In the media, while it is Politically Correct to depict witches and warlocks as being enemies of evil and friends of mankind; it is also Politically Correct to depict Christians who believe in the Scriptures as being either very stupid or very evil and by implication their God, Jesus Christ, is essentially depicted as either a false god, an evil influence or merely a weak person.

After Satan has polluted and permeated the culture with attitudes and actions that break down God's law and sully the reputation and Name of Jesus Christ, he then is ready to further subvert and weaken the Church as well. He can only do this if the Church has close ties with and desires to be acceptable to the culture and the world in which it lives. The world is already in Satan's hands but he will use the world to neutralize the power of God's people. He can do this the same way he has done in other countries: by the subtle altering of the Church's doctrine and practices. In the Old Testament Satan knew that God's people could only be defeated if they became a spiritually compromised people. He knew that then God would judge them for their sins. Because of this knowledge, he attempted to compromise them by the importation to Israel of heathen women who practiced idolatry. He knew if the Israelites fell to this temptation, married them and subsequently worshiped the gods of their wives along with worshipping Jehovah, then God would have to judge them. So today, Satan is tempting the Church with adulterous and idolatrous imagery and verbiage through the media and educational system. It is the Church's duty to separate herself from these evil practices. However, in fact, we have succumbed to these temptations and committed spiritual adultery.

Israel was eventually destroyed as a nation because she became idolatrous. Satan has used the tolerance and acceptance of other religions to tempt religiously correct Christians. He is tempting them to become tolerant of such cults as the Roman Catholic Church and Mormanism, two of our staunchest allies in the culture wars. If the Church does not fall on its face and repent of its failure to stand strong against the temptations of our culture, America will eventually be destroyed as a country. If America falls, it will be primarily because the Church has become so weak that it will not be able to stave off the attacks of Satan any longer. The God approved Church is the only organization that can successfully fend off and defeat the Enemy that wants to destroy America. As early as the 1940's and 50's, two great men of God, Leonard Ravenhill and A. W. Tozer warned the Church in America regarding how deeply she had fallen into compromise. <u>Why Revival Tarries</u> by Leonard Ravenhill is MUST reading for our generation! Many books, including <u>The Root of the Righteous</u> and <u>The Pursuit of God</u> by A. W. Tozer are equally recommended.

If Satan can twist and pervert the roles of men and women in the culture, the family or the Church he will successfully weakened the culture, the family and the Church. We must understand that even as the people of God in the Old Testament were weakened and punished severely, so the Church in America will be weakened and punished severely if it does not stand against the arguments and temptations of the enemy. Political Correctness and Religious Correctness are Satan's two most successful ways to weaken and destroy the United States of America and weaken and damage greatly the Church of Jesus Christ in America.

DEFINITION & AGENDA OF RELIGIOUS CORRECTNESS:

Some liberals use the term "Religious Correctness" to describe beliefs and activities of Christian Conservatives that are against the agenda of the Left. I am NOT using the term in this way. The Religious

Correctness that I am referring to is an outgrowth of the Political Correctness of the Left, but is practiced by people who would identify themselves as Evangelicals and/or Charismatics. This Religious Correctness however, is not spiritual and not scriptural.

In the religious culture of Evangelicals and Charismatics Religious Correctness is ultimately a more damaging influence than Political Correctness. As Political Correctness has a political and cultural agenda in mind, so Religious Correctness has a spiritual agenda in mind. Inadvertently many in the Saul Church today have fallen into the same blind obedience that has affected the adherents of Political Correctness.

Religious Correctness is often a group of written or unwritten ideas, words, or thoughts that are used to establish a code of conduct, or party line, that all must adhere to or suffer painful penalties. However, if one does adhere to Religious Correctness, the Church is quick to grant liberal rewards and great opportunity for advancement. As in Political Correctness there is an attempt to change conduct and ways of thinking in the body of Christ by, among other things, redefining, renaming and using terms or words in ways not used before.

The agenda of the Religiously Correct Church is much like that of Israel during the time of Samuel and Saul. The Israelites sincerely believed and felt it was necessary that they should have rulership that would help them to be like the nations. They felt it was necessary to be like the nations so that they could defeat the nations. Eventually they had their prayers answered, and God sent them a man after their own heart who did everything he could to be everything they wanted him to be. He chose the best things of the world for the purposes of worship and for the purposes of warfare. The Religiously Correct Church is doing the same thing. They are choosing the best of Political Correctness so they can have huge Churches with lots of people. They compromise doctrines so that they can add to their numbers, because they are afraid that if they don't, then people will never attend their church to hear their gospel preached or the people will leave. The Religiously Correct Church is the modern day counterpart of Israel under Saul. This Saul Church, like its namesake, WILL be defeated by the modern day Philistines that they looked to for new ideas and new methodology.

EXAMPLES OF RELIGIOUS CORRECTNESS:

The following are examples of words that have been introduced into the Christian vocabulary or have been redefined by those who adhere to the Religiously Correct viewpoint.

DOCTRINE:

This term has fallen into disrepute by the Religiously Correct. Particularly in the Charismatic Movement we have associated the term doctrine with tedious interpretations of the Word of God that are either unclear or unimportant because they are not basic to salvation. I have heard men say, "I don't teach doctrine, I just teach the Scriptures" as if doctrine was the faulty or overly complex interpretation of Scripture. The teaching of sound doctrine is considered extremely important by the Scriptures. Doctrine essentially means "teaching." I have heard other preachers or pastors say, "I don't believe doctrine is important; I teach relationship rather than religion." Today most Christians don't know what Scripture says about justification, sanctification, redemption or election. In fact, these words are fast falling out of use with most preachers and church goers alike. Most church goers are not familiar with biblical repentance, biblical discipleship, God's grace or even proper use of the law. What they have been taught is the need for unity with all religions that identify themselves as Christian, the importance of balance, how to get in touch with your feminine side, the need for a healthy and high sense of self-esteem, the need to have a covering, the importance of not "touching the Lord's anointed", warnings of being divisive and the importance of not judging others or even others judging them. To a large extent we have integrated the doctrines of Scripture with the philosophies of men. Of course, there are some great Churches that cover fundamental doctrines and teach appropriate application. I believe however, that for every Church that teaches solid doctrine there are at least twenty that do not do so. Most churches feel that the teaching of doctrine should be minimal. They are concerned that teaching too much doctrine might have a divisive effect on the congregation.

JUDGMENT:

Judgment is a touchy subject with the Religiously Correct. First of all, they have all heard about the preacher who beats his sheep up with threats of fire and brimstone. These messages are deemed inappropriate in the enlightened 21st century Church atmosphere. It is much more civilized to draw people to God with His love in a positive manner. I have even heard preachers refer to the Old Testament God of wrath and the New Testament God of love—as if God changed or grew or evolved.

The term judgment now is a negative term that is used only when dealing with people outside the Church. Final judgment and hell are usually referred to in passing but not as the major topic in a speaker's message. Everyone assumes that when someone preaches that America will be judged, it is only because of the damage done by the liberals, the Hollywood Left and the media elite.

The Church in America according to these people may "suffer for righteousness sake" but is in no real danger of being judged or punished by God for their sin or poor doctrine. The evangelical and charismatic Churches in America have a VERY high sense of self-esteem. When a prophetic message comes forth that warns the Church that it will be judged by God if it does not repent of its sin, that message is typically thought to be a manifestation of "the spirit of condemnation."

There is a frightening confidence and a blind braggadocio that is content to talk about the millions of converts, the HUGE churches, impressive outreach movements and the tremendous "growth" of charismatic and evangelical churches in America. The Church views itself as quite wealthy. One denomination almost casually discussed the quarter billion dollar sale they made of their radio station. The churches in America have indeed become very wealthy and confident that it is preaching the true gospel because of the great financial blessings they have received. In one sense, many believe that God is "confirming their message or word" by blessing them with large numbers of people and/or lots of money.

However, the Scriptures say, "I know your deeds, that you neither cold nor hot; I wish that you were either cold or hot. So because you are lukewarm, and neither hot nor cold, I will spit you out of My mouth.

Because you say, "I am rich, and have become wealthy and have need of nothing," and you do not know that you are wretched and miserable and poor and blind and naked, I advise you to buy from Me gold refined by fire so that you may become rich, and white garments so that you may clothe yourself, and the shame of your nakedness will not be revealed; and eye salve to anoint your eyes so that you may see. Those whom I love, I reprove and discipline; therefore be zealous and repent." Rev 3:15-19.

DIVISIVE:

This term applies to anyone who disagrees with the leadership regarding conduct or doctrine. Even if the concerned person merely wants to discuss the issues in private, often it is considered inappropriate to do so. The suggestion of leadership often takes the form of "if you don't agree with us, perhaps you should think about joining another Church." There seems to be no room for discussing the issues from a biblical viewpoint in the Religiously Correct Church. Gone are days when men would feel comfortable listening to a divergent viewpoint, and considering it from the standpoint of Scripture. The Scripture that is quoted is "mark them that cause division." This new application of the word is a tremendous tool of Satan to keep anyone from repenting or moving into greater light. Every revival or reformation in the last 500 years has been marked by men who questioned the conduct or the doctrine of current leadership. Martin Luther never wanted to leave the Catholic Church. He wanted the Catholic Church to leave the foul practices and doctrines of the Dark Ages. George Whitfield and John Wesley never wanted to leave the Church of England in the eighteenth century. They wanted the Anglican Church to embrace scriptural concepts such as "you must be born again." This view that identifies as divisive any man who disagrees with the conduct or doctrine of a Church, will most certainly keep that Church from experiencing great revival or reformation.

HARSH:

The Religiously Correct will apply this term to anyone in authority who raises their voice to someone under them. Particularly in reference to family matters. If a mother or father raises their voice in correcting their child, this is considered harsh and the prevailing attitude is that this will cause the child to be injured psychologically or spiritually. If a preacher raises his voice in criticism to activities that his hearers have committed, he will be judged as harsh. Jesus, of course, was harsh in His vocabulary and likely His tone, when He pronounced the seven Woes against the Scribes and the Pharisees. It is never appropriate to harangue or berate people especially our spouses or children, but there is a time for more volume and to speak in a tone of urgency or deep disfavor. The Religiously Correct are highly sensitive regarding the reception of criticism and will find a way of invalidating that criticism by referring to that criticism as harsh.

VERBALLY ABUSIVE:

This term is often used of men by Religiously Correct women as grounds for divorce. The Religiously Correct have added abuse, either verbal or physical, as grounds for divorce. The victim of verbal abuse, either real or imaginary, tends to define any negative comment as verbal abuse. Worse, they can stir up the potential abuse with soft spoken insults so that he or she will respond in a loud or inappropriate fashion. The needling of a person to illicit a sinful verbal or physical response should be taken into account when evaluating the respective guilt or innocence of either party. This has become one of Satan's greatest tools in the dissolution of marriages and the attendant suffering of children. It is worth noting that Scripture does not condone divorce on the grounds of such abuse.

COVERING:

Covering is a relatively latter day concept. This term although used earlier probably became popular in the early 1970's when it was taught that every sheep needed a shepherd, and every shepherd needed a covering ministry to whom he was accountable. This "covering" doctrine typically meant that one could not be ministering in obedience to the Lord except he be submitted or under another man of God or ministry. By doing so, he was protected from the enemy and the world by this covering of authority.

This doctrine of "covering ministry" has now reached the status of being Religiously Correct. In practically all of the Charismatic movement and in many Evangelical churches, this concept is accepted as Biblical.

The term covering, as it relates to our discussion, is only used once in the New Testament-- 1Cor 11:15 says, "...her hair is given to her for a covering." (NAS) This Scripture may possibly have some symbolic reference to the husband's authority over the wife, but there is no Scripture in the Bible that would defend the term "covering" to indicate that every legitimate ministry must be established under a man or a Church's authority. Neither are there any Scriptures that indicate that a man or a Church's authority will protect another ministry. 1 Cor 11:3 says, "Christ is the head of every man..." It does not suggest that every man needs a denomination or another minister to be his head or his covering if he is a man of God or a minister for the Lord. The Religiously Correct feel very uncomfortable with ministries that are not supervised or ministries that are not "accountable" to someone (accountability will be discussed in the next section). If the Religiously Correct are using this term to indicate Scriptural authority, accountability or protection, then that authority, accountability or protection would be in one way supplanting Christ as the Head of every man.

Historically speaking, the Roman Catholic Church taught that all Christians should be under their authority or covering. Even in 18th century, the Church of England believed that the circuit riders and preachers under both Whitfield and Wesley, because they were not authorized by the Church of England (under their covering and authority), were not really authorized by God.

In the Scriptures, Jesus and His disciples were vilified and even murdered because they would not directly submit to the authority of the rulers of Israel.

The covering doctrine is another example of elevating men and denigrating the authority of Jesus Christ in a man's life. Men in general and ministering men in particular, must learn to establish a personal relationship with Jesus Christ without ANY mediator or covering. They must also learn to depend upon the Scriptures and the Holy Spirit on their own. This does not go against any idea of learning from or listening to another man or ministry, but there are times when a man must go to Jesus without ANY mediator or assistance. By establishing covering as a necessity, we insert a Mediator, and there is no other Mediator between God and man except Jesus Christ. Covering in this sense does not sanction ANYTHING that a man does.

Jesus Christ, His Holy Spirit and the Word of God MUST sanction EVERYTHING that a man does, whether he is a husband or a minister of the Word. This doctrine of covering is not dissimilar to the Roman Catholic doctrine which indicates that every man must be under the Roman Catholic Church and the Pope. Jesus made it clear regarding covering. When His disciples indicated that others were ministering using the name of Jesus Christ, He did not discourage them from doing so: rather Mark 9:38-40 says, "John said to Him, 'Teacher, we saw someone casting out demons in Your name, and we tried to prevent him because he was not following us (he did not have our covering) but Jesus said, 'do not hinder him, for there is no one who will perform a miracle in My name, and be able soon afterward to speak evil of Me. For he who is not against us is for us.'" This makes it abundantly clear that we do not need a group or an individual to be over us so that we can function in obedience to our Lord. It is true that Paul went to Jerusalem to meet with the pillar apostles. That, however, was not so that he could get covering. That was so he could learn from them, fellowship with them and show them what God was doing in his ministry. Many men like Martin Luther, George Whitfield, John Calvin and Charles Finney functioned without covering and still succeeded to bless God, His people and the world.

The covering of any man, whether he is a pastor, prophet or husband is always and only the Lord Jesus Christ. He must be the one that directs him in his activities. He must do what the Father says and the Son confirms by the Holy Spirit. When he enters ministry, when he changes ministry and when he quits ministry. Jesus Christ is the Head of every man. As the man rules his family and ministers to his wife and children, Jesus is his Head. No pastor, divisional superintendent, elder, board member or bishop can instruct him apart from what the Lord tells him. He must be extremely careful not to obey any unscriptural directive that he receives from any of these people. He is responsible to God and NOT to them to interpret, teach and obey the letter and the spirit of Scripture.

ACCOUNTABILITY:

The accountability doctrine has some very good points and can be useful in developing and maintaining character. Like the covering doctrine, however, it has some problems that we need to mention. As was said in the previous section, men must learn to be accountable to the Scriptures and to God in a highly personal way. They must learn to look for all the answers to all their questions in the Scriptures, regarding their family, their job and every other facet of life. They must come to know the Person of Jesus Christ, the Holy Spirit and our heavenly Father by soaking up the Word of God and praying that God would open their eyes and asking Him through Jesus Christ to give them guidance through His Scriptures. When they need a directive concerning a path they should take or a choice they need to make, they should always go to the Lord first. Accountability doctrine can become a way of either lessening a man's relationship with the Lord or expanding his relationship with the Lord. If he learns to go to the Lord and the Scriptures first for help with any temptation or with any decision or with any need to understand His Word, then that is good. If his first choice is usually going to his accountability partner or mentor for help, then that is bad. A good accountability partner or mentor will always guide him to go to the Scriptures and to the Lord Himself first. Prayer partners can be good and accountability relationships can be good, but the other individual must himself be steeped in the Scriptures and not in the wisdom of men. He must be a man that always encourages greater relationship and greater understanding from the Scriptures and God Himself. In the Scriptures God makes it clear that we are always ultimately accountable to Him and Him alone, but He also tells us our need for counselors, ministers and men to come along side us in our struggles with the world, the flesh and the devil. Scripture also directs us to submit to those in the church that have authority over us, but NEVER if their directives or teachings go against the teachings of Scripture.

MUTUAL SUBMISSION:

The mutual submission doctrine was popularized in the Charismatic Movement in the 1960's and 1970's. This doctrine in some of the Charismatic Churches has been around for a long time, but in the 1960's and 1970's this doctrine became widespread. In simple terms, the doctrine says that even as the wife is to be subject to her husband, so the husband is to be subject to his wife. The two Scriptures that supposedly support this argument are found first in Eph 5:21, "…and be subject to one another in the fear of Christ." The other scriptural reference is in Gal 3:28, "There is neither Jew nor Greek, there is neither slave nor free man, there is <u>neither male or female</u>: for you are all one in Christ Jesus."

This interpretation of Scripture was likely helped along by the popularity of the women's movement in America. Early on, women had been fighting for, among other things, equal rights in the voting booth, and won a significant victory with the establishment of the 19th Amendment which allowed them to vote. There also was strong pressure by society to allow women to have a much greater voice in the household regarding family matters. Margaret Sanger, an early advocate of abortion and birth control, published a newspaper called "The Woman Rebel." The masthead of this publication said it ALL: "NO MASTERS, NO GODS!"

By the 1970's movies and television made it clear that men were typically both abusive and ignorant as they led their families. There were still popular images of men as good leaders in such television shows as Little House on the Prairie. But there were an equal number of demeaning male images in such television shows as All in the Family. By the late 1970's the authority of the husband in the family and the marriage relationship was greatly damaged. It was Politically Correct for a woman to be depicted as intellectually and morally superior to her husband. The culture accepted the fact that the husband was NOT to be the head of the wife as Christ is also the Head of the Church, as Eph 5:23 states. The Scripture that says, "as the Church is subject to Christ, so also the wives ought to be to their husbands in everything" (Eph 5:24) was also ignored.

From the 1980's on most fathers and husbands, in both television and the movies, were viewed as weak at best, and often the cause of the family's worst problems. Since then, men have generally been shown to be as immature, having no understanding of the marriage relationship. Typically they are not to be respected because they are not worthy of respect. They are always interested in sex, but never interested in love. The children are held in greater esteem than they are. The wife is much more likely to ask counsel, not from husband, but from her son or daughter regarding an important decision. Men are often depicted as merely little boys in grown up bodies. Even on Christian radio, one advertisement for Mother's Day had the woman saying about her husband, "He is really just one of my children."

The Church remained comparatively unscathed by these views until the 1970's. It was at that time that the Church began to draw more and more of its teaching from secular psychology. As was mentioned before, secular psychology for decades had held a view that marriage was a partnership, and that it was puritanical, old fashioned and harmful to the raising of children to allow the man to have such power over his wife and family. It was at that time that the mutual submission doctrine became popular in the Charismatic Movement. The Church chose to use the Scriptures mentioned earlier to validate the equality of the sexes with regard to authority one over the other ("be subject one to another" and "there is neither male nor female in Christ Jesus"). Looked at in their context, these two Scriptures have nothing to do with mutual submission.

The Scripture in Ephesians which says, "be subject to one another" does not indicate *mutual* submission but *respective* submission: children subject to parents, slaves subject to masters, and wives subject to husbands. Slaves according to Eph 6:5 are to be obedient to their masters (not masters being obedient to slaves) and children are to obey their parents according to Eph 6:1 (parents are not supposed to obey their children). So too, the wife is to be subject to her husband (not the husband to be subject to his wife). The husband's role is tough enough. He is to love his wife like Christ loves the Church.

Gal 3:26-29 says, "For you are all sons of God through faith in Christ Jesus. For all of you who were baptized into Christ have clothed yourselves with Christ. There is neither Jew nor Greek, there is neither slave nor free man, *there is neither male nor female;* for you are all one in Christ Jesus. And if you belong to Christ, then you are Abraham's descendents, heirs according to promise." Spiritually, being a Jew or a Greek, a slave or a free man, a male or a female does not exclude you from His kingdom: we are all heirs of Christ and Abraham's descendents according to God's promise. This does not mean that there are no Jews or Gentiles, slaves or free men, or males or females in the Church. Paul clearly indicates that there are roles in the relationship between masters and slaves and husbands and wives that must be obeyed in Scripture. As a master and a slave obey their respective scriptural directives and as a husband and a wife obey their respective scriptural directives concerning their conduct, they will be equally rewarded in the eternal realm.

The Religiously Correct, however, have completely taken away the authority of the husband as the head of the wife. I have heard it preached that Christ is the Head of both the husband and the wife and the husband had better recognize that, if he wants to have a good relationship with his wife, the implication being that the husband was somehow usurping the authority of Jesus Christ. Typically when reading and teaching the Scriptures in Ephesians most Charismatic pastors and speakers will make sure to mention that the husband should not take advantage of the Scriptures regarding his wife's submission to him. Men are always warned not to make her a "door mat." She too, is exhorted not to let her husband make her a door mat. When the subject of a husband loving his wife like Christ loves the Church is preached, it is usually pointed out that Christ was a servant-leader whose main role was to be a servant to the Church, and consequently, the main role of the husband was to be a servant for his wife. When discussing the husband's responsibility to love his wife like Christ loves the Church, it is NEVER mentioned that a wife should not take advantage of her husband's love for her and service that he is to give her. It is always assumed that it is only the husband that would ever abuse these Scriptures; it is tacitly assumed that the wife would never abuse her husband in that way.

The Scriptures, on the other hand, indicate that the man is the stronger vessel. Actually 1 Peter 3:7 says to husbands "…live with your wives in an understand way as with a WEAKER VESSEL since she is a woman; and grant her honor as a fellow heir of the grace of life, so that your prayers may not be hindered." It is important to note that this setting does not dictate that women should be berated for their weakness; rather they are, among other things, to be treated more delicately because of their weakness. Paul, when discussing ministry in 1 Timothy indicates that one aspect of that weakness is that they are more likely to be deceived than their husbands. He says in I Timothy 2:14, "and it was not Adam who was deceived, but the woman being quite deceived fell into transgression." Because of this Paul according to I Tim 2:12 did not "…allow a woman to teach or exercise authority over a man, but to remain quiet." (I Timothy 2:13 indicates that another reason for this is that Adam was first created and then Eve). God created men to lead and be the head of their wives, not the reverse. Our culture and the Religiously Correct teachers of the Church make it clear that they consider the woman to be at least equal with the man and in some ways even superior. A prominent conservative Bible teacher on the radio when preaching on prayer said "that there are no stronger prayers than those of a mother for her children." He then went on to expound at great length that a mother was actually emotionally and spiritually more equipped to pray for her children than her husband. He discussed how difficult life was for him after his mother died and he no longer was the recipient of her prayers. Scripturally we see very few if any examples of a woman's prayer for her children, but we see Jacob praying for his sons. Scripture in no way indicates that a mother's prayers are superior or inferior to her husband's.

Often the scriptural descriptions of a woman's comparative weakness, and the scriptural directive to submit to her husband are dismissed as the result of the culture that the apostles lived in and would not apply today. This is a direct attack on the reliability of the Scriptures. Any Christian generation that goes against these clear teachings in Scripture will be terribly weakened and eventually easily defeated.

INTUITION:

In the Religiously Correct Church of today women are reputed to have more intuition than men. This is a cultural myth that many people accept, but the word intuition is kind of a vague word at best. In this context does it mean more spiritual sensitivity? If that were so, then the preponderance of those who prophecy in the Scriptures would be women, but at least 90% of those who prophesy in the Scriptures are men. Samuel, David, Elijah, Elisha, Isaiah, Jeremiah, Ezekiel, Daniel, and all those mentioned in the minor prophets, Jesus, Agabus, John the Revelator and many other men in Scripture were all counted as prophets. Deborah was a prophetess in the Old Testament, Anna was a prophetess at the time of Jesus' birth and before, and Philip had daughters who also were prophetesses. This is not to discount the fact that women were included in the exhortation to prophesy in I Cor 14:1, "pursue love, yet desire earnestly spiritual gifts, but especially that you may prophesy." More compelling is Acts 2:17, "...your SONS AND YOUR DAUGHTERS shall prophesy..." However, there is NO INDICATION in ANY area of Scripture that women are either naturally or supernaturally superior to men in their ability to know the voice of God and speak it forth. In fact there is evidence in Scripture to indicate that even before the fall women were more likely than men to not hear correctly and to be deceived. As was mentioned in the last section, 1 Tim 2:14 says, "And it was not Adam who was deceived, but the woman being quite deceived, fell into transgression." In fact this apparent lack of ability to distinguish the truth from a lie is the fundamental reason why Paul did not "allow a woman to teach or exercise authority over the man…" A woman's "intuition" is nothing more than a fiction of the enemy to elevate the woman's authority above that of the man and turn God's order of authority upside down. As was mentioned earlier however, a woman has the authority of Jesus Christ, Himself, to prophesy a direct Word from God in the Church.

SERVANT-LEADER:

Concerning greatness in the kingdom, Matt 20:25-27 says, "But Jesus called them to Himself and said, 'you know that the rulers of the Gentiles lord it over them, and their great men exercise authority over them. It is not this way among you, but whosoever wishes to become great among you shall be your servant, and whoever wishes to be first among you shall be your slave.'"

In the Scriptures Jesus taught His disciples a great object lesson here. Jesus first said that the Gentile rulers, "lord it over," those under them. He also said that "He who will be servant among you will be the greatest among you." He did this to illustrate that being a good leader, whether you are a husband, a parent, a pastor or a boss, requires that you take good care of those that you lead or have authority over. He did not say this so that those under Him could order Him around or make pointed suggestions as to what He should do or somehow reverse roles with the master or leader. Once again, He did this to show them that a good leader takes good care of those under Him. He did not do this in any way to compromise His own authority or suggest the compromise of the authority of any leader. A husband leads his wife and children by loving her like Christ loves the Church, and loving them as the Father loves us. We must understand that at times this love is manifested in terms of correction or punishment. A good leader never sacrifices his God given authority as head of his wife and father of his children. Instead, he sacrifices his own desires and his own will as he is directed through prayerful reading of the Scriptures and his personal communication with the Lord Jesus Christ. Of course, he is never to "lord it over" those whom he leads. The religiously correct Saul Church implies that leadership involves a kind of servile submission to those whom you lead. Husbands and fathers are never to cast off their God given authority by being pressured to be servants by meeting the perceived needs of a wife or child. He is NEVER to submit to a wife or child because they whine or nag him to do something that he believes is against God's will for them. Their views certainly should be taken into consideration before God, but he is responsible to function on the basis of the authority of the Word of God. On judgment day He will not be able to excuse any action that is not pleasing to God by telling Him that he was only doing what his wife asked or told him to do. Unfortunately the servant-leader teaching has given some Christian women the false assumption that they should expect their husbands to be more responsive to their perceived needs. This in no way means that a husband should neglect treating his wife in a very special way and always do what is necessary to meet her REAL needs.

We must keep in mind that both the husband and the wife are fallen creatures, and at times, will take advantage of one another to serve their own desires. This is not limited to the husband "using his wife as a doormat." The wife, because she too is a fallen creature, can just as easily take advantage of her husband's role as a servant. It is not pleasing to the Lord when the wife takes upon herself the headship of the family and does not reverence and honor her husband as her head. An equally dangerous decision of the husband is to give her headship in the family and expect her to take care of him as Christ takes care of His Church.

The husband is to serve her needs and the needs of his children as the Lord directs him and not necessarily as they desire or even as the pastor or the "Christian" counselor directs him. This is to be done even if his wife and the children out vote him regarding his decision. Scripture does not define the marriage relationship, the family situation or the church as a democracy.

UNITY:

In the 17th chapter of The Gospel According to John, shortly before Jesus and His disciples went to the Garden of Gethsemane, Jesus prayed a prayer to His Father in the hearing of His disciples. Among other things, He prayed about unity. In verse 11 Jesus prays, "…Holy Father, keep them in Your name, the name which You have given Me, that they may be one even as We are." Verses 19-22 say, "For their sake I sanctify Myself, that they themselves also may be sanctified in the truth. I do not ask in behalf of these alone, but for those who also believe in Me through their word; that they may all be one; even as You, Father are in Me and I in You, that they also may be in Us, so that the world may believe that You sent Me. The glory which You have given Me I have given to them, that they may be one, just as We are one; I in them and You in Me, that they may be perfected in unity, so that the world may know that You sent Me, and loved them, even as You have loved Me."

It's important to note that the unity that Jesus is praying for is accomplished solely by the Father. Verse 17-21 says, "Sanctify them in the truth…that they may all be one…" Before they are to be one they must be sanctified in the TRUTH by the Father, and the purpose of this sanctification in the truth is so they may be all one. When they become one, then the result will be that the world may believe that the Father sent Jesus (vs. 21). In verse 22 Jesus says, "The glory which you have given Me, I have given to them that they may be one, just as We are one." Jesus states there clearly, that He gave His own glory to them that the Father gave Him so that His people may be one. He goes on to say in verse 23 that the purpose of them becoming one was so that they would be perfected in unity. And the purpose from the viewpoint of the world was so that the world would know that the Father sent Jesus and loved His disciples even as the Father has loved Jesus.

This oneness is something that is not accomplished by men, but is solely accomplished by our heavenly Father and His Son, Jesus Christ. Men are not able to orchestrate the glory of God. This prayer of our Lord's will most definitely be answered in His time, in His way. This is not a unity or a oneness that will come into being by the machinations of men. We cannot organize or excite ourselves into this unity. We are not even sure who is really His and who is not really His. First we must be sanctified in THE TRUTH and then experience His glory. THEN we will become one, even as He and the Father are one.

The oneness that the Saul Church has attempted to accomplish in the Body of Christ is a false unity or oneness that is not of the Father but is of the flesh. TRUTH has become an unimportant commodity with the Saul Church. There is little concern regarding the truth of Scripture. The Saul Church values unity much more than truth. Calling conferences for the purpose of unifying the Body of Christ is basically of the flesh. Getting tens of thousands of men to meet together in a show of unity at a demonstration or event is of the flesh. Establishing organizations that unite Evangelicals and Roman Catholics is particularly sad. Five hundred years ago the Protestants broke away from the Roman Catholic Church because of their false gospel of faith plus works, their dependence upon penance as a way to deal with sin, their indulgences which released their loved ones from thousands of years of purgatory, their reliance upon Mary as a co-mediatrix, their support of the Pope as the Vicar or earthy representative of Jesus Christ and many other contradictions with Scripture. The Catholic Church still believes and practices and demands the same things that she did five hundred years ago. The Catholic Church is not a group of people with which we should want to be unified. The people of the Catholic Church should be people that we share the true gospel with and do everything that we can to see them come to the Lord Jesus Christ by faith in His shed blood alone. Catholics and Evangelicals Together is not an organization that was founded by the prompting of the Holy Spirit, rather it was an attempt to further an unscriptural unity that will not merely produce no fruit, but in fact will produce very bad fruit. When members of the Catholic Church are sanctified in the truth and when members of the Religiously Correct Evangelicals and Charismatics are sanctified in truth, then we will be on our way to becoming one in Christ.

Another Scripture that many quote as they call for unity in the Body of Christ is from the Book of Acts. Acts 1:14 says, "These all with one mind were continually devoting themselves to prayer, along with the women, and Mary the mother of Jesus, and with His brothers."

It is EXTREMELY important to note that they were "ALL OF ONE MIND." Most, if not all of them, had sat under the teaching of Jesus Christ, Himself, for three years. It is likely that they all believed that He was the Messiah sent from God. It is also important to notice that there were only 120 of them in the Upper Room. Most of the 7,000 who had seen Him miraculously feed them were not there. Of the 500 who watched Him leave in a cloud, less than 25% of them were there. There was no solicitation by the disciples to have a unity conference. There was no cry for the multitudes to come and join in. This was a sovereignly chosen group of people that were in attendance. This group was chosen by our heavenly Father and not one person was missing, and not one too many was present. Once again, this meeting was totally and solely arranged by God, so that these men and women would experience His glory and His sanctification in the truth.

The Saul Church is not unlike the world which rejects and denigrates true Christians who will not recognize the gods of the Hindus, Muslims and Buddhists. The Saul Church does not want to appear narrow minded to other Christian faiths so they do not reject Roman Catholics and in some cases Mormons who preach another Jesus and another Gospel. They no longer agree with Paul who said in Galatians 1:6-12, "I am amazed that you are so quickly deserting Him who called you by the grace of Christ, for a different gospel; which is really not another; only there are some who are disturbing you and want to distort the gospel of Christ. But even if we, or an angel from heaven, should preach to you a gospel contrary to what we have preached to you, he is to be accursed! As we have said before, so I say again now, if any man is preaching to you a gospel contrary to what you received, he is to be accursed! For am I now seeking the favor of men, or of God? Or am I striving to please men? If I were still trying to please men, I would not be a bond-servant of Christ. For I would have you know, brethren, that the gospel which was preached by me is not according to man. For I neither received it from man, nor was I taught it, but I received it through a revelation of Jesus Christ."

The pathetic attempt of men to create unity by solicitation that is not approved by God has accomplished nothing except false hope and failure. The unity they have striven for has not been accomplished and will not be accomplished until God's perfect timing. Not only that, NOTHING in this world will keep that unity from occurring. It is enough for us to preach the pure and total Word of God and to do all that He requires of us and has taught us.

The attempt of the Saul Church to artificially create unity is strikingly similar to the same attempt of The World Council of Churches in the mid 20th century. This organization also is not very concerned about doctrine and wants to unite in spite of our differences, so we can bless the earth with our unity. At one time Charismatics and Evangelicals recognized that this group was not of God. I don't know how they view the World Council of Churches today.

BALANCED:

"Balanced" at one time meant that a man was able to preach judgment and blessing, eternal punishment and eternal rewards, and the ravages of sin and the blessings of holiness. Like other Religiously Correct words the meaning of this word has also changed radically.

Perhaps at one point in Church history, balance meant "balance your total hatred of sin with a total love for God", or "balance your understanding of the use of the law in Scripture with your understanding of the use of grace." But that is not what many proponents of the teaching of balance are teaching us today.

A "balanced man" has come to mean a man who understands and depends upon both the Scriptures and understands and uses the BEST ways of the world. The proponents of this view do not suggest that the Bible is not the answer to man's problems. They firmly believe that it is the answer to our problems. It is just that they say we also need to recognize the importance of the wisdom that the world has to offer. They justify this viewpoint with the phrase, "All truth is God's truth." They take the "best" that psychology and psychiatry have to offer, and then along with the Bible, present balanced Christian counseling. In my undergraduate Christian psychology course my teacher who was a licensed psychiatrist said that Jay Adams, the writer of our class text book, was out of balance and behind the times because he did not incorporate modern psychology and psychiatry into his teachings. As was mentioned earlier, he even said that if Paul the Apostle knew as much as we do about modern psychology, he would have had an even greater ministry.

Later, when I pursued my Master's Degree in seminary, I was chided for my views regarding the writings of Sigmund Freud and Carl Jung. I suggested that their views were confusing, often contradictory to one another and their general theories regarding human behavior were worse than useless. I felt these views were satanic. My teacher felt that I was quite out of balance and did not understand the importance of the teachings of these men and other intellectual giants in the world of psychiatry and psychology. The problem is that what they consider to be the best often contradicts or falls short of Scripture. Balancing secular psychology with biblical counseling often removes the fear of the Lord and promotes a desire to esteem self more highly than others. In fact, securing a high sense of self esteem can replace or discourage meekness, humility and self denial.

The "balanced" man recognizes that one must have understanding of the world to balance his understanding of things spiritual. I have heard dozens of pastors refer to an individual as being "so heavenly minded that he is of no earthly good." This individual is apparently so consumed by his passion for heaven and being with our Lord Jesus Christ that he has become out of touch with day to day living and cannot relate well with the general population. They believe that this type of asceticism would make him an ineffectual witness for the Lord. In the Saul Church, Old Testament prophets, John the Baptist and even Jesus would be considered out of balance.

The "balanced" Christian is supposed to balance his political life with his spiritual life. Many believe and teach that Christians are to blame for the demise of morality, justice and clear political thinking in America because they have not been politically active. They believe that this demise has come about because Christians have not voted enough and have not supported conservative candidates properly. They believe we need to balance our spiritual life with a healthy political life. I firmly believe that many individuals, both Christian and non-Christian, are called to participate in the political and cultural wars that are now being waged. But the Church as an entity is not to commit her energy to politics and the cultural war. We need to do our job, which is to preach Jesus Christ and Him crucified, and to make disciples of all the nations, baptizing them in the name of the Father, and the Son and the Holy Spirit, teaching them to observe all that Jesus commanded. We are *never* to ignore *ANY* perversion of the Scriptures and we must speak out as Christians against the murder of unborn children and the redefinition of sodomy as an alternative lifestyle. He DID NOT, however, command us to be politically involved. We should not feel guilty for majoring on the Word, the whole Word and nothing but the Word.

The balanced man rationalization makes it seem that we are second class if we do not involve ourselves in some way in the political and cultural wars.

The reason we have failed is not because we have failed to support conservative candidates or failed to vote. The reason we have failed is because we have become double-minded like Saul and the people of Israel during his time. Because of our lack of single hearted commitment to the Word of God and the power of the Holy Spirit, we have left a void for Satan to fill and as always, he has done so. We need to focus on our own failure as a representative of Jesus Christ on this earth. Unfortunately, anyone who "sighs and groans over the abominations which are being committed in the midst of Jerusalem (the Church)" (Ezekiel 9:4) is considered radical and way out of balance.

Balance is NOT the issue in Scripture. The issue is COMPLETENESS! Col. 2:10 says, "And in HIM you have been made COMPLETE." Also in Tim 3:16 it says, "All scripture is inspired by God and profitable for teaching, for reproof, for correction, for training in righteousness and IS SUFFICIENT."

DEFEATING RELIGIOUS CORRECTNESS:

The defeat of Religious Correctness will most certainly be difficult and painful. It will cost us as much today as it cost the Protestant reformers in the 16th century. Many were persecuted for righteousness sake, some were killed and ALL were considered ANATHAMA by the Roman Catholic Church.

Until Jesus comes, there will always remain elements of Religious Correctness. There will always be churches that will please men by using the teachings of men that they get from the World and the religions of the World. Even after the Great Reformation of the 16th century was accomplished, the most religiously correct institutions of that time STILL flourished. The Roman Catholic Church lost some ground in northern Europe, but still retained great power in the world system. The Roman Catholic Church was essentially shelved by God as being any kind of vessel for Revival and never dominated Christendom again. Even to this day however, it is considered by some to be the largest denomination in the world. Others, more correctly judge it as being the largest "Christian" cult in the world. So too, the Saul Church is no longer a vessel for real Revival as she has been in the past. The time will come when the David Church will be God's vessel for Revival and a manifestation of His great power and love. This in no way should discourage us from exposing and defeating Religious Correctness in these last generations.

In order to defeat Religious Correctness we must know first of all that it is a weapon of Satan and not merely a cultural aberration. The second thing we must do is start to look for Religious Correctness in our own lives, our own churches and our own denominations. We must NOT assume the attitude that we must not judge ministries as to what they say or what they do. We MUST judge righteous judgment. We must judge false doctrine and false teachers. Third, we must recognize just how dangerous Religious Correctness is and how much it has damaged God's people and our effectiveness against the enemy. Fourth, we must be aware of the fact that Religious Correctness is merely an outgrowth of our desire to please people. All of us want to please people. We all want to fit in, whether we are in high school or whether we are in the ministry. We want our words and our actions to be approved of men because we live in perhaps the most self-conscious and man pleasing of all generations. Our self-consciousness has to do with how we look, how we sound and how we act. If we live a Religiously Correct life we will be most praised by men and least ridiculed by them. In order to defeat Religious Correctness, we must have an entirely different agenda than the Religiously Correct have. For at least the last 200 years of Church history the focus slowly has been shifting from an emphasis on God's desire, God's power, God's sovereignty and His glory to an emphasis on man's desires, man's power and man's needs. We have been taught that if we adhere to a strict regimen of prayer and fasting, and if we gather around us many others, regardless of doctrine and then unite, we will see great culture changing revival. We firmly believe that it is up to us. We have taken the responsibility away from the Lord and we have taken it upon ourselves to save mankind. We have advertised extensively our revivals, we have collected billions of dollars to see the world changed for Jesus Christ and we have changed our clothing, so as not to offend seekers; we have done surveys to determine what they really want, we have toned down our message so as not to offend them, we have drastically altered our doctrine to include many of the beliefs of the world, and if we open our eyes honestly and widely, we can clearly see that the culture in America is further away from Jesus Christ than it has ever been! Accommodating men has NOT worked and NEVER will!

I Chron 7:14 say, "If my people who are called by my name will repent of their sins and cry out to me, then I will heal their land." We have been incorrectly taught that "our land" is the country in which we live (United States of America). WE CHRISTIANS are a HOLY NATION. WE are the PEOPLE OF GOD (I Peter 2:9-10). Our land is the kingdom of God, spiritual Israel, the Church of Jesus Christ. THE CHURCH NEEDS TO BE HEALED of its divided heart; then we will see God move dramatically in our country. We must repent of the grievous sin of pleasing men and not pleasing God. We must re-focus ourselves to understand that even evangelism is not essentially for men and the unsaved; rather evangelism should be for the glory of God; we should witness to people and pray they get saved primarily for God's glory and God's pleasure. We build a church for God's glory and God's pleasure. We hold fellowship dinners for God's glory and God's pleasure. We preach messages for God's glory and God's pleasure. We pray for the sick not just so people will be healed but so God will be glorified. We preach the gospel not just so that people will be saved and not have to go to hell, but for God's glory and God's pleasure. The focus of the Church must once again be upon Jesus Christ. He must be the issue of our salvation, our sanctification, our glorification in heaven and any gift or power that He gives us. We must be a spiritually and scripturally correct people who recognize that the Word of God is sufficient and that God's grace is sufficient, and that the faith that God gives us is sufficient: Sola Scriptura, Sola Gratia, Sola Fida. Everything we have is of God and for God. OF COURSE, we are magnificently blessed and others are magnificently blessed, but we don't get the full joy or even the full power of our salvation until we understand it is primarily for Jesus Christ, the Holy Spirit and our Heavenly Father. We are NOT primarily the issue, HE IS, and Scripture declares this clearly from Genesis to Revelation. When we stop esteeming ourselves, our church or our denomination highly and start esteeming Jesus Christ highly, then we will have taken the first step towards defeating Religious Correctness and Satan himself.

THE NECESSITY OF DEFEATING RELIGIOUS CORRECTNESS

Satan has no opponents in the world. All in the world are his children and under his rule. Even the most moral are his. He is the god of this world. His only enemy on this earth is Jesus Christ and His true Church. His true Church is made up of those who are born again by the Spirit of God into a new life. If Satan is able to keep this Church compromised and neutralized in America, he will destroy this country.

Satan's strategy has always been to weaken or destroy the effectiveness of God's people, and he uses the culture in which they live to those ends. In the last generation he has been extra-ordinarily successful. We must recognize this strategy so we can be a part of the powerful remnant in this world that will most assuredly ultimately defeat Satan and all that are his. In order to do so, we must abandon and defeat Religious Correctness.

CHAPTER 9

BEWARE THE LEAVEN OF RATIONALIZATION

I Samuel 15:13-15, 18-21, ""And Samuel came to Saul, and Saul said to him, "Blessed are you of the Lord! I have carried out the command of the Lord." But Samuel said, "What then is this bleating of the sheep in my ears, and the lowing of the oxen which I hear?" And Saul said, "They have brought them from the Amalekites, for THE PEOPLE spared the best of the sheep and oxen, to sacrifice to the Lord your God; but the rest we have utterly destroyed... and (Samuel said) the Lord sent you on a mission, and said, 'Go and utterly destroy the sinners, the Amalekites, and fight against them until they are exterminated.' Why then did you not obey the voice of the Lord, but rushed upon the spoil and did what was evil in the sight of the Lord?" Then Saul said to Samuel, "I DID OBEY the voice of the Lord, and went on the mission on which the Lord sent me, and have brought back Agag the king of Amalek, and have utterly destroyed the Amalekites. But THE PEOPLE took some of the spoil, sheep and oxen, the choicest of the things devoted to destruction, to sacrifice to the Lord your God at Gilgal..""

When Samuel discovered that Saul had not obeyed the Lord's directive to utterly destroy all the Amalekites and their possessions, he confronted him with his sin. Saul's response was to justify and make excuses for his disobedience. First, he blamed the people. Next, he excused his sin by appealing to Samuel's devotion to God by saying that the animals were to be used for religious purposes as a sacrifice to the Lord. He rationalized his disobedience by shifting the blame to others and by claiming that the religious value made the apparent disobedience excusable.

Shortly after being saved by the Lord Jesus Christ, the Lord spoke to me about my walk. He said, "Beware of the leaven of rationalization." In Matthew 14:26 Jesus says, "Beware of the leaven of the Pharisees", but this was different. The Lord spoke to me about rationalizing because I, both before and after I was saved by Him, had an uncanny ability to find good reasons for my various rebellious activities. I even had scientific support for this rationale. First, college psychology taught me that my outbursts of anger were necessary because I needed to release my frustrations. Psychologists, refer to this as the hydraulic principle. The idea goes like this: if you hold anger in and don't find a vent for it, then you are in danger of experiencing a variety of internal afflictions, which include getting an ulcer or developing high blood pressure. Second, my problems with authority were supposedly my father's fault because he disciplined me too harshly (in experience, this was totally untrue).

God, however, would not let me live such unscriptural lies. He showed me that I could not rationalize away my Scriptural responsibilities to exercise self-control and obey those who are in authority over me.

The Saul Church is a rationalizing Church. We have infused the secular view of man into our thinking and have looked at man basically as a victim of his circumstances or heritage. Like Saul, certain of our activities are identified in Scripture as sin and rebellion, but we refute those accusations. We now consistently label alcoholism and drug addiction as diseases rather than sins. Please understand I am aware that many sins can turn into bondages that need drastic spiritual remedies and radical repentance. We excuse our own bitterness, unforgiveness, and selfish sensitivity by pointing out, often in the midst of unrepentant tears, that we have been "hurt" terribly. We usually blame spouses, ex-spouses, pastors, ex-pastors, parents, prejudiced people, or bosses who have never really understood us. Notice that many of the people who hurt us were authorities in our lives. One of the most common reasons for our being hurt is that these authorities in our lives were too critical or did not correct us with enough love. We realize that unforgiveness and bitterness are not acceptable to God, but our method for disposing of these problems is to either pray for an inner healing or get Christian psychological counseling, which usually reinforces our suspicions that our parents or our ex-spouses are largely to blame for our sins. Please understand, parents and other people over us may well have been verbally, physically or even sexually abusive. But the solution has to do not with my hurts or pain but with my unacceptable attitude of bitterness or unforgiveness. Often Christians use their parents as scapegoats for their own rebellion. This attitude is unacceptable to God. When we recognize our sin of unforgiveness, and repent of it, then we are clear with God. We receive God's forgiveness; we obey His commandment to forgive others, not on the basis of what they have done or will do to us, but on the basis of what Jesus did for us on the cross.

Another solution, which is common in some Charismatic churches, is to go through psychologically oriented counseling sessions that are liberally mixed with deliverance ministry. We then are told to love our parents, but we also are dragged through even more hours of "therapy" which more and more shows us how truly rotten and unloving they really were. Oftentimes we blame our own problems on "inherited sin." This notion completely ignores the facts that we have been born again and are now new creatures in Christ. We ignore 2 Cor 5:17 which declares, "Therefore if anyone is in Christ he is a new creature; the old things passed away; behold, new things have come." We have had books written, sermons preached, radio and television programs broadcast, all reinforcing our rationalization - that our problem is ESSENTIALLY SOMEBODY ELSE'S FAULT. Usually the therapy leads us to conclude that we were affected by SOMEONE ELSE'S SIN and we are instructed only to forgive them. Forgiving them is very important, but we are typically not clearly shown our own need to repent of our sin of unforgiveness. We need to receive God's forgiveness for our part in the matter. Often our poor work habits or unthankful complaining attitudes were what triggered our boss's verbal abuse. I remember as a child being very "wise" and sarcastic with my father and mother when asked to do chores. I also remember convincing my mother of my faultlessness in a situation, so I could get her on my side. I am talking about convincing her of something that was not true. I knew I was at fault, but I also knew that I could get her to sympathize with me against my father. There were times when he would lash out in anger and call me names. Other times he would rip off his belt and give me a licking. Looking back I can see now that my acts of rebellion and manipulation were my fault. It is true that my father's anger was his fault but I was not merely a victim. Many psychological counselors will discount or ignore the child's sin in such a matter, but it is absolutely necessary for Christians as adults to recognize their own sinfulness in situations with their parents, and to repent of these activities. A good counselor will try and get the whole story. A good Biblical counselor will understand that the issue is not inner healing, but taking responsibility for our own actions, receiving His forgiveness and being cleansed by properly apprehending the efficacy of the blood of Jesus Christ. In summation, we are not CLEARLY shown our own need to repent of our sins and receive God's forgiveness.

Years ago, in an inner healing service my wife inadvertently attended at a denominational camp meeting for women, the women who had been hurt in the past and still suffered the effects were told to "visualize" the offending party of the past begging for forgiveness at their feet. The women were led to say, "I forgive you" to the imaginary groveling offenders. The women were never told to repent of their own sin of unforgiveness, and, as in most cases, they were never told to see if they, in any way, had contributed to the other party's disobedience, or to see if they had responded in a sinful manner. They were brought to a place where there was no room for personal repentance or responsibility. They were given instruction in the fine art of rationalizing away their sin and placing it on someone else.

In chapter 13 of 1 Corinthians, the profound love chapter of Scripture, the Apostle Paul discusses the essence of love in detail. First, he lays down the foundation that this divine virtue MUST attend all our works, good deeds and religious activity. If it does not, those activities are WORTHLESS. Some of the attributes that he mentions that are particularly pertinent for our discussion are the following: "love is not provoked, love does not take into account a wrong" (1 Cor 13:5), "love bears all things, love endures all things" (1 Cor 13:7). These attributes indicate to us that we need to put up with a lot from other people. This portion of Scripture indicates that if these attributes do not exist in our hearts, then we have become a noisy gong or a clanging cymbal. If we do not have these attributes in our life then whatever we do, profits us NOTHING (1 Cor 13:1-3). These aspects are there because we have been forgiven from the most expensive debt of all (see Matt 18:21-35). This debt is calculated in these verses as being billions of dollars. This is an unpayable debt. All other debts are miniscule compared to the debt that we owe to the Lord Jesus Christ because He died on the cross for our sins, forgave us and paid the price for our sins with His blood. It is clear from Scripture that we are to forgive solely on the basis of what He has done for us. Our forgiveness is NEVER based on what others have done to us (whether these acts were real or imaginary). We forgive because of His forgiveness of our sins and consequent love for us. When an individual truly understands the depth of his sins against the totally innocent Lamb of God, he will have no need to rationalize his concern about being offended, no matter how serious the offense has been. I have seen my wife, who was molested and abused as a child by her step-father for years completely forgive and love him. This was not done because his attitude had changed in the least; this was done because she had seen the magnificent and complete forgiveness of her own sins through the work of the Son of God on the cross.

Rationalization, along with being a terrible sin, is also an insidious trap. When psychologically applied, it causes us to NEED something besides the Cross of Jesus Christ for our sanctification. We are not told to forgive people merely on the basis of His great and wondrous and loving work of forgiveness and redemption on the cross. We are told we must add to that work a recounting, or "visualization", of situations and people who caused us so much pain which resulted in "unhealed hurts." We are not taught to apply Matthew 18 which clearly teaches that we are to forgive others SOLELY on the basis of the FACT that we deserve only hell, and have been forgiven of our sins by God. We are not told that our acts of sin against a Holy God are much more terrible than anything anyone could have ever done to us. Jesus says in Matthew 5:44 to love our enemies. The understanding is that we are to love them willingly and gladly, BECAUSE OF THE LOVE WE HAVE BEEN SHOWN BY THE FATHER in the face of our own terrible sins against Him. Instead, in the Saul Church, we are taught to apply the fleshly, deadly doctrines of psychology and inner healing as expounded by the scripturally inept or demonically confused. We now are given PSYCHOLOGICAL solutions to spiritual problems, and spiritual solutions are typically ignored.

We do not merely rationalize our sin and blame others with a Christian psychology rationale; we also rationalize our sin by accusing the accuser. We appeal to the fact that they don't understand! This statement is usually followed by "God knows my heart" or "You don't have the right to judge me!" Both of these ploys are particularly effective because they put the offensive accuser (or corrector) on the defensive. This tactic also gives us time to think of some further excuses for our judged conduct. Another excuse is that "our motives were good anyway", or "it may be true that I did make a bad mistake, BUT it is nothing compared to your virtually unforgivable sin of JUDGING ME!" In the political realm we see these tactics: when Bill Clinton was accused of his perverse sins, he switched the attention of the media, to the supposedly cruel inquisition led by Ken Star and the ruthless Republicans. This last tactic which categorizes any form of verbal correction as "judging" is particularly effective. Many in the Church are certain that no one has the right to judge anyone else. They come to this conclusion by a superficial and carnal understanding of the Scripture, which says, "judge not lest ye be judged." They were never taught what the Scripture actually meant. They were never taught that it meant "condemn not lest ye be condemned." In no way do these Scriptures indicate that we are not to differentiate whether a person's act is good or bad.

Several years ago, I was involved with a prison ministry that a man set up after he had been incarcerated for political crimes. He was deeply moved by the painful condition and lack of spirituality among the men that he did time with. He decided to start ministering Jesus Christ to these men and developed a program that is recognized as one of the most successful Christian prison ministry in the nation. I became interested in prison ministry through a friend and was introduced to this program. In order to qualify to teach in this program, I had to take a number of classes and in doing so I read the ministry books that were a part of his curriculum. I was quite surprised to find that most of these books contained a great deal of self-esteem teaching for the prisoners. The premises of these textbooks was that the men needed to have more self-esteem and needed to love themselves more, in order to be truly successful in their pursuit of Christianity. The author taught that most of these men grew up in abusive households and thought little of themselves, and because of this they could not truly love others. He contended that these men, along with being guilty criminals, were also victims of households that deeply damaged their self-images and caused them to think ill of themselves.

My experience with these men in the prisons and men like them outside the prisons was much different. In my twenties before I was saved by the Lord Jesus Christ, I was involved in the criminal element from two standpoints: I was heavily involved with gambling and met many individuals who were card cheats, scam artists and generally speaking, con men that looked for an edge anywhere they could find it. I certainly was no better than they were; after several years of making a small living at playing poker in the clubs, I succumbed to the temptation of becoming a card cheat and worked with other card players in scamming in low stakes poker games. My experience taught me that we all thought much more of ourselves than we did of our victims. We used to discuss the fact that the suckers were going to lose anyway, and they might as well lose quickly. Most of the card cheats were fairly intelligent and looked upon the others as either stupid or "sick" because they were masochists who seemed to have a desire to be punished. We were the very willing punishers. We were the winners; they were the losers. We were the manipulators; they were the ones who were manipulated. We were the sharks; they were the fish.

Another realm of criminal activity that I was involved with was buying and selling drugs. I couldn't help but notice that many drug dealers; both small time and big time had no concern for the people that were victims of the drugs they sold. Many KNEW what heroine or speed or psychedelics did to the people to whom they sold. They really could care less. They esteemed themselves very highly, and cared little for their clients. Because of the type of people who sold drugs and cheated at cards, I came to know quite a number of professional thieves. One in particular, a very personable man who had a great a sense of humor and could be very generous when he wanted to, had a credit card scam that for its time was quite large. He made it clear that he could care less about the victims and rationalized his crimes by noting that everybody is a thief and liar, and he was just a little smarter than the rest.

When I became a pastor and was counseling a woman in our congregation and her boyfriend, regarding their upcoming marriage, I had a chance to hear some stories from her fiancé who was getting ready to go back to prison for armed robbery. His most telling story was about an armed robbery of a home in the suburbs. He had staked out this home and he was sure that the family was on vacation. The reason he knew this was because he said that he had watched the house for four nights in a row, and he noticed that the lights automatically turned on at nine o'clock all four of those nights. He deduced that this was a timer that was set up to make it look like someone was living in the house. On the fifth night he entered the premises about eleven o'clock, after the automatic lights had turned off. While he was rummaging through one of the bedrooms, he heard the front door open and a man came in. It was the owner of the home. He told me that he waited behind the door, with his gun drawn, and if the man walked through the door into the room where he was, that he would shoot the man and kill him. He said, he did not want to go back to prison and he would do anything to save himself from life behind bars. He made it abundantly clear that he esteemed his life infinitely more than he esteemed the life of his possible victim. It turned out he did not need to kill the man because the man went to the other end of the house and my robber friend made his escape through the window. He made it clear he would have felt bad about killing the man, but it was the right thing to do, because he wasn't going to let him stand in the way of his freedom.

Criminals who rob, rape, murder, cheat, or sell drugs esteem themselves MUCH more than their victims, and love themselves MUCH more than their victims. The Bible is still correct when it says, "no man hateth his own flesh, but cherisheth it" and we are called to "esteem others MORE HIGHLY than ourselves." In working with Prison Fellowship I noticed that this self-esteem teaching and self-love teaching was much more popular than the teaching which warned of the punishment of God and encouraged unselfish conduct. Most of the prisoners loved hearing about their status as victims, and many used these so-called truths to manipulate the system. The greatest grief was that many "Christian" ministries merely reinforced their rationalization that they were victims.

We are becoming much more like Israel's northern kingdom (Samaria) which embraced the God of the Jews and His ways, and also embraced many of the local gods. The self-esteem and self-love teaching is not from Scripture, but from the secular psychology of the humanistic culture in which we live. It is of the world and for the world, and when it is practiced by Christians, it is spiritual adultery.

The Saul Church commits the sacrilegious act of rationalizing their disobedient acts because of benefits brought to the Church. In the

1970's a large church prepared one of its staff members to take secular psychology classes for a Masters in Psychology because the church was told by people in the legal community that the church was less likely to be sued by a disgruntled counselee if the church had a licensed psychologist on staff.

Back in the 1980's we all witnessed the grievous spectacle of a minister telling the people that if he did not collect a large sum of money (in the millions) that God would have to take him home (kill him). He received a check for at least $1,000,000 from a race track owner in Florida. Of course the gambling revenues that constituted the bulk of the $1,000,000 were gotten from people who were in many cases in bondage to gambling. This man felt that it was ok because the money was to be used for God's work. As was to be expected, his work went bankrupt several years later. The gambler's blood money did not help at all.

Many church leaders have taught members of their congregation to rationalize the pursuit of money as a laudable spiritual endeavor. The rationalization goes like this: God needs the money to build His Kingdom, and He needs moneymakers or "givers" to give money to the kingdom builders; therefore, certain people have a calling to be moneymakers or givers. Therefore, because much money is needed to build the kingdom of God, many people are needed to make all the money that God needs. I have met people who sincerely told me they were pursuing wealth because they were called to be givers, and that in order to do so, they had to be wealthy. They apparently were completely unaware that they were violating I Timothy 6:9 which says, "but those who want to get rich fall into temptation and a snare and many foolish and harmful desires which plunge men into ruin and destruction." They also were taught that luxurious living was a part of being one of God's children, and they needed to show the world what it was like to be a child of the King. In my experience and observation, most of the people that labored to become wealthy for these reasons NEVER became wealthy and in fact struggled for years. The result of this rationalization is that tens of thousands of people have ended up laboring for the things that perish. They serve Mammon with the excuse that they are building the kingdom. Their pursuit of wealth and riches and comfort and prestige is nothing more than a self-deceiving, on-going rationalization. Scripture makes it clear that God blesses some with material wealth but it is our attitude regarding money that defines us as either obedient or disobedient. Many Christians never sought after wealth but God did make them wealthy anyway.

One of the most popular rationalizations for not doing what we are told is best explained by this statement, "I don't like the way you told me to do that. If you were really a godly man (or woman) speaking by the Spirit, you would have said that WITH MORE LOVE! You didn't say it right, therefore it can't be God, and I won't do it." They believe that if the tone of voice is harsh or impatient that automatically disqualifies the validity of the word spoken because that is not how the Holy Spirit speaks. Even if the offended individual later realizes that what was told him WAS correct, he is able to blame the person who told him, by appealing once again to the excuse that "It was not said with love."

The implied notion is that when a godly person gives correction or rebuke, he will do so with politeness, love and a soft voice. However, even a casual look at Scripture reveals that prophets did not always speak with honey dripping from every word. Sometimes they were harsh to God's disobedient and/or illegitimate children. In the New Testament we read the words of Stephen, "You men who are stiff-necked and uncircumcised in heart and ears are always resisting the Holy Spirit; you are doing just as your fathers did (these words all by themselves without reference to a tone of voice would be considered UNKIND). Which one of the prophets did your fathers not persecute? And they killed those who had previously announced the coming of the Righteous One, whose betrayers and murderers you have now become; you who received the law as ordained by angels, and yet did not keep it." (Acts 7:51-53). Jesus also sprinkled His teaching with hard words, especially when dealing with religious phonies. Matthew 23:13-33 is a good example, "....woe to you, Scribes and Pharisees, hypocrites, because you shut off the kingdom of heaven from men; for you do not enter in yourselves, nor do you allow these who are entering to go in. Woe to you Scribes and Pharisees, hypocrites, because you devour widows' houses, even while for a pretense you make long prayers... you travel about on sea and land to make one proselyte; and when he becomes one, you make him twice as much a son of hell as yourselves. Woe to you blind guides...You fools and blind men...Woe to you Scribes and Pharisees, hypocrites...You clean the outside of the cup and of the dish, but inside they are full of robbery and self indulgence...You are like white washed tombs which on the outside appear beautiful, but inside they are full of dead men's bones and all uncleanness...You serpents, you brood of vipers, how shall you escape the sentence of hell?" It would be difficult, if not impossible, to speak these words with a sweet, kind, loving understanding tone of voice. There had to have been a force of warning and judgment in the tone of Jesus' words. Even to His own disciples He said, in Matthew 17:17, "....O unbelieving and perverted generation, how long shall I be with you? How long shall I put up with you?" And when Jesus drove the money changers out of the temple with a whip, he likely was not soft spoken.

Even carnal enemies can be used by God in a most insulting way to convey truth to us. II Samuel 16:5-11 notes that Shimei was a bad spirited, hateful man who insulted David in a most degrading way: """"When King David came to Bahahurim, behold, there came out from there a man of the family of the house of Saul whose name was Shimei, the son of Gera; he came out cursing continually as he came. And he threw stones at David and at all the servants of King David; and all the people and all the mighty men were at his right hand and at his left. And thus Shimei said when he cursed, "Get out, get out, you man of bloodshed, and worthless fellow! The Lord has returned upon you all the bloodshed of the house of Saul".... Then Abishai the son of Zeruiah said to the king, "Why should this dead dog curse the lord my king? Let me go over now, and cut off his head." But the king said, ""What have I to do with you...If he curses, and if the Lord has told him, "Curse David", then who shall say, "Why have you done so...Let him alone, and let him curse, for the Lord has told him..""" Notice in this quote that David could say, "Let him go...God is speaking through him to me." He did not refuse to listen to the message even though it was not said "in love."

David had the wonderful ability to hear the correction of God even in a carnal hate-filled man. If the prophets, Shimei, who was a carnal enemy, Stephen, and Jesus Himself could speak harsh words of rebuke, certainly, in the midst of a rebellious and deluded church age, we can expect God to speak with force, anger, and sometimes even with insult to us. Scripture proves that the way in which a message is delivered is not the issue. The issue is the message. Yet we have an entire generation, because of the infiltration of humanistic psychology into our churches, that is so selfishly sensitive that the people feel quite justified in rejecting a word of correction, because it was not delivered "with love" and causes them to have low self esteem.

Of course, we recognize the responsibility to speak properly and to have great love. II Tim 2:25 says, "with gentleness correcting those who are in opposition..." That is NEVER, however, to be the criteria to judge whether or not a word is to be received. We MUST LEARN to deny ourselves and let the cross do its work of dealing death to our flesh, whether it is a perfect word from one who loves us, or an ill-intentioned word from one who hates us. We must never rationalize disobedience on the basis of the messenger. We must learn to hear and obey the message regardless of the messenger. Sometimes God's greatest display of love is a stern, penetrating word that turns us away from sin. God's word may come to us from a brother or sister in Christ; or even a worldly sinner like Shimei that just happens to be at least partially right.

All of this over-sensitivity must go. Church members who have been offended by the tough sermons or harsh words of their pastors must learn to hear because their pastors are concerned for them and sees that their lifestyle makes their calling and election VERY unsure. Often, God speaks through willing men words that warn listeners that they are tip toeing on the brink of the pit of Hell.

Rationalization for Saul was really the covering that blinded his eyes to the rebellion that was so prominent in his heart. He excused sin and blamed others, and ultimately dressed up his excuses so well that he may in some cases have actually believed them. The great problem is, as long as he could hide behind his excuses, he was really blind to the forgiveness of God. He had so rationalized and excused himself before God that his heart told him that he really was not guilty, just misunderstood, and because he was not guilty, he obviously needed no forgiveness. Because he felt he needed no forgiveness, he did not ask for forgiveness and because he did not ask for forgiveness, he RECEIVED none.

The Saul Church today, like its namesake, has rationalized sin so well that it has come to believe and teach lies. They believe and teach the lie that blames others for their sin. They believe and teach the lie that calls sin "disease." They believe and teach the lie that disguises lust for money and the love of the world in the religious cloth of "building the kingdom" or proving and manifesting our faith in a generous God. A church or individual that rationalizes away the fact that a particular deed or attitude is sin cannot receive forgiveness for that sinful deed or attitude. Recognition of sin and repentance of sin is always necessary for true change to take place. They MUST repent of their selfish sensitivity and let the SWORD of the Lord, the Word of God, pierce them to the Death so they can receive Life! Like the leaven of yeast in bread about to be baked the leaven of rationalization eventually permeates the entire man and The Excuse becomes a way of life. As with Saul, the central issue is SELF-JUSTIFICATION. The rationalizing, excuse-making attitude, whether it comes from psychology or is just something that was learned as a child and never given up, can even dilute the doctrine of justification by faith in the shed Blood of Jesus Christ alone. The possibility thinkers and psychological positivists in the Saul Church say that "we are not really as bad as all that." They do not like Scriptures such as "our righteousness is as filthy rags." We must make no excuse or rationalization or justification whatsoever, before God for our sins. We must totally depend upon the finished work of the cross of Jesus Christ for our justification and sanctification. We must understand that GOD CANNOT FORGIVE A HURT; we cannot justify ourselves. We cannot come to Him merely as a victim or a hurting person; we must come to Him as a sinner. The Saul Church is filled with men and women who because they have never been brought to look at the exceeding sinfulness of their hearts, don't really know Christ as Savior. Jesus Christ came to save us from our sin, not merely to heal our hurts. The Saul Church seems to have rationalized that in the twenty first century, we don't really need to discuss issues like sin and judgment and hell, because we have surmised that this generation will not tolerate such radical extreme out of balanced teaching. We are much more likely to either discuss "mistakes" and "hurts" than to teach or preach messages that convict people of the terrible consequence and offence of their sin and the uncompromising judgment of God on those who do not come to Him as Forgiver of their sins. For the same reasons, if sin IS mentioned, in most churches, it plays a very minor part in the message. We never want people to "come under condemnation." Seldom, if ever, do we read or hear messages like those of George Whitfield, John Wesley, Charles Spurgeon or Charles Finney. In all likelihood we would laugh off the platform Jonathan Edwards if today he preached "Sinners in the Hands of an Angry God." Even worse, we possibly would just sit there in embarrassed silence and avoid him after he spoke. We excuse this mentality because we honestly believe that people are basically victims of the sin of others.

Romans 7:11-13, speaking of the law and sin says, "…sin, taking an opportunity through the commandment, deceived me, and through it killed me. So then, the Law is holy, and the commandment is holy and righteous and good. Therefore did that which is good become a cause of death for me? May it never be! Rather it was sin, in order that it might be shown to be sin by effecting my death through that which is good, that through the commandment SIN MIGHT BECOME UTTERLY SINFUL."

The King James Version says, "....sin might become EXCEEDING sinful." This Scripture makes it clear that the purpose of the law was NOT to drive people to despair or condemnation; rather it was to force people to see their sin MAGNIFIED. The law is to be used so that people can see just how terrible, harmful and dangerous sin is. The purpose of the law is to help us see the true nature of our sin. Once we have this wonderful revelation of our sinful condition, we are then presented with the grace of God through the shed blood of Jesus Christ, and because we see how terrible our sin is, we should be quick to repent of our sin and receive His forgiveness. Unfortunately, the Saul Church is so afraid of driving people away by preaching this message that they make sin exceeding watered down and are much more likely to present a therapeutic Gospel which appeals NOT to people who are plagued by their sin but to hurting people who are concerned about their bad feelings. This rationalization of causing sin to appear less and less in our messages and put the emphasis on our pain and our suffering has caused MANY to never understand their desperate condition.

CHAPTER 10

REBELLION AND WORSE

I Samuel 15:3 "Now go and strike Amalek and utterly destroy all that he has, and do not spare him; but put to death both man and woman, child and infant, ox and sheep, camel and donkey."

I Samuel 15:8-11 ""He captured Agag the king of the Amalekites alive, and utterly destroyed all the people with the edge of the sword. 9) But Saul and the people spared Agag and the best of the sheep, the oxen, the fatlings, the lambs, and all that was good, and were not willing to destroy them utterly; but everything despised and worthless, that they utterly destroyed. 10) Then the word of the LORD came to Samuel, saying, 11) "I regret that I have made Saul king, for he has turned back from following Me and has not carried out My commands And Samuel was distressed and cried out to the LORD all night.""

I Samuel 15:17-19 Samuel said, ""Is it not true, though you were little in your own eyes, you were made the head of the tribes of Israel? And the LORD anointed you king over Israel, 18) and the LORD sent you on a mission, and said, "Go and utterly destroy the sinners, the Amalekites, and fight against them until they are exterminated." 19) Why then did you not obey the voice of the LORD, but rushed upon the spoil and did what was evil in the sight of the LORD?""

I Samuel 15:22-23 Samuel said "Has the LORD as much delight in burnt offerings and sacrifices. As in obeying the voice of the LORD? Behold, to obey is better than sacrifice, And to heed than the fat of rams. 23) For rebellion is as the sin of divination, and insubordination is as iniquity and idolatry. Because you have rejected the word of the LORD, He has also rejected you from being king."

I Samuel 15:28 "...so Samuel said to him, The LORD has torn the kingdom of Israel from you today and has given it to your neighbor, who is better than you.'"

Earlier in 1 Samuel 13:13-14 Samuel said to Saul, "You have acted foolishly; you have not kept the commandment of the LORD your God, which He commanded you, for now the LORD would have established your kingdom over Israel forever. But now your kingdom shall not endure. The LORD has sought out for Himself a man after His own heart, and the LORD has appointed him as ruler over His people, because you have not kept what the LORD commanded you."

In this section of Scripture Saul was told, because of his disobedience, that his kingdom would not endure. Had he been obedient, his kingdom would have endured through him and his son and his son's sons. In I Samuel 15:28, Saul was specifically told he was no longer the leader of Israel. I Samuel 15:23 says, "For rebellion is as the sin of divination (witchcraft), and insubordination is as iniquity and idolatry. Because you have rejected the word of the Lord, He has also rejected you from being king." Saul lost his rulership because of rebellion - rebellion against God's direct command to utterly destroy all the Amalekites and all of their possessions. God did not give Saul an A minus because he accomplished 92% of what he was told to do. God flunked him and gave him an F. Saul utterly failed because his partial obedience was an act of total rebellion. Rebels flunk completely in God's school. Rebellion is one of the most serious of crimes against the Cross of Jesus Christ, and is dealt with severely by the Lord. The punishment of all unrepentant rebels is hell itself. Rebellion is considered by God to be as serious a sin as divination (witchcraft in the KJV version).

When we look at Saul, at first glance, we don't see a rebel. We can sympathize with him in regard to the Amalekite situation. He did an excellent job. He did not take the beautiful women, he did not take the strong young men, and he did not even let the sympathetic look of an innocent child deter his sword from the obedient act of slaughter. He did what he truly felt was best: he spared Agag their king and the best of everything else. He acted from the most practical of motives. But God called it rebellion. Why would God accuse this simple man, who acted with good intentions, of the most serious of sins? It is because Saul acted from SELF-WILL. Saul did what HE thought was best,

NOT what he was told to do by God. Saul was practical, but he was not spiritual. Saul was carnal, self-willed, and rebellious. His heart was not given over to God. He obeyed when he felt that obedience was sensible. He disobeyed whenever the situation indicated that obedience was unreasonable. Saul was a rebel. To be sure, he was a RELIGIOUS rebel, but he was still a rebel. His rebellion ultimately cost him his leadership and the direction of God, and what's more important, God took the anointing of His Holy Spirit from Saul.

Today, if any one single word could best describe the state of the world, that word would be Rebellion. "I Did It My Way" is a song popularized by two of the world's finest rebels: Frank Sinatra and Elvis Presley. The Saul Church too, because it is a Church that mixes the "best" of the world with what it desires of the Spirit, is also a Church in rebellion. Rebellion has permeated the Church as leaven permeates the dough. Rebellion has infected the Church in the same way it has infected the world. We are now a lump that is greatly polluted with the leaven of rebellion.

Rebellion is the opposite of submission. In Scripture we are told to submit to the authorities who are over us. Saul would not submit to Samuel because he felt it was not necessary. Similarly in the Saul Church of today, we have Christians who function regularly in the selfish, deadly sin of rebellion. Many in the Church change jobs, husbands, wives or churches whenever they are told to do something they don't want to do; especially when they believe they have been told in an inappropriate manner. They claim their "rights" and refuse to submit to directive or rebuke. In a job situation most people, including Christians, quit because they decide they have been hurt, abused, or not appreciated. The result is that most Christians quit because they would not submit to the dealings of God. They are rebelling against the cross that Jesus told them they are to take up daily. They are rebelling against the notion of denying themselves, going the extra mile, loving their enemies, and turning the other cheek. They are not at all sensitive to what the Holy Spirit is doing; they are only sensitive. They get hurt easily, they complain, and they rebel against any authority, whether it is from the Church or the world, that tells them to submit to the situation, directive, or rebuke. A common response to a situation that the Holy Spirit has set up for their maturation as a Christian is "I don't need to take that kind of stuff anymore...I quit!" When we resist what the Holy Spirit has prepared for us, we are resisting the Holy Spirit and rebelling against God. One of the reasons he is able to resist and rebel so easily is because of current demonic teaching which instructs the so-called Christians to remove themselves from situations where their self-esteem, self-confidence, self-image, and self-respect are being damaged. They are actually being counseled in how to be good rebels. They are counseled concerning their rights and how to assert those rights, just as people in the world are counseled to assert their rights. Gone is the counsel of the Sermon on the Mount which instructs God's people to turn the other cheek, go the extra mile, bless them that curse you, pray for those who despitefully use you, and love your enemies. Gone is the counsel in I Corinthians 13 which tells us to "not take into account the wrong being suffered, to bear all things, and to endure all things." (I Cor. 13:15, 17). The greatest tragedy is in the realm of marriage. All too quickly a dissatisfied wife or husband is willing to abandon the marriage relationship because they feel that they are experiencing abuse, either physical or psychological. Families are destroyed and children are condemned to a single parent or 2 or 3 "fathers." Because of this their hearts become divided and confused. All this occurs because one parent would not obey or embrace chapter 13 of I Corinthians.

Notice what happened when Jeremiah ministered to Israel during a time of great rebelliousness. He warned her for years about the judgment that God would bring upon her because of her unrepentance. Another prophet, Hananiah, who ministered in this time spoke this message to the people in Jeremiah 28:2-4, ""Thus says the Lord of hosts, the God of Israel, "I have broken the yoke of the king of Babylon. Within two years I am going to bring back to this place all the vessels of the Lord's house, which Nebuchadnezzar, king of Babylon, took away from this place and carried to Babylon. I am also going to bring back to this place Jeconiah, the son of Jehoiakim, king of Judah, and all the exiles of Judah who went to Babylon", declares the Lord, "for I will break the yoke of the king of Babylon..""

Jeremiah's response, from Jeremiah 28:5-9, was at first appropriately sarcastic and then extremely serious: ""Then the prophet Jeremiah spoke to the prophet Hananiah in the presence of the priests and in the presence of all the people who were standing in the house of the Lord,

REBELLION AND WORSE 111

and the prophet Jeremiah said, "Amen! May the Lord do so; may the Lord confirm your words which you have prophesied to bring back the vessels of the Lord's house and all the exiles, from Babylon to this place. Yet, hear now this word which I am about to speak in your hearing and in the hearing of all the people. The prophets who were before me and before you from ancient times prophesied against many lands and against great kingdoms of war and of calamity and of pestilence. The prophet who prophesies of peace, when the word of the prophet shall come to pass, then that prophet will be known as one whom the Lord has truly sent..""

Hananiah's response noted in Jeremiah 28:10-11 was, """"Then Hananiah the prophet took the yoke from the neck of Jeremiah the prophet and broke it. And Hananiah spoke in the presence of all the people, saying, """Thus says the Lord, "Even so will I break within two full years, the yoke of Nebuchadnezzar, king of Babylon, from the neck of all the nations..""" Then the prophet Jeremiah went his way.""" But Jeremiah had the final word, as recorded in Jeremiah 28:12-17, """"And the word of the Lord came to Jeremiah, after Hananiah the prophet had broken the yoke from off the neck of the prophet Jeremiah, saying, """Go and speak to Hananiah, saying, "Thus says the Lord, 'You have broken the yokes of wood, but you have made instead of them yokes of iron.' "For thus says the Lord of hosts, the God of Israel, 'I have put a yoke of iron on the neck of all these nations, that they may serve Nebuchadnezzar, king of Babylon; and they shall serve him. And I have also given him the beasts of the field.'" Then Jeremiah the prophet said to Hananiah the prophet, """Listen now, Hananiah, the Lord has not sent you, and YOU HAVE MADE THIS PEOPLE TRUST IN A LIE. Therefore, thus says the Lord, "Behold I am about to remove you from the face of the earth. This year you are going to die because you have COUNSELED REBELLION against the Lord."""" Notice particularly Jeremiah 28:16, "....This year you are going to die because you have COUNSELED REBELLION AGAINST THE LORD." Hananiah was punished severely for counseling rebellion, as Saul was punished severely for engaging in rebellion, and the Church of Saul in our generation will also be punished severely because we have both counseled and engaged in rebellion. Notice that Scripture says that Hananiah COUNSELED REBELLION. If we read Jeremiah 28 carefully, we do not see Hananiah directly telling anyone to resist or hate or disobey God. In fact, Hananiah seems to be a very nice, positive prophet. He even uses visual aids to emphasize what he probably very sincerely believes the Lord is saying to His people about the freedom from bondage that the Jews were supposedly about to experience. He has high hopes and a good word. Yet the Lord, through Jeremiah and through Scripture, brands him a teacher or counselor of rebellion. Why does the Lord so accuse this positive, hopeful, probably sincere man of God? He accuses him because he was not speaking by the Holy Spirit but by his own human compassion, and what's worse, he was ministering human compassion in the place of the word of judgment that God had for His people. The fact that this word was a word of judgment should never have been the issue with Hananiah, but it probably was. He was a misguided patriot. He was loyal in an unholy way. What's worse, he was an optimist. God has no room for prophets who are Optimists or Pessimists. He only desires that prophets be Reveal-ists. He only desires that the prophet reveal His Word for His people at precisely the proper time. God wants His prophets to be ready in season or out of season. He demands His prophets to speak the truth, the WHOLE truth, and nothing but the truth. The prophet can have no sides to take; he may only speak God's words. If the movement is lukewarm or polluted and God directs him to speak His word of judgment, he MUST do so.

Hananiah and his kind, both then and now take sides. They are FOR THE MOVEMENT; they never see the need for God's people to repent. They are AGAINST God judging His people. They are AGAINST divisive prophets like Jeremiah who are so negative. They are AGAINST the confusion and the unsettling feelings that hard words from these negative men bring to God's people. They are AGAINST the prophets who prophesy defeat for God's people - even if great blessing and victory is on the other side of that defeat. The problem is that God labeled Hananiah, and all who repeat his error, counselors of REBELLION.

Who are the counselors of rebellion in the Saul Church of today? They are the men and women who bring a word of comfort to those who need to hear a word of correction, warning, or judgment. They are the men and women who edit the Bible by removing or neutralizing words of correction, warning and judgment with their carnal preaching and teaching. These men and women make it appear that God no longer demands holiness, hates sin or requires discipleship and obedience. They are quite certain that the current state of affairs in the Church would never call for God's judgment. They are completely unaware of the lukewarmness and the self satisfaction that exists among most churches in America. They are the preachers who cause the visible Church to live its daydreams of "Everything is going to be ok." They are the unity mongers who would sacrifice holiness and sound doctrine for "togetherness."

These men and women are the prophets and prophetesses you find in many Charismatic churches who, on a regular basis, have a word of comfort for the people at the assembly. Their so-called words from God virtually always tell of God's love, the fact that He is pleased with the people, and the fact that He is healing their relationships and blessing materially. The people are virtually never warned of judgment or corrected regarding their sin. The credo they are taught is "let's not be negative." They seem to have a frivolous attitude toward Jesus Christ. They excuse and even counsel divorce on the basis of sympathy for an apparently abused spouse. They do not counsel on the basis of the Word of God. They are the modern evangelists who smugly mock old fashioned preachers who cause their people to be uncomfortable by their convicting messages. They say to the people that it is not necessary to have those words spoken to them directly from the pulpit because it is not their job to be the Holy Spirit; it is much better to let the Spirit of God deal with each individual in a private manner, forgetting the admonition in Ezekiel 3:17-18, "Son of man, I have appointed you a watchman to the house of Israel; whenever you hear a word from My mouth, warn them from Me. When I say to the wicked, "You shall surely die"; and you do not warn him or speak out to warn the wicked from his wicked way that he may live, that wicked man shall die in his iniquity, but his blood I will require at your hand..."" They have also forgotten that it is the shepherd's job to keep the sheep out of danger. Most shepherds do not believe that the sheep are in any real danger, and in today's Church if a prophet or prophetess would speak about the dangerous plight of many of God's people, the pastor might well reject that word because it is a negative word that does not comfort his people. Many leaders in the Church today are practitioners and purveyors of the philosophy that "you can catch more flies with honey than you can with vinegar" forgetting that one of Satan's names is "Lord of the Flies."

If rebels like Saul are under a terrible curse, counselors of rebellion are under an even greater one. Even as the shepherds counsel rebellion, so the sheep have learned, and learned well, current Psycho-Christian doctrines. Many listen religiously to the Psycho-Babel on Christian radio, read a few Psycho-books, and feel obligated to "counsel" all their friends and little brothers and sisters on how to enhance their self-esteem, self-worth, self-confidence, and self-love. For every Christian lay person counseling the biblical injunction that says, "You must take up your cross, deny yourself and follow Jesus", you have a hundred Psycho-Christians mouthing the old humanistic, a-Scriptural platitudes: "You just need to love yourself more. After all, everybody knows "you need to love yourself before you can love anyone else", or "you don't need to take that kind of talk from him (or her)." Look what is happening to your self-image and self-respect. God CERTAINLY would not want you to have to put up with THAT sort of abuse anymore. For THE SAKE OF YOUR SELF-RESPECT, leave her (or him)!"

The Saul Church was born in the midst of rebellion. God's people, both thousands of years ago when Samuel judged them for the Lord, and decades ago when the Church grew dissatisfied with its station in the world, rejected God and rebelled against His ways. Their shallow materialism was rebellion against a deep revelation of Himself that He strove to work in their hearts. Their partial obedience to His Word by rejecting much of the world but keeping the best was rebellion against His Holiness and His Holy Spirit. Their excuses and rationalizations for their sin merely compounded their rebellion and their judgment. The kingdom of Israel under Saul was finally destroyed right after Saul's ultimate rebellion, seeking counsel from a witch. So the Saul Church of today is on the brink of judgment because of its rebellion and its acceptance of false teachers and false prophets and its desperate seeking of counsel from the world and even worse. Rebellion is a serious deadly sin and has serious deadly consequences. By obeying only part of the Word of God, Saul was tried and convicted and punished terribly by God for committing the sin of rebellion.

The Saul Church in the latter part of the twentieth century was also under the judging hand of God for its rebellion. We saw the exposure of our leadership with many headlines and stories about their greed, lust and what is worse, their excuses and partial repentances in the newspapers, television, and weekly magazines. The judgment that God brought at that time was relatively moderate. We experienced some shame, a loss of standing in the world's eyes, a few monitory set backs and most serious of all, because we did not repent fully, the Church experienced the judgment of an even deeper blindness. Unfortunately we have learned virtually nothing since that time that God dealt with His people because we would not repent. Because of this our hearts have been further hardened.

In the last decade a major Charismatic denomination, because of the folly of its president and the love of money, lost 15 million dollars through suspect investments that turned out to be scams. Several years previous, the former president of that denomination was asked to resign because of financial improprieties. They felt the solution was to get a President of impeccable qualifications. They chose the most popular and most highly thought of leader in that denomination. They did not understand that the problem was not with the head of that denomination but the problem was with the foundation of that denomination. The foundation is made up of good and bad elements. There are elements of the Word of God in that foundation but these elements are liberally mixed with teachings of rebellion to God's Word. This organization has been on the cutting edge of the NEW GOSPEL of unity regardless of truth and has been a moderate proponent of the gospel of self-esteem. This denomination has ignored or rationalized away Scriptures regarding God's view of divorce. In the name of balance they have chosen Scriptures that would not offend the people and ignored Scriptures that they felt would "hamper unbelievers from coming to Christ." They have taught rebellion to millions in this country and even spread this rebellion through missionaries all across the world.

That foundation is built with a Saul mentality and must be changed. This denomination and others like it must repent of the grievous sin of teaching rebellion if it is to be spared the devastation of the great shaking that will surely come to God's people. Each church or denomination or movement is like a building. Some are very tall, some are short, but regardless of the height or size, a proper foundation must be under them all if they expect to survive the great shaking.

Deep repentance regarding Saul Church attitudes that goes to the very foundation of each denomination, church and leader must occur for God to prepare them to survive the judgment and be a part of the next great move of God. The Revival/Reformation that will surely come, will include only leaders and members who have a desire to wholly please God and have a heart after Him and His ways and are willing to do so even if it costs them their ministries or the respect of their denominations or piers.

CHAPTER 11

SWEET SMELLING MONEY

I Samuel 16:14 says, "Now the Spirit of the Lord departed from Saul"....

When the Holy Spirit of God leaves or is leaving, there is always one thing that will be very evident in the Visible Church. The Church will begin to cry out for something to give her power. She will look for something to help as the Holy Spirit formerly helped. And a Church, such as the Saul Church which has already chosen to be like the world, understands exactly what it needs. The Saul Church will cry out for this power giver as if its life depended on it. The power giver they desire is the power giver that the world has known about and sought after for centuries. The power giver is MONEY. In the past generation, as the anointing of the Lord has been steadily disappearing, we have been hearing an increasingly desperate cry for money. From virtually every TV ministry this cry has become almost deafening. These great men and women of Faith seem to put their whole trust in their ability to collect money for their respective works.

George Mueller did not ask men for help but instead he cried out to God to meet every need and saw God mightily and abundantly provide. This spirit is all but gone today. George Mueller's faith, which primarily addressed God regarding the need, is declared impractical by the ruling kingdom builders of the Saul Church. They need, cry out for, and seek Big Money from men because they have LITTLE faith in God: they have little faith in the Spirit of God to accomplish the works of God without money.

When a man or ministry starts to cry out for money, in many cases, it is because he has been so busy with Saul's work that he has forgotten how to cry out to God and trust Him to provide. He may still cry out for God's Holy Spirit to touch his heart to love God more and also to touch his ministry that it might truly be anointed, but he is double-minded. He is still worried about failure. He is still worried about having sufficient funds to build the kingdom, the work or the denomination. His heart is not right and his cry to God is muffled by his anxiety for mammon. Many cry out for their TV audience to send in money as if God was not in charge but the TV audience was in charge. TV evangelists say things like, "The very future of World Evangelism and our ministry is in your hands. Do your best!" This may be a sincere appeal for money but they DO NOT understand! God's ministries will survive and flourish, as He desires and when a man is willing to trust in Him plus NOTHING and NO ONE! The tragedy is you cannot serve both God and mammon. You will finally choose one or the other. If you are double-minded, eventually mammon will be what you seek and what you fear losing. You will even have good reasons for getting more, and you may never use a penny for your own comfort, but you will essentially be depending on it for your ministry. You will feel "without money, this work of God will fail", whereas at one time you would have said, with a single-minded heart, "Without His anointing and direction this work will fail."

When the Spirit of the Lord begins to depart men get desperate. More and more church growth seminars must be attended. More and flashier entertainment must be found. More people must attend the church and be taught to give. The church must look respectable so respectable people will attend. No loud messages in tongues, no unusual manifestations can be tolerated. No negative prophecies can be delivered. More and more secularized education must be obtained. More degrees, more Ph.D.'s, more psychological counseling, more programs, more sports, more movies, more bands, more specials, more humor, more activity, more radio ministry, more television ministry is necessary. And we must not forget the most important principle of all, WHEN THE ANOINTING GOES, WE CAN ALWAYS BUILD THE KINGDOM WITH MONEY. The Saul Church's lifeblood is money. Whether Charismatic or Evangelical, MONEY becomes a KEY issue when the anointing leaves. The Church becomes "practical", materialistic and money conscious. The continued cry for money is a sure sign that a ministry has begun to lose or has lost the anointing of God.

Previously in Chapter 8, I spoke of a denomination that had some leadership difficulties and eventually lost $15,000,000 to religious con men. They were able to solve their $15,000,000 loss with one simple act. They sold the denominational radio station that they had used for ministry for 75 years. They sold the property at a phenomenal profit. It first transmitted the gospel in the 1920's and was originally purchased for a small fraction of its selling price in the 21st century. Some sources said, it sold for a quarter of a BILLION dollars. With this money they easily covered the $15,000,000 loss to the scam artists and they put money back into other denominational programs. It is likely not merely a coincidence that this sale was made after the $15,000,000 debacle. I am sure that they legitimately helped many ministries that were in the red and needed a transfusion of money. And I am in NO WAY looking upon the sale itself as an evil venture. BUT, it must be noted that the money gathered from that sale took care of a large number of financial problems and left them with a very healthy bank balance. It may have been a sound financial decision, but it is sad that the difficulties that were overcome and the problems that were solved were essentially financial. They completely ignored the spiritual problems. The problem with the denomination was foundational. They had a wrong view of the value of money and how to use it for the kingdom. This denomination greatly valued men and ministers who were able to raise large amounts of money and build churches that raised large amounts of money. They valued money gatherers more than they valued men who preached a pure and powerful Word from the Lord.

But men that greatly value money will cry, "You don't understand! Times are different now! The modern kingdom of God NEEDS money and lots of it!" That's true, the Saul Church DOES need lots of money; especially lately, because the Anointing is going and soon will be completely gone.

We can see in the Church today how our appeals for money have become much more sophisticated and much stronger. At first, the appeal was usually based on guilt, "If you don't give, many will be lost forever and you will bear the responsibility of not having given to this ministry." The appeal to guilt has been replaced by the appeal to greed. Greed has now become one of the best methods of gathering money. Modern Christian psychology has taught us that positive motivation is better than negative motivation. "If you give...you'll get..."

We even have doctrines which encourage greed, such as seed faith; prosperity doctrines, etc. Misrepresentation is also extremely effective. We SELL tapes for a "DONATION"! That is a contradiction in terms;

it is either a gift or a donation that you give from your heart to the ministry, or it is a sales transaction (you PURCHASE the tape or you PURCHASE the book). Of course, they call it a "gift" so they don't need to pay taxes on the profit received as a non-profit organization. This is scripturally wrong: we must render unto Caesar that which is Caesar's and render unto God, that which is God's. Our part in this is uncomplicated obedience in representing a purchase as a purchase and not as a gift or donation.

It is a serious thing to cheat the government out of their rightful taxes and the Lord speaks clearly about those who handle money properly. He says in Luke 16:10-11, "He who is faithful in that which is least is also faithful in much; and he that is unjust in the least is unjust also in much. If therefore ye have not been faithful in the unrighteous mammon (the least), who will commit to your trust the true riches (spiritual riches)." Another way of putting it is if you don't know how to deal correctly with unrighteous mammon (the least), how can you be expected to be given the responsibility of dealing with godly or spiritual matters (the true riches)? This Scripture clearly indicates the importance of handling money with integrity and godly wisdom.

Possibly the reason God is so concerned about the way we handle money is because money is to the world as faith is to the Christian. The world believes that the more money you have the more influence, pleasure, power and important things you will be able to get. The world also knows that without money it is impossible to please the people. The Bible makes it clear that selfless faith is the way to apprehend the true riches of the kingdom and without faith it is impossible to please God.

When we deal deceitfully in the realm of offerings or donations, which the Bible indicates is a form of worship, we are perverting one of our most sacred and fundamental ways of relating to God. When we give from the heart to Him and His work, we are worshipping Him and showing our love, our trust and our thankful hearts for taking care of us and loving us so much. When ministries demand a "freewill offering" but are actually selling something, the ministry perverts and/or erases the worship aspect of giving and we grieve the heart of God.

Gifts and donations certainly can be solicited for concerts, church services or special meetings either for the visiting speaker or any other need. But they must be free-will offerings and not mandatory payments. If it is mandatory payment, then these are purchases and must be considered as profit for the sponsoring organization and also must be considered payment (not donations) by the payee. You can deduct a donation or offering from your taxes but you cannot deduct a non-business related purchase.

The Early Church of the first generation of Christians as represented in Scripture gave no notice that any of their ministers charged money for any of their ministry. Paul requested donations and gifts for some of the churches, but never charged money for any ministry. Even the Didichae (one of the earliest Christian writings) warned that if a prophet asked for money for his ministry he was to be considered a false prophet. We see then that there were people who charged for their ministry, but they were looked down upon.

From at least the Middle Ages on, the Catholic Church has charged her people for services rendered. One of their most grievous practices was discussed at length by Martin Luther in his 91 Thesis which he hammered on the Wittenberg Door in 1517. Indulgences were purchased from the Church for either great sums of money or smaller sums of money dependent upon the need of the church or the ability of the giver. These indulgences would grant extended periods of relief from the pains of purgatory to relatives or friends of the purchaser. Also, the people could purchase letters that would forgive them for specific sins. The purchase of relics for obtaining special powers against Satan or special ability in prayer was also wide spread. These relics were represented as anything from John the Baptist's toe bone to small pieces of the True Cross. Luther made it clear that the purchase of indulgences and relics never enriched the purchaser, only the seller (the Catholic Church).

These practices ceased entirely in the Reformation Church that protested the heresies of the Roman Catholic Church. However, in the 20th century these practices under different guises began to emerge again. The Protestant Evangelicals began to negotiate payments with major speakers and singers. Then (probably in the 1950's or 1960's) a new phenomenon appeared: the Christian concert. The Church noted that secular concerts not only drew large crowds but also large amounts of money. Ticket prices of Christian concerts were fairly consistent with concerts of mildly successful secular groups. There have been some groups or singers that only took a donation to cover operational expenses, but most charged money for their services. To be fair if these were merely entertainments that represented themselves as having no spiritual value, perhaps this would be fine. Some of these groups however; represented their groups as being there for the purpose of either reviving God's people or reaching out to the unsaved. They justified their charges on the basis of a need to cover advertising expenses, hall rentals and general wear and tear. In all likelihood they really did not believe that God would provide for their needs as ministers of His Gospel. How different this is from the ministry of men like Jonathan Edwards, George Whitfield, John Wesley and Charles Spurgeon. Whitfield did solicit donations for the care of orphans but spent his life for the gospel and never established any wealth for himself. The other three men likewise made the world and the Church a much better place but ministered freely and with great faith and power. One may argue that musicians and singers are different than revivalists and evangelists. However, if they really consider themselves as those who bring God's people into worship of the Lord or desire to bring the unsaved into His kingdom, then they are ministers of the Lord. Because they are His ministers, they can expect God to provide for their needs. He may never make them famous. He may never give them "Rock Star" status, but He will save souls and lift God's people into the heavenly realm to love Him more purely and more passionately. Both ministers that preach and ministers that play music and sing must have a single mind and trust God to lead them into His will and provide for them as they do His will and His work.

I believe this Saul mentality that charges for ministry is changing and we are seeing more and more singers and musicians involved in leading WORSHIP without charge and not merely entertaining for money. Especially in the field of music, we are beginning to see a division of the David Church from the Saul Church. Those who trust that God will provide are being divided from those who trust in ticket sales. Those leaders who want people to enter into God's presence are being divided from those who want to entertain people.

Another group of people that feel it is important to charge money, particularly in a crisis situation, is the Christian counseling ministry. Their rationale is that it cost money for their education and they need to be paid on an hourly basis in order to continue to perform their duties. For some reason, unlike most pastoral ministry, they feel that an offering either directly to them or through a church facility as a monthly income is not enough. It is inconceivable that Paul or John or Peter or Jesus would EVER charge money to a desperate person to help him or her grow in grace or be set free from some trap set by the Enemy. The ministry of the Biblical counselor should either be through the local church and paid for by the offerings of the local church or it should be gifts and offerings that are not demanded by the counselor or even suggested by him from those to whom he ministers. No TRUE Christian should EVER turn away someone who came to be ministered to in a time of need because he could not afford the ministry.

Indulgences are still bought by desperate Catholics. Also they will probably be purchased until Jesus comes. Men and women who demand or strongly suggest that they should receive money for prayer cloths, anointing oil or counseling fees are no better than those who sell indulgences.

Because the Anointing of God has slowly but steadily been going away over the last 50 years or more, these unscriptural practices of gathering money have continued and even increased. Perhaps, however, it is because we ask for or demand money for services rendered that the anointing is leaving. Money has been the mortar that has held the bricks of our house of ministry together. Money has brought us comfort and money has allowed ministry to continue and even flourish. Unfortunately, when judgment hits the people of God, the ministries whose mortar is money will collapse. The only ministries that will stand are the ministries that selflessly trust God to provide for their needs and to provide the Anointing of His Holy Spirit.

The Charismatic Church will have NO REVIVAL until she renounces her dependence upon and love of MONEY. If she will not do so, God will take away her candlestick of godly authority. Over the centuries He has removed the authority of the Roman Catholic Church and many Protestant denominations that depended more on people and money than they did on God. Very possibly we will not again be able to say with any degree of Real faith and Real expectancy, "such as I have (healing for the man at the Gate Beautiful) I give unto you", until we can say with equal conviction, "Silver and gold have I none!"

We want to minister like Peter and John but we don't want to live like them. Many of us have become infected with the LAODICEAN spirit of the Saul Church.

God is not against honest requests to fill real needs. He is not against men and women being paid a decent salary. The workman IS worthy of his hire. But He IS against any so-called ministry that is motivated by any other reason than to glorify God and to feed His sheep. But He does ask the preacher and the teacher to exercise mercy and faith in God's provision as they respond to needs and requests for ministry. He does not even mind if a man gets blessed financially, but it is AN ABOMINATION the way we plead for money; especially while the pleader has a $500,000 home, a $3,000 a month housing allowance, an ample expense account, and a $100,000 a year salary. Sell your home - get a smaller one - take a cut in pay, especially that expense account and housing allowance; and THEN ask for money. OR SHUT UP and trust God to supply. But He probably will not allow you to move into truly spiritual teaching and ministry of the Holy Spirit until you deny yourself a bit of that financial security, and start trusting Him more on a day-to-day basis. Remember "Not by might (Money), not by power (What Money Supposedly Enables), but by My Spirit says the Lord" Zech. 4:6.

Can you imagine Paul, Peter, John or Jesus crying for money like we do? We Charismatics are particularly guilty. On the one hand we all cry for a return to New Testament Book of Acts Christianity, but on the other hand we feel we need lots of money to spread the Gospel. We do not merely ask for money but we beg, plead, lie, con, mislead and entice for money. On radio and TV sometimes we steal tithe or offering money from the local churches. The Saul Church does whatever it takes to get as much as it can to fulfill their destiny. Oral Roberts, the man who made one of the most outrageous appeals for money in the history of the Church, has been the almost perfect example of the Saul Church attitude regarding money.

Oral Roberts started ministering in the mid-to-late 1940's with one of the most amazing healing anointings of the last several generations. Many blind eyes and deaf ears were opened, many lame people walked, many growths disappeared. Then, several decades later, the anointing of God started to dry up, so Oral, as the years went by, became interested in television as a way to reach the people. He preached about seed faith and brought us some of the first televised Christian entertainment. Oral taught us to give to his ministry and people began to give and give generously.

Later he started massive building programs. He built a school and he built a hospital. The cost was tremendous but he raised hundreds of millions to build and support Oral Roberts University and The City of Faith hospital. The Anointing of God to heal for the most part had left him, but he was very busy on great projects and gathered millions for his kingdom. Money became not merely a means to an end, but something to seek after with a passion.

About twenty-five years ago at a denominational pastor's conference which I attended in California, Oral told the assembled pastors that it took half a million dollars a day or a week or a month to finance his ministry. After this confession, he gave a rousing sermon on the value of money: the text was a ludicrous misrepresentation of Scripture from Philippians 4. He even went as far as to lead at least a thousand pastors in the chant of, "Sweet smelling money." Then with a "Louder! For the Lord!" they repeated it. Then with a "One more time" the cries were deafening: "SWEET SMELLING MONEY!" The leader of the conference assured us that Oral's teaching on money from Philippians 4 was the most balanced teaching on money or prosperity that he had ever heard, and we were all encouraged to clap for Oral and generously give to his ministry.

This was followed by Oral's insistence that the pastors "claim from God what they truly deserved." He said that many of us made $18,000 a year ($1,500 a month) and we should rightly claim $80,000 a year ($7,500 a month). After this confession of faith, we would receive this great blessing and we could then live and minister in a manner befitting our efforts. As a body, the ministers stood to their feet crying out to God to get what they deserved. And, to God's great despair, many probably did.

When the anointing goes....

Get all the money you can....

You'll need it.

CHAPTER 12

EVIL UNDER THE SON

I Samuel 15:22-23, ""And Samuel said, "has the Lord as much delight in burnt offerings and sacrifices as in obeying the voice of the Lord? Behold to obey is better than sacrifice, and to heed than the fat of rams. For rebellion is as the sin of divination (witchcraft in KJV), and insubordination is as iniquity and idolatry. Because you have rejected the word of the Lord, He has also rejected you from being king.""

When final judgment was pronounced by God, Saul had no idea what that meant. He must have understood that he would perhaps someday no longer be king over Israel, but that did not seem to upset him. As was spoken earlier, the main thing that bothered him was that he might not receive the honor of the elders and the people. Even though he was told that he was rejected by God from being king; even though his sin was compared to that of divination (witchcraft), Saul was apparently not disturbed about this. He was not aware of what the words rebellion, iniquity, insubordination, idolatry, and REJECTION ultimately implied. His shallow, people-pleasing mind could not comprehend how his actions had been viewed by God. Saul apparently did not see his actions as rebellion. He did not seem to get the point of God's word through Samuel. We hear no cry from his heart to "take not Thy Holy Spirit from me." He seems to feel no great loss. Perhaps he felt that things would go along much as they had previously. After all, when he was told that his kingdom would not endure, nothing much really seemed to change. Saul was not aware of the terrible chain of events that would begin to happen over the years to come, as the evil spirit came and tormented him because of his rebellion.

Chapter 16:14 of I Samuel contains one of the most terrifying verses in the Bible: "Now the Spirit of the Lord DEPARTED from Saul and an EVIL SPIRIT FROM THE LORD terrorized him." We see Saul for the rest of his life function under the double judgment of God. First, the Holy Spirit of God leaves him. Second, he is sent a demon (an evil spirit) from Jehovah God Himself. We watch Saul, paranoid and conniving, try desperately to hold on to what he knows he is losing. We see Saul scheme against God by trying to destroy a man whom he knows now possesses the anointing of God that he once possessed. The last days of Saul's life were a mocking commentary on Samuel's pronouncement. I Samuel 15:23 says, "For rebellion is as the sin of divination (witchcraft)." Saul's sin was compared to witchcraft and, at the end of his life, in a desperate attempt to obtain supernatural assistance after failing to contact God, and with apparent total ignorance of the implications of what he was doing, he seeks and finds a medium or a witch to help him. I Samuel 28:6-8 says, ""When Saul inquired of the Lord, the Lord did not answer him, either by dreams or by Urim or by prophets. Then Saul said to his servants, "Seek for me a woman who is a medium that I may go to her and inquire of her." And his servants said to him, "behold there is a woman who is a medium at En-dor." Then Saul disguised himself by putting on other clothes, and went, he and two other men with him, and they came to the woman by night; and he said, "Conjure up for me, please, and bring up for me whom I shall name to you..""" He named Samuel and when Samuel came, he prophesied the final defeat of Saul's kingdom, and he prophesied the death of his sons and Saul's own death. All of this was fulfilled the next day when Saul commits suicide by falling on his sword so the Philistines will not humiliate him. I Samuel 31:4 says, ""Then Saul said to his armor bearer, "draw your sword and pierce me through with it, lest these uncircumcised come and pierce me through and make sport of me." But his armor bearer would not, for he was greatly afraid. So Saul took his sword and fell on it.""

The consequences of rebellion have been slowly unfolding for the Charismatic church of the last generation. In many Charismatic churches most healings are now not even real. More and more we are hearing such things as, "you lost your healing", or "you are healed, it just hasn't manifested yet." Some even feel they were healed for a week or so, but then they are as afflicted as they were before they "got healed." They are counseled that "the symptoms have returned but you are still healed." There are some legitimate healings but most are now phony. Gone are the glory days of Smith Wigglesworth and others. We are psychologically hyped into an expectation that never is fulfilled.

Healings are called out and nobody responds. Unseen cancers are declared healed, the crowd cries and praises God, but six months later the poor misled cancer victim drops dead more confused than before he/she encountered "the power of the spirit."

In countless churches dozens of people ritualistically go forward to be prayed for, claim their healing amidst cheers and shouts of "Praise the Lord", and keep coming back, time after time, never having truly received their healing. Preachers lie and say, "God told me you would be healed." The poor seekers lie when they say they know God healed them. Both lie because they believe their "confession of faith" pleases God. Abomination in the House of God! Lies are called faith. Many Charismatic churches now emphasize an even more unproveable kind of healing: the inner healing. Once again the same, seemingly tireless group, on a monthly or bi-monthly basis, goes forward for an inner healing or deliverance. Always thirsty, never filled, continuously deluded, but are satisfied with experiencing the tingling sensation of hands being laid on them as they are "slain-in-the-spirit." This swoon however never really seems to change anything. They always say it does, but they are seldom any different and they keep coming back. Time after time. They claim, they testify. But there is no change. Later the pastor comments that the services were tremendous. He says "The presence of God was so thick; you could have cut it with a knife." Everybody cheers. Everybody "gives glory to Jesus." Very few of the announced 100's are really changed by God. Perhaps some are, but only a few. Many are too embarrassed to admit that nothing happened. Others are content to be phonies, understanding that their pastors know they are phonies, but that they do not want them to tell the truth because it "might hurt someone's faith." People are "delivered from the bondage of Satan." Again and again. The same crowd. The same bondages. Time after time. The same claims. The same unspoken failures. The same clenched teeth smiles, "praising God." The same lies. The same unspoken encouragement to lie. But nothing really changes. Unbelievers come to visit these churches and in many cases, their greatest suspicions are confirmed: this "Christianity" is totally phony.

Several decades ago we began to see another manifestation of the deteriorating Saul Church. I Samuel 16:14 says, "Now the Spirit of the Lord departed from Saul and AN EVIL SPIRIT FROM THE LORD terrorized him." The aforementioned Oral Roberts made the startling and well publicized announcement that he heard a supernatural being tell him that he had to raise $4,000,000 in a several month period or this being (which claimed to be God) would kill him. To any discerning individual, spiritual or not, this remark was absurd. Many felt that this was a clever way to raise money. Others felt it was really God. But the answer is simple and very sad. This was NOT the Holy Spirit. The Holy Spirit does not need the money. The voice he heard was an evil spirit. The voice really threatened him. This being really wanted this man to raise millions, but the voice was demonic. The voice brought shame to the Real Jesus Christ because many undiscerning people really believed this was the character of our loving Savior. They actually believed that God would terrorize a man into pleading for millions of dollars so his life could be spared. Publicly, this gentleman was the first gross manifestation of what has been happening in the whole Saul Church. When his television ministry was established and began to use peace-filled, "nice" preaching and entertainment to attract people to Jesus, we could discern the sickly sweet odor of strange flesh being offered. But when he pled for money the unmistakable stench of the Evil One was present with the threat of death if money wasn't given to placate this spirit. The Spirit of God was gone, and a new, terrible spirit came to be in charge of this man's ministry.

Evil spirits have entered other lives where the Anointing is gone, and have found a willing ear that will listen to any new ideas that might enlarge their kingdom. They whisper doctrines of demons into these empty hearts and fill them with their lies. I Timothy 4:1, "But the Spirit explicitly says that in later times some will fall away from the faith, paying attention to deceitful spirits and doctrines of demons." The Saul Church has embraced the demonic lies of psychology and sorcery, including: visualization, name it and claim it without any real faith, some kinds of inner healing, and the power of self, and have been terrorized into believing that if they abandon these ungodly pursuits, they will lose their success. Some of our churches and ministries have become the dwelling place of the demonic.

Years ago, I asked a more experienced pastor friend of mine if it was possible for a demonic spirit to heal. He told me about a personal encounter he had with a man that he knew. This man at one time had a very successful healing ministry but lost it after he got involved in adulterous relationships and became quite backslidden. He said that this man had been out of the healing ministry for about ten years and had greatly desired to once again minister healing to God's people. One day this man was talking to my friend and asked him if he still had one arm shorter than the other. My friend said that he did, but also mentioned that he really didn't want his arm lengthened because then he would have to have all his shirts and coats altered. The man insisted that my friend give glory to God and allow him to pray that his arm would be lengthened. Under a lot of urging my friend finally submitted to the man and let him lay hands on his arm and pray. His arm immediately began to grow out of his sleeve. But as this continued he became very uncomfortable in his spirit and prayed under his breath "God if this is not of You, let my arm return to the length it was before." Immediately his arm shrunk back to its former length. I asked him what had happened and he said that the man was so desperate to minister the miraculous gift of healing that he didn't care where the power came from. He said that he believed that his arm was being lengthened by a demonic power."

Saul didn't care where the supernatural guidance came from; he just wanted to know what was going to happen! As a last resort he called for a medium or a witch to give him supernatural counsel. I am concerned today that many in the Saul church similarly don't care where the power comes from. They just want to see power.

In the 18th century during the Great Awakening in America and England, under the ministry of George Whitfield, John Wesley and others, MANY of their hearers fell down under the power of the Holy Spirit. These people were under tremendous conviction because of their sin against God and fell to the ground without being prompted by the speaker, especially under the ministry of George Whitfield. Often they were dealt with by God for hours and cried out for His mercy and forgiveness. Others would come to these people who were in great distress and prayerfully counseled them concerning the relief that Jesus Christ could give for their sin and despair. These people preached the gospel to those in spiritual agony and MANY became born-again and experienced real conversions that changed their lives forever. Hundreds of preachers were born-again during these meetings and consequently ministered to tens of thousands of people whose lives were miraculously changed in both America and England.

Many today go to Charismatic meetings so they can be prayed for, fall over and have an experience. Many do have experiences. Some feel light headed, some tingle all over, some laugh uproariously, some feel exhilaration. Very few experience conviction of sin, or an increased love for their Savior Jesus Christ. They just want to experience a kind of "spiritual" high. I am concerned that they want an experience, any pleasurable experience so badly, that it might not always be the Holy Spirit that they experience.

Another example of evil spirits at work with Charismatics that I have witnessed occurred at a home meeting that my wife and I attended a few years ago. The leader of the group turned the meeting over to his wife who had just been to a woman's conference where the theme had something to do with "Taking the City for Christ Through Spiritual Warfare and Worship." She was excited to share with us the new teachings that she had just learned. She had been taught the importance of using drums in worship and in warfare. She told us that for thousands of years heathen peoples have used drums to drive away evil spirits and to contact their gods. She said that it was time for God's people to take advantage of this powerful spiritual weapon. We Christians in America have been far too subdued in our warfare and needed to become deeply involved emotionally. Drums were said to be a very effective way of stirring our emotions and allowed us to become much more involved in worship and warfare. She said loud voices, singing or praying along with the loud rhythmic drums helped focus our minds and hearts in worship to God and warfare against Satan. She gave us an example of this technique by rhythmically beating on a tom-tom. She cried out in a sing-song way that was strangely reminiscent of American Indian chanting that I had seen in Western movies. Soon many in the meeting were crying out and chanting to the beat of the tom toms and were marching around single file. As she chanted and sang she went around the room praying for people in both English and in an unknown tongue. When she came to me I felt very strange and uncomfortable. As she prayed, I prayed in tongues in opposition to her prayers which I felt strongly were not of God. As I prayed, God assured me that this experience was not of Him, but was a demonic spirit attempting to recapture the hearts and minds in a geographical area where this demon had once held many hearts captive. My wife and I abruptly left the meeting. Several days later we contacted the couple and spoke to them our views. At first they were reluctant to listen and the husband strongly defended his wife. After repeated warnings the wife acknowledged that what we had said was probably true, and indicated that she would give the issue much prayer. Church Listen! THIS IS MORE THAN JUST FLESH! This not merely the spirit of unregenerate man! This is SATANIC! This is an EVIL SPIRIT that comes to confuse and capture the hearts of God's people. We do not need drums or volume to contact the Lord for His favor in battle. The scene I just related is much more representative of the priests of Baal that battled Elijah and cut themselves and shrieked out to their god and worked themselves into a fervor of religious "ecstasy" but were totally unsuccessful. Elijah meanwhile, dug trenches and poured water over the sacrifice and merely called to God to show whose god was real and whose god was phony. Fifty years ago Christians would have immediately recognized that the drum beating warfare was not of God. But our world culture, because of its own demonic quality, has infused the same heathen spirit into parts of the Church.

The Anointing of God is gone completely now in some Saul Charismatic churches. In others, it is fading fast. I Samuel 16:14 says, "Now the Spirit of the Lord departed from Saul."

Many Charismatic churches have responded to the emotional silliness of people like we just discussed and have decided that they will put an end to all of these machinations. In these churches, the pendulum has swung fully to the other side. They are highly suspicious of any message in tongues or prophetic utterance. In fact, because they have seen or heard about abuses of the gifts, they have decided that they will oversee the delivery of the gifts. They will screen the prophecy to be delivered if it is not from someone they trust to deliver a word that would be uplifting and positive. Typically they will weed out any negative references because they believe that prophetic utterances are always to be encouraging and edifying in a positive way. They do not follow the scriptural injunction to listen to the prophecy first and then to judge whether it is of God or not. Unfortunately, this position has led to a virtual stifling of the gifts of the Spirit in both community churches and denominational charismatic churches. These same churches are concerned about any negative utterance that might come forth. Some churches are also concerned that messages in tongues might confuse new Christians and unbelievers and suggest that they be delivered only in small groups or home meetings. The Scriptures, however, clearly state that "...tongues are for a sign, not to those who believe, but to unbelievers..." (I Cor 14:22).

Many Evangelical churches never believed in, or depended upon, the supernatural manifestation of the gifts of the Holy Spirit through God's people. Many have believed that God no longer gives His people supernatural gifts as are recorded in the New Testament. But they have believed and relied upon the Holy Spirit to convict of sin and reveal Jesus Christ as Lord and Savior in a way that would forever confirm their faith and grant them supernatural power to preach and teach the Gospel and the rest of Scripture. Many Evangelicals were touched by God in such a mighty way that they were literally floored by His Presence. George Whitfield, Charles Finney and D. L. Moody are just three of many evangelicals who have been mightily filled with God's Holy Spirit and preached anointed messages of conviction that persuaded people supernaturally. Most non-Charismatic Evangelical Saul Church leaders believe that they were filled with the Holy Spirit when they were born-again and consequently most of them do not seek for any subsequent empowerment of the Holy Spirit.

Today's leaders major on learning church growth principles, having talented worship leaders and appropriate psychological counseling techniques. Also Christian self-help books are quite popular. Often they do not view unsaved people essentially as sinners, but they view the unsaved as hurting people who need Jesus to make them healthy and whole. Consequently, a fervent love for God, a raging hatred of evil and lukewarmness, and a power to deeply touch the spirits of their flock is for the most part gone.

The Anointing of God is gone completely now in some Saul Evangelical churches. In others it is fading fast. I Samuel 16:14 says, "Now the Spirit of the Lord departed from Saul."

The leaders of the Church of Saul have pursued the kingdom of God and gathered people to populate their versions of it for decades now. They have exhausted virtually every worldly method. They are losing the Spirit very quickly - from the head on down. Even as the anointing oil poured down over Aaron from the head to the body (Psalms 133), so the anointing has been leaving the Saul Church from the leaders on down. Because of double-minded, half-hearted obedience, the anointing is virtually all gone. Already we see the evil presence of Satan and his demons being manifested in some of the leaders and people. The Christian leadership scandals that were front page news in the 1980's and 1990's exposed great sin and terrible problems that existed in high profile ministries that had huge followings. Even into the 21st century we have seen unthinkable sin exposed at the national leadership level in the Church.

In the late 1990's we saw Charismatic churches and denominations lose millions to scam artists because of their greedy foolish hearts. We must remember that most of the people who were scammed were men of prayer who really believed they heard from God regarding their participation in these phony money making schemes.

God has sent an evil spirit to the Saul Church even as Saul was similarly plagued by the Lord. There is a terrible price to pay for ministering in the flesh in the Name of Jesus. There is a terrible judgment that comes from God upon those who lose sight of the real issue of being a Christian which is, ""Jesus answered, "The foremost (commandment) is, 'HEAR O ISRAEL! THE LORD OUR GOD IS ONE LORD; AND YOU SHALL LOVE THE LORD YOUR GOD WITH ALL YOUR HEART, AND WITH ALL YOUR SOUL, AND WITH ALL YOUR MIND, AND WITH ALL YOUR STRENGTH.' 'The second is this, 'YOU SHALL LOVE YOUR NEIGHBOR AS YOURSELF.' There is no other greater commandment other than these"" (Mark 12:29-31). When God and His whole Word is the focus of God's people, we will be strong. When man's desires and apparent needs are the issue, we will be desperately weak. The evil spirit that now is coming upon the Saul Church IS a judgment from God Himself.

The victories that Saul gained were for the most part temporary victories. In I Samuel 31:7, "And when the men of Israel who were on the other side of the valley with those who were beyond the Jordan, saw that the men of Israel had fled and that Saul and his sons were dead, they abandoned the cities and fled; then the Philistines came and lived in them." We see that in one battle the Philistines took back much of what Saul had fought for and won over the previously forty years. And so today we are beginning to see the Saul Church lose much of what it has fought for and won. Even as the victories of Saul were for the most part lost when Saul died, so the victories of the Saul Church will prove to be, for the most part, temporary victories.

Losing the Anointing of God, losing hard fought victories, and ultimately being turned over to an evil spirit, are terrible, but just compensation to a man or a people with an unrepentant, rebellious heart. The manifested evil of the spirit of extortion, demonic healings, heathen worship, and falling victim to scams that rob God's people of millions of dollars have been present for years in the Saul Church. In the decades to come, as in the final days of Saul, God will tear it all down and begin to build a Church that is after His own heart.

CHAPTER 13

THE KING IS DEAD; LONG LIVE THE KING

I Samuel 31:4-7, ""Then Saul said to his armor bearer, "draw your sword and pierce me through with it, lest these uncircumcised come and pierce me through and make sport of me." But his armor bearer would not for he was greatly afraid. So Saul took his sword and fell on it. And when his armor bearer saw that Saul was dead, he also fell on his sword and died with him. Then Saul died with his three sons, his armor bearer, and all his men on that day together. And when the men of Israel who were on the other side of the valley, and those who were beyond the Jordan saw that the men of Israel had fled and that Saul and his sons were dead, they abandoned the cities and fled; then the Philistines came and lived in them..""

Saul died just as Samuel had prophesied from the grave. And now the visible fulfillment of the spiritual fact that Saul had lost the kingdom was at hand. Not only did he lose the kingdom, he lost his life and his family as well. Not only did Israel lose their leader, they lost much of their freedom as well. Saul started out right in God's eyes. He was, at the beginning, according to I Samuel 15:17, "little in his own eyes." He was legitimately surprised to be chosen for leadership, and he was so touched by the Holy Spirit that he was "changed into another man" (I Samuel 10:6). God changed his heart and gave him miraculous spiritual abilities. He even prophesied with the prophets: I Samuel 10:9-10, "Then it happened when he turned his back to leave Samuel, God changed his heart; and all those signs came about on that day. When they came to the hill there, behold, a group of prophets met him and the Spirit of God came upon him mightily, so that he prophesied among them." Even though Saul's end was terrible and his last years were a pain-filled, paranoid finish to a disobedient life, earlier in his life he had concern for others, zeal for his people, and he was even able to instill the fear of the Lord into them and unify them with that fear. God also gave him supernatural strength: I Samuel 11:4-7, """Then the messengers came to Gibeah of Saul and spoke these words in the hearing of the people, and all the people lifted up their voices and wept. Now behold Saul coming from the field behind the oxen and he said, "What is the matter with the people that they weep?" So they related to him the words of the men of Jabesh. Then the Spirit of God came upon Saul mightily when he heard these words, and he became very angry. And he took a yoke of oxen and cut them in pieces, and sent them throughout the territory of Israel by the hand of messengers, saying, "Whoever does not come out after Saul and after Samuel, so shall it be done to his oxen." Then the dread of the Lord fell on the people, and they came out as one man...""" As long as Saul had the anointing of God he was a spiritual, mighty man of the Lord.

Remember David's tribute to Saul, from I Samuel 1:19-24: "Your beauty, O Israel, is slain on your high places! How have the mighty fallen! Tell it not in Gath; proclaim it not in the streets of Ashkelon; lest the daughters of the Philistines rejoice, lest the daughters of the uncircumcised exult. O mountains of Gilboa, let not dew or rain be on you, nor fields of offerings; for there the shield of the mighty was defiled, the shield of Saul, not anointed with oil. From the blood of the slain, from the fat of the mighty, the bow of Jonathan did not turn back, and the sword of Saul did not return empty. Saul and Jonathan, beloved and pleasant in their life, and in their death they were not parted, they were swifter than eagles, they were stronger than lions. O daughters of Israel, weep over Saul, who clothed you luxuriously in scarlet, who put ornaments of gold on your apparel."

David's tribute to Saul tells us much about Saul and why he failed so miserably. His popularity is mentioned - he found great favor with his subjects: he was beloved. His ability as a warrior is mentioned: his sword did not return empty, - he is called swift and strong. His ability to provide material blessing is mentioned: he clothed his subjects LUXURIOUSLY in scarlet and gold. All the qualities that David mentions are outer, carnal qualities. Nothing is mentioned of God's love for him, his love for God, his dependence on God, or his faith in God. He was given power by God, but it was not used to best advantage. Saul never really understood the great gift that God had given him. Saul never seemed to understand why he was given such power. He never seemed to understand that it was to do the will of God and bring glory to God. He seemed to think the power was merely to bless God's people and himself. Even though his heart was changed, it seems that it was not changed completely. Saul was a man with a divided heart. Saul wanted to minister for God, but on his own terms. He was given strength and ability, but he seemed content to see shallow victories and carnal blessings. HE DID NOT DELIVER HIS PEOPLE TO BE FREE TO LOVE GOD; HE MERELY DELIVERED HIS PEOPLE TO BE TEMPORARILY FREE FROM THE PHILISTINES! He did not provide their hearts with a single-minded devotion to Jehovah their God; he merely reinforced their desire to use God to get their own way by seeing the enemy defeated and being able to live in luxurious comfort. Saul never saw the heart of the issue. He never understood that the Philistines were not the issue; God was the issue. Even when he spoke to the spirit of Samuel, he missed the point, "Then Samuel said to Saul, "Why have you disturbed me by bringing me up?" And Saul answered, "I am greatly distressed; for the Philistines are waging war against me, and God has departed from me and answers me no more, either through prophets or by dreams; therefore I have called you that you may make known to me what I should do." (I Samuel 28:15). Saul was worried about the Philistines. Samuel tried to show him that the real issue was that God had departed from him, and had become his enemy! Saul would never cry as David cried in Psalms 51, "take not Thy Holy Spirit from me." He did not value the Holy Spirit. He valued the carnal. His heart was not after God. His heart was after the carnal. Carnal victories! Carnal luxury! Carnal honor! But not after God for <u>Himself</u> <u>alone</u>. We do not see at any point in his life Saul express a single-minded love for God or fear of losing His Holy Spirit.

The leadership in the Saul Church in our day has been showing signs that it too has lost the anointing of God, and also no longer fears losing the Holy Spirit of God. There is a Laodecian presumptuousness that this church is doing fine and need not fear judgment. The only fear they express is that they will not be able to finance the tremendous monuments they have erected to themselves and their denominations. They fear failure, not loss of relationship with God. They seem to be oblivious of the fact that the Philistines (the world) gains victory after victory and the Church loses ground in the culture. They are oblivious to the gains of the cults, such as the Jehovah Witnesses, the Mormons and even the false religion of the Muslims. The Saul Church is dying BY CHOICE because it will not see! The eyes and the brain of the Saul church are no longer functioning properly. There is double vision in the leadership, and the thinking process of men in authority no longer seems to be able to discern right from wrong.

Even as early as the 1980's the Charismatic leadership of the Saul Church would not immediately rebuke a man who blasphemously depicted God as a tyrant who threatened him with death if he did not raise huge sums of money for works that he was associated with. It is unbelievable that leaders and pastors of huge Charismatic ministries would not speak out against this unscriptural display of greed or folly or both. It should have been clear that this man had lost touch with God. There should have been a unified cry to Christians and the secular public that this man was wrong. They should have spoken to him in private and if he would not be corrected, they should have warned the Church and the public that he had been misled by an evil spirit. They should have discouraged people from giving to his work until he repented of his words. They should have clearly stated that the statements he made could not have possibly been inspired by God. Terms like "abomination" would have been fitting for the remarks he made. This man was a great hindrance to what God was doing in America and should have been dealt with severely using pressure to have him step aside from his leadership. Because he was not dealt with by men, within several years, God dealt with him and one of his great works was shut down. The Charismatics, however, would not let the Sword of the Word touch him. This once great man's spiritual failure described above is topped only by the terrible sin of the leadership neglecting to warn the sheep of his false prophecies. How could these shepherds be so blind and spiritually ignorant? The Saul Church is killing itself by rejecting the sword of the Lord, the Word of God. Consequently, it is becoming blinder and almost brain-dead.

The death of Saul was a great tragedy for the people of God and their new leader, David. David did not gloat or point to the terrible spiritual decline of the old king. We too, if we truly desire to be men after God's own heart, must NEVER revel in the fall of any anointed or previously anointed man of God. The ministry of Saul was set aside by God because of his failures, and the new leader, David, was patiently waiting for God to raise him up. Even today, all in the emerging David Church want leadership that is fully, passionately, and radically after God's own heart! We want leadership that invites the Sword of the Lord to cut away all that would hurt His Body, whether it is people, doctrines or sin. Even if the sword of the Lord which is the Word of God, cuts deeply into our own hearts, we prefer that God would do His work and NOT allow the disease of sin to fester in His Body. We want leadership that is so in love with Jesus that they would rather die than cause Him shame.

We want leadership that knows there is a cancer that is destroying the people of God and their culture and knows the operation will hurt PERSONALLY, but for the sake of the Lord Jesus Christ is desirous of having the SAULISH INFECTION cut away from both the Body at large and each individual heart. This is necessary if the whole Body which God will raise up will be composed of men and women with pure hearts. This is necessary if we are to see a Church that is made up of men and women who are after God's own heart.

DAVID'S LOVE AND HONOR FOR SAUL

As was just mentioned, in the first chapter of II Samuel we see a beautiful song of praise directed to God's people regarding Saul, their recently fallen king. David wrote this psalm and as its content reveals, loved and honored the life and ministry of Saul. He was not unaware of the fact that Saul had lost the anointing of the Holy Spirit and was terribly afflicted by an evil spirit. He was personally touched by his paranoia, by his jealousy and his murderous intentions. In spite of this, David still honored Saul and the anointing and power of God that once flowed through him.

Often critics of the Charismatic Movement don't recognize that a man who commits terrible crimes against God and men can still have once carried the mighty anointing of God, even as Saul at one time was mightily anointed by God. These men will reference with great accuracy the demonic or insane utterances of men who once ministered God's healing power. But they wholly neglect to recognize the mantel of healing that once rested on them. They cannot understand nor do they have any love for men and women who once carried this anointing of God and then have lost it. Many have ministered healing, have prophesied and have preached great sermons and were powerfully used by God for His glory, and then failed God. Many critics, however, because of the inappropriate lifestyles, false doctrines or false prophecies of these men and women, have completely discounted every facet of the anointing of God that they once possessed and categorize all that they have said or done as "of the devil." They seem to be completely ignorant of the fact that God has in Scripture AND in the life of the Church, anointed men who have done things which pleased themselves and the people but often were not concerned about pleasing God.

Scriptural examples of the failures of men anointed by God include Balaam, Samson and Peter. Balaam, who was at the end an enemy of God and His people because of his own greed, had to be recognized as a man through whom God had spoken many times. Samson, when he was in the Spirit, magnified the Lord spectacularly with his God given gifts of strength. Other times, however, he was a man of lust, rebellion and self-conceit. Peter, in the New Testament, both before and after the powerful Holy Spirit illuminated his mind and life with tongues of fire that rushed through his soul and his spirit like a mighty wind, also let the Lord down. In Scripture at least two situations are mentioned. After Peter went out with the seventy and healed the sick in the Name of Jesus, he denied Him three times. After the day of Pentecost, he denied the heart of the Gospel in front of Paul and others by his unwillingness to eat with Gentiles because he feared offending his Jewish brothers. We must not entirely discount a man's ministry or message on the basis of his sinful attitudes, actions or even poor doctrine. Even when these attitudes, actions or beliefs are wrong, we still MUST recognize the anointing from God that rested on individuals that God used and honor them accordingly.

The non-Charismatics who are completely convinced that the supernatural gifts and ministries of the Spirit are absolutely and unalterably NOT for today believe that ALL these gifts and ministries are either of the flesh or worse yet, of Satan himself. Because of this belief it is almost impossible for them to honor anything supernatural that God has done through Pentecostals or Charismatics. This lack of charity and total condemnation of supernatural Charismatic and Pentecostal ministry CANNOT be excused by their ignorance. In spirit, it is not much different than the wrong headed and hateful attitude of some Protestants in the 16th century who tortured the Ana-Baptists who re-baptized by immersion those who became believers.

The true David spirit is a spirit that is wise as a serpent; those in the David Church know that the enemy can get a foothold in a Christian's life and that a man can become an enemy of God because of his beliefs, his teachings or his immorality. But David was gentle as a dove in his love for Saul and had mercy upon him when he could have killed him. Today some of the most articulate critics of the Charismatic Movement lack the spiritual ability to see the anointing of the Lord in MANY of those that they so vehemently criticize. Often they are correct in pointing out the error and sin that they see, but they are absolutely unable to honor anything in the lives of these men and women. This is not to suggest that all persons that they criticize are men or women of God. Many in that day will say Lord Lord we ministered supernaturally in your Name, and He will say to them, "I never knew you." BUT, He will NOT say that to EVERYONE who ministered supernaturally.

It is extremely important to recognize the tension that always exists between truth and love. The Bible never fails to point out errors of judgment and sins against God that great men have committed, but always acknowledges the power of God that flows through them during their time of effective ministry. Good writers of church history also will not flinch at mentioning the foolish doctrines and sinful deeds of great men and women of God. Poor writers and dishonest scholars typically paint an idealistic picture of the heroes of the denomination or movement that they support. The reverse can be said about unloving men of little discernment who neglect to mention or praise the great doctrines or great deeds of those who are not part of the movement or denomination that they support. This is equally dishonest and displeasing to God.

There will come a time when David must separate himself from Saul. but the true David will never lose his love nor his respect for the ministries that have been anointed by God to serve His purposes. It is important, as these men and women are directed by God, that they leave the Saul Church, but it is even more important that they honor what God has done through the lives of men and women that have fallen short or men and women who have not yet seen the tragic damaging error of the Saul Church.

SECTION II

PEARL HARBOR

CHAPTER 14

TO JUDGE OR NOT TO JUDGE

Suppose that you wanted to totally incapacitate or kill a strong, healthy young girl. Now suppose that you had access to a strain of cancer that could accomplish your purpose. Obviously you would need a carefully thought out plan. First you would have to come up with a way to make contact with your victim. Perhaps you could disguise yourself as a doctor. You could then tell her that you had a new diet that would cause her to grow faster, become stronger, and also feel better than she had ever felt before. Perhaps you could mix the deadly strain of cancer with a powerful steroid and cocaine. This would give her strength, a feeling of euphoria and a sense of mental sharpness. You could put the deadly mixture in a milk shake to make it pleasantly palatable for her. She would learn to trust you as a friend and to enjoy your little visits because of the good feelings and the sense of mental alertness and strength that she experienced.

But even with the best laid plans there can be hindrances that would keep you from achieving your goal. Suppose she had caring relatives who loved her very much and could see that she was deteriorating and suspect there was something wrong with her. What if her older brother from college came home and saw her condition? He might see that her new diet made her alternately euphoric and then irritable and paranoid. He might notice that her "growth" was not a natural or a healthy growth but was unnatural and unhealthy. Her friends also would likely notice that something was wrong. After investigation they might determine that there was something terribly wrong with the diet of this young girl. At this point it would look like your little scheme was about to be exposed for what it was. But because you were smart you would have a properly well-thought-out response to their concerns and conclusions.

As criticism and suspicions would mount towards your methods and the diet that you had prescribed for her it would be necessary to come up with a believable response to this criticism. The answer is both simple and very obvious: you could tell her very calmly, firmly and lovingly that these overly suspicious intruders had no need nor right to judge her. After all, she is old enough to know the truth from a lie. What is more important, the others have no right to judge with whom she associates nor to question the methods that her highly respected doctor is using to make her feel better and become stronger. After all, you tell her, that she does not judge them does she? Of course not. No one should judge anyone. It is not right. After all, EVEN THE BIBLE SAYS: JUDGE NOT! You tell her to consider the results that she has experienced. See the growth! Notice how good she feels! See the increased strength that she has! ANYWAY, they have NO RIGHT TO JUDGE A SISTER!

No Right to Judge

Judge Not

Judge not lest YOU BE JUDGED!

Don't criticize

You have a CRITICAL SPIRIT

These phrases have become the litany of the cancer riddled steroid pumped pleasure drugged dying (but growing!) Saul Church. This DON'T JUDGE doctrine has prevented the real doctor with the scalpel/sword to come and cut away the cancerous growth and take away the steroids and the cocaine. Very likely, in the Halls of Hell there is a demon strutting around with a giant medal hanging around his neck because of his discovery of the Ultimate Doctrine of Demons. This doctrine however is not really new. It is a rerun of the old Roman Catholic doctrine. It is a new application of an old doctrine that is still in use. That doctrine says that we must not judge the Holy Father the Pope, and certainly we are not to judge Mother Church and her teachings. Particularly we are not to judge teachings on Mary, on salvation by faith plus works and sanctification by doing penance and many other doctrines that come from traditions of men that the Catholic Church values as equal to Scripture.

The Reformation dealt a severe blow regarding the placing of men and doctrines above judgment. Every revival since then has reinforced this great truth. The First Great Awakening reminded the dying Church of England that "you must be born again." The beginnings of the Second Great Awakening reminded the Church, among other things that she could not be complete without the power of the Holy Spirit. The Pentecostal Revival of the early 20th century reminded the weakened Church that the gifts and ministries of the Holy Spirit were for the people of God today. Every revival reclaims Scripture that has been rationalized away by complacent and scripturally blind leaders.

Unfortunately in America in the 21st century, we have seen most revival fires die down to virtually nothing. And even the old dead doctrine of the Roman Catholic Church has risen up out of the mire and mist to weaken and blind God's people in their fight against the enemy. We now consider the Roman Catholics to be our brothers in the battle. Like the Roman Catholics we too now have our extra Scriptural "authority." We value and function as if "psychological insight" is equal with Scripture. Also in this New Age of Popes, we have thousands of protestant popes, all who cannot be judged because they are the Lord's anointed: both Evangelical popes and Charismatic popes. All are supposed to be the anointed of the Lord and all are not to be touched by criticism. What is even worse, since Martin Luther re-established the biblical truth that we who believe in Christ are ALL anointed by God, we can now apply this doctrine (judge not) to ALL Christians. Everyone who goes by the title of Christian, according to this New Age doctrine, is not to be judged by a brother or a sister.

It is Not IF We Judge but HOW and WHO and WHAT We Judge!

In this New Age of deception Matt 7:1 is one of the most misapplied Scriptures in the Bible. This Scripture is usually only partially quoted as, "judge not", and even when it is quoted in it's entirety it is misunderstood both as to intent and context. The context of this verse is that it is the first verse of the third chapter of the Sermon on the Mount. It is preceded by chapters five and six. Matt. 7:1 is the first sentence of an entire chapter devoted to telling God's people How, Who and What they should judge. The whole chapter is an exhortation on judging or evaluating. The chapter relates to judging so-called Christians and doctrines which are supposed to be Christian.

The first section, Matt. 7:1-5, tells us that we need to judge with the right attitude. "Do not judge lest you be judged. For in the way you judge, you will be judged; and by your standard of measure, it will be measured to you. And why do you look at the speck that is in your brother's eye, but do not notice the log that is in your own eye? Or how can you say to your brother, 'Let me take the speck out of your eye,' and behold, the log is in your own eye? You hypocrite, first Take the log out of your own eye, and then you will see clearly to take the speck out of your brother's eye." We must not be critical merely to put someone down or make ourselves look better by comparison. The "log" that is in the eye of the one who judges may well be the JUDGMENTAL, CONDEMNATORY attitude we see in many people. It may also be any sin that causes us to defensively attack another because we feel so guilty about our own sin or merely because we do not like the person. It is the attitude that takes pleasure in exposing someone as a sinner; it is NOT the attitude that wants to see a fallen brother truly repent or a deceived brother return to the truth; it is only interested in "getting" the other guy. The Lord warns us that if we treat others in that manner, then HE HIMSELF will see to it that we are dealt with in the same way. This Scripture tells us that if we are overly concerned about other people's sins, and are quick to point out their faults, and speak without mercy we are in danger. We can expect to be dealt with in the same manner BY THE LORD. We must understand that if we are concerned about God's holiness and also concerned about a brother trapped in sin, we must function with mercy. If we correctly show mercy to others, then God will show us mercy. One reason many leaders in our churches do not want to deal with other people's sins is because they do not want their OWN sins to be dealt with. We must understand that when we go about cleaning up the Body of Christ, we too will be cleaned up and exposed by God. This is NOT a grievous thing to a man who TRULY desires God's holiness in his own life and wants God's will more than his own will. This man KNOWS that God is fully aware of his sins and, if God chooses to expose his sins to others, he is not too concerned because he longs to be holy at any cost. But the admonition by the Lord in chapter 7 of Matthew is to judge as WE would like to be judged – with wisdom, love and mercy, but WHERE NECESSARY, with severity and even public exposure.

Matt 7:6 is not merely a random interjection into the teaching: this Scripture has to do with judging to whom we minister. "Do not give what is holy to dogs, and do not throw your pearls before swine, lest they trample them under their feet, and turn and tear you to pieces."

The words of God are precious and holy and at times must be protected. We must realize that some men are dogs and some men are swine. When we come to recognize this truth, if the people to whom we are ministering these pure, precious, holy words of God are dogs or swine, we typically are not to minister this truth to them. It is not just that you may well be attacked by these people, it has to do with what these people do to the Word of God. When they treat His Word with distain or insult and turn these holy words into something ugly, you MUST, in most cases, cease your ministry to them.

There are times however, when you are to minister as a prophet and regardless of how they respond, you must deliver a word of judgment or warning to them. Often these words will harden their hearts and they may turn on you but there are times when God directs us to minister in this way. Isaiah 6:9-10, which is referred to and quoted in four sections of the New Testament, is a good example of this usage. ""And (the Lord) said, "go and tell this people, "keep on listening but do not perceive; Keep on looking but do not understand." "Render the hearts of this people insensitive, Their ears dull, And their eyes dim, Lest they see with their eyes, Hear with their ears, Understand with their hearts, And return and be healed.""

Another major section in this chapter on judging (Matt 7) deals with WHAT to judge. It deals with judging doctrine (Matt. 7:13-14, "Enter by the narrow gate; for the gate is wide, and the way is broad that leads to destruction, and many are those who enter by it. For the gate is small, and the way is narrow that leads to life, and few are those who find it."). For two previous chapters, Jesus has been teaching us some of the greatest foundational doctrine in the Bible. He has been telling us what HIS WAY is. Now He tells us that we need to be very careful. He says that the entrance point into His kingdom is the Narrow Gate. He says that even the way that we live is NARROW. He warns us that the Road to Destruction is BROAD and many walk this way. Chapters five and six of Matthew have been a description of the narrow gate and narrow road. He tells us here that WE NEED TO JUDGE WHAT WE HEAR. Is it the Narrow Way or the Broad Way that is being taught? He says that we must judge what we hear and only receive doctrine that opens the narrow gate, and leads us on the narrow way. Jesus tells us here to JUDGE AS IF OUR LIFE DEPENDED ON IT because it does! The WAY we choose to walk will determine WHERE we end up.

Next Jesus tells us to BEWARE (Matt. 7:15-23, "Beware of the false prophets, who come to you in sheep's clothing, but inwardly are ravenous wolves. You will know them by their fruits. Grapes are not gathered from thorn bushes, nor figs from thistles, are they? Even so, every good tree bears good fruit; but the bad tree bears bad fruit. Every tree that does not bear good fruit is cut down and thrown into the fire. So then, you will know them by their fruits.

Beware means to <u>watch out for</u>. It implies that we must be more than careful. Beware means there is danger to avoid. He tells us to BEWARE of false prophets. In this section, He tells us WHO to judge. He warns us against prophets and teachers that will lead us to or teach us the BROAD way which leads to destruction. We must BEWARE of those who speak for God that don't warn us about danger, or prophets that almost ALWAYS have a positive nice word that tickles the flesh. If they do not teach or prophesy like Jesus, they may well be false ministers. A helpful spiritual exercise would be to get a red letter edition of the Bible and JUST READ THE WORDS OF JESUS. In the midst of the words of hope and love you will see many warnings and judgments.

We MUST judge these men regarding what they speak and how they act. Jesus warns us NOT to judge by outward appearance. These men are disguised to look like sheep. When their heart is exposed, however, it IS the heart of a hungry, blood-thirsty, murderous wolf. He tells us to JUDGE these men on the basis of their fruit. Are they gentle, loving, selfless, holy, giving men of God who are concerned with the needs of the flock? Or are they merely smiling, selfish, impure TAKERS who cater to the desires of the unsuspecting sheep so they can have a large flock and be looked upon as successful? Jesus tells us we MUST judge ministers of the gospel. Again, we judge because our spiritual lives depend on it! We must judge the fruit of their lips and the fruit of their lives. Do they stress the material and the psychological or do they stress the spiritual? Do they encourage people to love themselves and seek comfort or do they encourage people to love Jesus enough to obey Him and follow Him wherever He takes us.

In the next section, Jesus warns not to judge apparent ministry abilities or successes as any indication of relationship with Him. Matt 7:21-23 says, ""Not everyone who says to Me, "Lord, Lord" will enter the kingdom of heaven"; but he who does the will of My Father who is in heaven. Many will say to Me on that day, "Lord, Lord, did we not prophesy in Your Name, and in Your Name cast out demons, and in Your Name perform many miracles?" ""And then I will declare to them, "I never knew you: depart from Me you who practice lawlessness.""

Just because a man apparently or even actually prophesies, casts out demons, works miracles and does it all using the name of the Lord, it does not mean that these gifts are an indication that he is the Lord's. Once again, we see the word LAWLESSNESS to describe the false prophets and teachers and miracles workers. They do not have a love for the law; they do not care enough about Jesus to obey Him. They are JUDGED by Jesus to be phonies and are told to DEPART from Him. We too must not judge a man by his ministry success, but judge him by his fruit of loving obedience to our Lord and his teaching about the narrow gate and the narrow way.

The last section of this chapter once again refers not only to ministers but to all who would apparently follow Jesus. Here the Lord gives us the example of the two foundations. Matt. 7:24-27, "Therefore everyone who hears these words of Mine, and acts upon them, may be compared to a wise man, who built his house upon the rock. And the rain descended, and the floods came, and the winds blew, and burst against that house, and yet it did not fall, for it had been founded upon the rock. And everyone who hears these words of Mine, and does not act upon them, will be like a foolish man, who built his house upon the sand. And the rain descended, and the floods came, and the winds blew, and burst against that house; and it fell, and great was its fall."

Hearing the words of Jesus is NOT enough: we must HEED them; we must DO them. In this section of Scripture, the rock is not merely encountering our Lord Jesus Christ, but clearly is OBEDIENCE to the words of Jesus Christ.

His sheep WILL hear His voice and WILL follow Him! John 10:27 says, "My sheep hear My voice and I know them and they follow Me." Matt 7:24-27 clearly exhorts us to judge ourselves and make sure that we are obeying the words of our Lord Jesus Christ, so that when the storm comes we will not fall away. II Cor. 13:5 says, "Examine yourselves to see whether ye be in the faith—test yourselves." The Lord tells us to judge ourselves by our response to His Word. True believers will believe Him ENOUGH TO OBEY HIM and REPENT a lot! Phonies DO NOT understand that real faith ALWAYS ultimately has the fruit of obedience to Him. Jesus tells us to JUDGE ourselves and to see if we are hearers only or DOERS of his Word.

DON'T TOUCH THE ANOINTED OF GOD

I spoke earlier about how Jesus JUDGED the Pharisees, even though they represented the spiritual leadership of the Jews. He judged them, PUBLICALLY and ANGRILY, as being HYPOCRITES. Paul judges Peter, PUBLICALLY, as being a phony around Jewish Christians. This account is presented in Gal. 2:11, 14, ""But when Cephas (Peter) came to Antioch, I opposed him to his face, because he stood condemned…But when I saw that they were not straight-forward about the truth of the gospel, I said to Cephas in the presence of all "If you being a Jew live like the Gentiles and not like the Jews, how is it that you compel the Gentiles to live like Jews?"" Also in the Old Testament, we see prophets judging both kings and the people of God whenever they were told by the Lord to do so. We MUST judge leadership and at times speak out against what they teach and what they do, and even what they don't teach and don't do. It is not a privilege, it is a responsibility.

PROPHETS ARE LOST

The enemy has enjoyed a major victory for hundreds of years. Even as he continues to fool billions into believing that he does not exist, he also deceives hundreds of millions of apparent Christians into believing that prophets no longer exist. The Evangelicals and Fundamentalists still do not believe that, in our day, a man can hear from God and bring a warning or word by inspiration, dream, or vision to God's people. They continue to be deceived into believing that this type of ministry (the supernatural gifts and ministries as described in Acts, 1 Corinthians, Book of Revelation, etc.) ceased once the Bible was completed. This, of course, is deception and even the HARD NOSED Fundamentalists, if they keep loving Jesus Christ for Himself alone, and live long enough, will see how much they were fooled.

The Charismatics and Pentecostals, on the other hand, conditionally accept the ministry of the prophet. But their idea of a prophet is a man who tells us essentially GOOD things. Today many Charismatics and Pentecostals will not believe or accept men who have the anointing of a prophet like John the Baptist or John the Revelator. John the Baptist railed against the religious hypocrites and John the Revelator foretold the severe dealings of God with His people in the second and third chapters of the Revelation.

Charismatics and Pentecostals have come to believe that all prophetic messages are supposed to be encouraging and edifying in a positive sense. Most quote from I Cor 14:3. Most quote either from the New International Version which says, "But everyone who prophesies speaks to men for their strengthening, encouragement and comfort" or the New Living Translation which says, "But one who prophesies is helping others grow in the Lord, encouraging and comforting them." They believe and teach that all prophetic messages should be positive. I have personally experienced pastors who rejected the message that I delivered because it was a warning and not a positive word of encouragement. They quoted this Scripture to me in defense of their actions. This doctrine is WIDESPREAD in the Charismatic Movement. They do not accept the N.A.S.B. translation which says, "But who prophesies speaks to men for edification and EXHORTATION and consolation." Even the King James Version says, "But he that prophesieth speaketh unto men to edification and EXHORTATION and comfort." The Apostle John is an excellent example of one who prophesies in exhortation form. Please note John's exhortations to the seven Churches in the Book of Revelation. Five of these exhortations judge the five Churches to be in great danger and calls for them to repent or experience terrible judgment.

Many churches and ministers reject any prophet or prophecy that would JUDGE their people, their churches, the ministers themselves or their denominations. They would also reject any prophetic call to repent. They believe that they do not need any judgment and in fact, many churches and denominations teach that God would never judge His own people.

In both the Old Testament and the New Testament we see prophets of God judging the doctrine and conduct of God's people. If the conduct of the people of the Lord or their leaders is found to be unrighteous or unholy, the prophets, by the guidance of Scripture and the Holy Spirit calls the people to repent of their sin of going astray from God's Word. Typically the prophet warns the people of the judgment that will most certainly come if they do not repent and change their ways.

JUDGMENT BEGINS IN THE HOUSE OF THE LORD!

In our time, a time when the Greatest Deception of all times is being perpetrated upon the world and the Church, a time when if it were possible EVEN THE ELECT would be deceived—the enemy has managed to slip into the visible Church of Jesus Christ a doctrine of demons which says that judging of false doctrine and false teachers will not be tolerated "in the spirit of unity." Just at a time when the Greatest Deception of all times is twisting and shaping doctrines to fit the image of the desires of our flesh, and the image of the desires of the enemy, the attitude of "don't worry about doctrine", or "don't judge the other man's doctrine—just love him for the sake of unity" appears on the Christian scene.

We NEED TO JUDGE AND BE JUDGED NOW more than ever before! Judgment must cover everything that is happening in the Church. Years ago at a meeting of ministers, the Lord spoke to me about the need for Christians to judge righteous judgment. He showed me a fountain gushing out of the earth and a stream that came forth from that fountain. From a distance the fountain looked relatively clear. However, when I got closer to it, I could see debris in the fountain. The fountain contained clods of dirt, tin cans, refuse, and garbage – but the debris did not make the water undrinkable, you just had to be careful. Then I saw the fountain split and there were two fountains. One of the fountains was becoming clearer; there was less and less debris and refuse as it continued streaming forth. The other fountain got more and more filthy until eventually all that came out of it was a horrible smelling, sludge-like material. Eventually the smelly, sludge-like material just stopped and that fountain ran dry. The stream that was getting progressively clearer became perfectly clear and this stream flooded over everything and even the fountain of filth was swept away. Then the pure stream became an ocean and covered the whole earth.

I asked the Lord the meaning of the vision and He said that the single undivided fountain and the stream that came from it was the move of the Holy Spirit on the earth as it existed at the time of the vision. He said that the stream would split into two streams, because He was going to bring division. He said that there would then be two "apparent" moves of His Holy Spirit upon the earth. One stream, the stream that becomes progressively more pure, would be made up of people who HONESTLY look at the stream of the Holy Spirit in their own lives and in the life of His Church. He said that those who see the doctrinal impurities & person sins, acknowledge the doctrinal impurities & personal sins, confess the doctrinal impurities & personal sins and repent of the impurities/sins will be a part of the move of His Spirit and will become progressively more like Jesus. The stream that gets dirtier, until it is completely filthy, is made up of people who will NOT see the impurities in their own lives or in the life of the Church. These people will stubbornly choose NOT to let God's Word and God's men JUDGE their hearts and doctrine. They will take the position that they do not need cleansing and that it is not necessary to JUDGE the CHURCH with regards to matters of doctrine or the practices of its leaders and sheep. These people are SATISFIED to remain in their current condition and are confident that God will put this unacknowledged and unrepented sin and carnal ministry "under the Blood." They feel sure that His love will cover their multitude of sins. These unrepentant, presumptuous people will become progressively more impure until they are totally filthy and the movement that they are involved with will also become totally defiled and useless to God.

The Lord said that soon He will raise up men who will expose the filthiness in the Church, both doctrinal filth and personal filth. He said that it is NECESSARY that we listen to these men. Those who speak against and mock or IGNORE them are in danger of being part of the FILTHINESSS described above. But all who fall on their faces before God repent of their terrible carnality, and cry out against the abominations that are being committed in His Holy Temple will be spared the filth and the judgment that follows. In our day it will be as prophesied by Ezekiel in chapter 9, ""And the Lord said to him, "Go through the midst of the city, even through the midst of Jerusalem, and put a mark on the foreheads of the men who *SIGH AND GROAN OVER ALL THE ABOMINATIONS* which are being committed in its midst." We MUST open our eyes and SEE the true condition and weakness of God's people in our time!

It is absolutely necessary that we JUDGE what God's truth is and what is not true concerning the doctrines taught by each minister and ministry so that we can experience all of Him! Bad doctrine and/or sinful lifestyles are an abomination to God. In fact, often bad doctrine (spiritual adultery) leads to sinful lifestyles (adultery and homosexuality). God has made it clear through His Word that both shepherds and sheep must be discerning people, careful to hear and quick to change.

CHAPTER 15

IF POSSIBLE - EVEN THE ELECT

Matthew 24:24 quotes Jesus Christ as He teaches about the time of the end. He says, "For false Christs and false prophets will arise and will show great signs and wonders SO AS TO MISLEAD, IF POSSIBLE, EVEN THE ELECT." In response to the disciples' question about the sign of His coming and of the end of the age, Jesus prefaced His remarks with, "See to it that NO ONE MISLEADS YOU." In Matt 24:5 He says, "....many will come in my name saying, "I am the Christ" and will MISLEAD MANY.'" He goes on to say, in verse eleven, "Many false prophets will arise and will MISLEAD MANY." Jesus' main point is that the time of the end will be marked by a subtle and extremely effective delusion and deception. All who are called by His name will be enticed, tempted, and bombarded by these clever errors and doctrines of demons. If this is indeed the time of the end we must be extremely careful.

In II Thessalonians 2:3-4, when discussing the day of the Lord, Paul starts his teaching with, "LET NO ONE DECEIVE YOU IN ANY WAY, *it will not come* unless the apostasy comes first, and the man of lawlessness is revealed, the son of destruction In verses 7-12 he says, "For the mystery of lawlessness is already at work; only he who now restrains will do so until he is taken out of the way. Then that lawless one will be revealed whom the Lord will slay with the breath of His mouth and bring to an end by the appearance of His coming; *that is,* the one whose coming is in accord with the activity of Satan, with all power and signs and false wonders, and with ALL THE DECEPTION of wickedness for those who perish, because they did not receive the love of the truth so as to be saved. For this reason GOD WILL SEND UPON THEM A DELUDING INFLUENCE SO THAT THEY WILL BELIEVE WHAT IS FALSE IN ORDER THAT THEY ALL MAY

BE JUDGED WHO DID NOT BELIEVE THE TRUTH, BUT TAKE PLEASURE IN WICKEDNESS." Here Paul warns of great deception and delusion, *SOME EVEN SENT BY GOD*, in the last days. In the same vein, I Timothy 4:1-2, Paul says, "But the Spirit explicitly says that in later times some will fall away from the faith, paying attention to DECEITFUL SPIRITS and DOCTRINES OF DEMONS by means of the HYPOCRISY OF LIARS, seared in their own conscience as with a branding iron."

We are currently experiencing tremendous deception. We hear the lie that murdering babies is merely freedom of choice. Television commercials even joke about how they deceive us into buying their products. Salesmen are taught the fine art of persuasion using misrepresentation, half truths, and even outright lies in order to close the sale. Our everyday lives are filled with lies that are no longer even considered wrong, because our consciences are so seared. We "call in sick" when we are either too lazy to go to work, have other plans or we are too sick for work but are not sick enough to miss a trip to the beach. "Tell them I'm not here" is what we tell our children to say to someone who calls us on the telephone and we don't want to talk to them. Our income tax returns typically do not tell "the truth, the whole truth and nothing but the truth." We are a nation of liars in a world that has for millennia considered and even applauded lying. Meanwhile, our children are deceived into taking drugs for peace. We are deceived into buying cars we cannot afford. The public school children are being lied to about everything from sex to evolution to God Himself. The mass media tells us, through sitcom after sitcom, and drama after drama, that "the little white lie" is a necessary part of life and SOMETIMES there is no alternative but to tell a blatant, selfish, hurtful lie - IT ALWAYS DEPENDS ON THE SITUATION. Situational ethics has created the "GOOD" LIE and we have absorbed this teaching into our culture, our country, our personal lives, AND EVEN THE CHURCH!

The white lie, subtle deception, misrepresentation and even the big lie are now an everyday reality in the life of the Saul Church in America. Already discussed were the psychologically crafted techniques of manipulative, deceptive methods of raising money, ranging from "personal letters" "signed" by greedy big-name preachers to the trick of soliciting money for one purpose and then using it for another purpose. A good example of this is when an offering for missions is taken and at a later date, the missionary's money is used to pay the everyday bills for running the church. The Saul Church is especially good at speaking only a part of the truth. When the pastor wants you to spend $2,500 to go to Europe or Israel with him, he may neglect to tell you that if they get ten of you to go, then he goes free. He implies that his dual purpose in extending the invitation is that he LIKES you, and is intensely interested in your spiritual growth. Openness is not the strong suit of the Saul Church. The Saul Church is shamefully involved in deception. This slack attitude regarding lies has affected many charismatic denominations. The world says "what goes around comes around" and the Bible says "you will reap according to what you sow." That is why it is no surprise that one of the great charismatic denominations lost 15 million dollars to a con man who worked a Ponzi scheme.

IS IT ANY WONDER THAT DELUDING SPIRITS AND DOCTRINES OF DEMONS ARE IN THEIR CHURCHES? Gal. 6:7 says, "DO NOT BE DECEIVED. God is not mocked; for whatsoever a man sows this he will also reap." The Saul Church has sown lies and now it is reaping lies. The Saul Church has become so permeated with the world's attitude about truth and falsehood that it is now on the verge of experiencing II Thess. 2:10-11, "....because they did not receive THE LOVE OF THE TRUTH so as to be saved. And for this reason God will send upon them a deluding influence so that they might believe what is false." So-called Christians, whether Evangelical or Charismatic, who do not LOVE the truth, both in the Scriptures and the truth worked out in their own lives, are dangerously defining themselves as candidates for the words of our Lord in chapter seven of Matthew which say, "Depart from Me you workers of iniquity; I NEVER KNEW YOU!"

We MUST have a passionate love for truth. True born-again Christians are dwelling places for the Holy Spirit. He is the One who guides us into ALL truth. We must want truth regardless of what it cost. We must set aside our pride and be willing to lose ministries, money, friends, and family for THE SAKE OF THE TRUTH. How cheaply some sell out to the Father of Lies. How terribly some grieve the Holy Spirit by their disregard for the truth. The truth is more than mere words. The truth is embodied in our Lord and Savior Jesus Christ. He said, "I am the way, the TRUTH and the life." How do we worship God? The Bible says, "In Spirit and IN TRUTH." What sets us free? "THE TRUTH shall set you free."

Why is the Saul Church so lax with truth and so filled with deception? It is very obvious. It is because it does not love the truth. If we LOVE Jesus Christ, we must LOVE THE TRUTH, even to our own hurt. If we do not, we are in danger of not being His. Saul was not willing to pay the price of humility. He should have known and repented of disobeying God by sparing the best of the flock and the king he had conquered. He excused himself and blamed others. How can people who lead God's people be so spiritually stupid and blind?

The answer is simple. They did not receive the love of the truth. They tolerated small lies and they were slightly deceived. This hardened their hearts to small lies. Then they tolerated medium sized lies and they were moderately deceived, and their hearts were correspondingly hardened. Then they quite easily put up with gross lies and they were then grossly deceived and ripe for Great Deception.

The Saul Church tolerated the lie that allowed them to use the methods of the world to preach Jesus. Then they embraced the lies about seeking material wealth AND the Kingdom of God. Furthermore, they adjusted their viewpoints to accept the love yourself doctrine of the world in place of the deny yourself doctrine of Scripture. IS IT ANY WONDER some have openly embraced New Age doctrines and methodology in their churches? Is it any wonder that some VISUALIZE, POSITIVIZE and make agreements with worshippers of Mary? WE MUST UNDERSTAND that they also made adjustments to the truth in their personal lives. First it was, "Tell them I'm not here, honey." Then it was, "It isn't necessary to tell the government about this outside income - I'll use it to help build the Kingdom." And finally, lying and half truths became a way of life so that even "In the Name of Jesus", they could lie about a supposed healing or "Word from God." Throughout the Charismatic Movement we now have big time preachers calling out healings in large crowds, knowing that a response is certain because of the size of the crowd. Either a person will come forward whom they can declare as "healed", or the person can even go along with the whole thing and pretend to be healed. People who go up to be prayed for are badgered into "confessing" their healing, even if it is not so or worse yet, they feel the very real pressure of the evangelist to answer positively the statement "you ARE healed, aren't you?" IS IT ANY WONDER that the enemy could gain a foothold in such lie infested groups of people? IS IT POSSIBLE that the ENEMY MIGHT BE THE ONE behind some "supposed" miracles that are worked in Jesus Name? Take a look at the Catholic Church and the "miracles" that occurred at Lourdes and Fatima where "the Blessed Mother of God" appeared to many of the "faithful." In the Name of Jesus Christ many were "healed" to confirm the word of Mary's special place with God as the perfect Mother of God, the eternal virgin, the ascended one, the co-mediatrix along with Jesus and all the other heretical lies that goes along with the Catholic Church and Maryolotry. WHO WAS CONFIRMING the blasphemous teachings and "manifestations" of Mary? WAS IT GOD? OF COURSE NOT! It was Satan! And if you believe that the enemy would not have the right to "assist" liars in their desire to "confirm their word" about prosperity, lawlessness, psycho-Christianity, visualization or name it and claim it teaching, you are not familiar with Scriptures.

Listen to what the Lord says in Deuteronomy 13:1-5, "If a prophet or a dreamer of dreams arises among you and gives you a sign or a wonder, and the SIGN OR THE WONDER COMES TRUE, concerning which he spoke to you saying "Let us go after other gods (whom you have not known) and let us serve them; you shall not listen to the words of that prophet or that dreamer of dreams; FOR THE LORD YOUR GOD IS TESTING YOU TO FIND OUT IF YOU LOVE THE LORD YOUR GOD WITH ALL YOUR HEART AND ALL YOUR SOUL...that prophet or dreamer of dreams...has counseled rebellion against the Lord your God...to seduce you from the way in which the Lord your God commanded you to walk."

Just because a sign or a wonder "confirms" the word spoken does not mean it is from God. If you are told it is OK to worship Mary and a miracle follows - DON'T DO IT! Mary worship is not in the Scriptures! It is NOT the way of the Lord. We are not to follow after men who encourage "covetousness which is idolatry" (Col. 3:5) EVEN if there are miracles in their midst "confirming" their word. So it is with men who mix psychology or any other worldly philosophy that leads us from utter dependence upon the pure unadulterated truth of God's Word. We must realize that when we see SIGNS AND WONDERS following men or women who preach another way other than the narrow road of Scripture, God is TESTING US to find out if we LOVE HIM WITH ALL OUR HEARTS. If these Scriptures regarding signs coming to pass from Deuteronomy were important for God's people in the Old Testament, HOW MUCH MORE are they important to us, the generation that is experiencing what may well prove to be the greatest deception of all time.

Although there are still some real healings in the Charismatic Movement, the deluding influence is already here. Saul has lost the authority of God and the Lord has sent an evil spirit (I Sam. 16:14). The Saul Church does not love the truth and God has sent them a deluding influence so that they might believe what is false (II Thess. 2:10-11).

As important as it is to identify New Age methods and doctrines that have infiltrated the Church, EVEN MORE IMPORTANT is to love the truth and to live the truth. We must learn to be a people who consistently tell the truth, even to our own hurt, and are without guile or deception in our conversations and actions. OUR ABILITY TO PERCEIVE TRUTH IS DEPENDENT UPON HIS GRACE WHERE IT IS MANIFESTED IN OUR LOVE FOR HIS TRUTH AND OUR PURSUIT OF HIS TRUTH. If we live and speak lies, we will believe lies. ONE test of the soundness of your doctrine is to check how completely honest and guileless you are. If you are a sneaky liar, your doctrine will be faulty. But if you repent of being a liar and do all you can to repair the damage caused by your lies, you will be able to see and hear the truth more clearly.

Deception is not only sinful, it is DANGEROUS. Those who are hardened to everyday lies have been defined by God as liars and liars have no part in the Kingdom of God. Preachers who practice deception and will not repent of this may be deceived by GOD HIMSELF! We must be careful lovers of truth! We are living in the most deceptive time in history and we must cling to truth like life Himself! The more we remain in our white lie mentality, the more deceived we will become. We must receive the love of the truth! Then we must, with God's help, test every teaching to see if it is consistent with God's truth from His Scriptures.

Years ago, at a pastor's meeting the speaker was talking about revival. He made it sound like revival was going to be a lot of fun and that everything would be rosy when God poured out His Spirit on all of us. I had a prophetic word about the fact that God was going to send revival but it was not going to be a Christmas-like atmosphere as they supposed, where everybody gets gifts and celebrates. The Lord said that it would be like Good Friday and Easter - death and resurrection, and that we should expect death before resurrection. I did not deliver the message because of fear of being laughed at, ignored or misunderstood. And later, when I was confessing my fear of man and my selfish pride to God, I asked Him if they would have received the message. He did not answer me but He did speak this to me. He said, "The Church has chained its prophets to the walls because they do not want to hear the truth, and the prophets will stay chained until they become small in their own sight." He said that the prophets, for the most part, were like those to whom they would minister - people with a high regard for themselves - but that when they become small in their own sight, they will slip through the handcuffs that hold them chained to the walls. Then they will go forth one by one until there is a mighty army of prophets speaking the Word of God with the authority of the Holy Spirit. They will speak the truth and warn of judgment to come. They will correct false doctrines and bring forth personal truth that hurts. Along with these difficult words, they will speak words of hope, words of promise and words of great blessings. All of this is for the purpose of raising up a people who love the truth and are willing to live the truth regardless of the cost. What if speaking or preaching the truth, the whole truth and nothing but the truth cost you your job or your income? Would you do it? What if the truth cost you your ministry? Would you do it? What if it cost you your spouse or your family? Would you do it? Many will be tested in just such fashion. God is looking for truly honest men and women who will not deceive! They will not do so simply because they love Him too much to grieve Him with a lie.

We must let the sword of the Spirit cut away our lying hearts and give us new hearts. We must realize that we are deceitful lying individuals in the midst of a nation of liars and let God touch our lips and our hearts with a stinging burning coal that will purify us, and allow us to hear His words of correction—correcting both our lives and our doctrines.

During and before the 18th century whenever ships went on long voyages the crews and passengers often would be afflicted with a dread disease called SCURVY. Neither ship captains nor doctors were able to figure out what caused this ravaging ailment. In 1741 an English doctor discovered that men became sick after they had run out of fruit. After that time the British government made sure that all ships were well supplied with lemons and especially limes. All on board who ate these lemons and limes were not affected by the scurvy. The practice became so prevalent that British sailors came to be known as "Limies" and eventually all English people were called "Limies." I believe that God wants His people in America to become Limies of the Spirit. The following is a Word that God compellingly committed to my heart on November 3, 2005.

The Lord says to the Church of Jesus Christ in America: """I will take you on a long journey of the Spirit across a great ocean of challenges, conflicts and attacks. You will be in many spiritual battles and must be prepared! Both before and during this great conflict and trial, you must learn to eat sour fruit such as lemons and limes of the Spirit. These are not the lemons and limes that are sweetened with sugar to make lemonade or limeade; rather these are lemons and limes that My prophets will feed to many people that are called by My Name. These will be words that will be sour to the taste and sometimes sour to the stomach, but will be strength and health to your spirits, your hearts and your walk.

Many will resist and say, ""NO! We don't like the sour words of "Repent, Sin Not and Obey." We have learned to love the ice-cream words such as, "I love you and have wonderful things for you."" The Lord says, "If you do not learn to love the limes and lemons of the Spirit, you will be afflicted with scurvy of the Spirit. Your teeth and gums will rot and you will be unable to chew meat. Your legs and muscles will ache and you will not be able to walk right or run or fight. You will be weakened terribly, and will be easily defeated by the Enemy.

The journey will be long and dangerous and filled with storms and attacks. Some will think it will never end, but My people who trust Me and desire the sour, but health giving Words of My prophets, will fight and defeat the Enemy with health and strength they have never known and will be exhilarated because of the many victories over sin and

Satan, and will REJOICE as I prepare and perfect My people. In turn, many of those who eat and learn to enjoy the flavor of the sour words of the Spirit and appreciate their effects will then prophesy to others who will become healthy, strong warriors.""

The Bible says that IF POSSIBLE EVEN THE ELECT will be deceived. For this deception to be effective, ANOTHER Jesus Christ will be presented. This alternative to the real Jesus Christ will have to be very attractive. The alternative will fit the desires of the religious people. This alternative will likely be an undemanding, soft and somewhat feminine Jesus similar to the artistic representations of Jesus in the Middle Ages. The "other Jesus" strategy is not new for Satan. Many groups offer another Jesus - among them are the Jehovah Witnesses, the Mormons, the Catholics, Unity and many modern liberal churches. Now we see another Jesus being offered who preaches a lawless gospel and is more concerned about the hurts that His people have than He is about their sin. This Jesus is now being offered to the so-called Evangelical and Charismatic churches.

WE MUST UNDERSTAND that this deception is extremely effective and can only be avoided by having a heart like David's - one that is after God's heart and will do all His will regardless of the cost to our pride, ego, flesh, or ministry. Those who are like David, the single-hearted lovers of God for Himself Alone, will not only be spared from deception but blessed with the Real Jesus Christ for all eternity!

Zeph. 3:13 says, "The remnant of Israel will do no wrong and TELL NO LIES, nor will a deceitful tongue be found in their mouth." Oh that we may desire and pray with all of our hearts, to be a part of the remnant that will know the Living Truth (Jesus Christ) forever and ever.

CHAPTER 16

APOSTASY: THE KEY IS LAWLESSNESS

Sometime in the future we will see the Body of Christ subjected to terrible difficulties – judgment because of lukewarmness, persecution and betrayal. The counterfeit Christians however, who are materialistic, man-pleasing and self-pleasing will have no part of these dealing of God. They will run from the dealings and say whatever is necessary in order to be spared from these difficulties. They will be exposed as those who are spiritual dilatants that don't want to delve deeply into the heart of our Lord and Savior Jesus Christ, but are satisfied to "taste" the things of the Spirit. They may fall over at the touch of a hand; they might get healed by the Lord; they might experience goose bumps and even laugh uproariously. Eventually however, they will be exposed as those who are only along for the ride. When the ride becomes too expensive and too rough, they will leave for the company of others more sympathetic to their desire for comfort, peace and safety. When once again it becomes dangerous to be a Christian in the dark days to come, we will see many rebel against God's call to endure to the end. This apostasy will be a final manifestation of the great division that God is creating to prepare a pure and unified people.

Apostasy is not merely refusing to identify with Jesus Christ in His death, but also a sovereign work of God to purify His Body. Rev. 3:16 illuminates our sovereign Lord's involvement in apostasy. In this verse Jesus says, "So because you are lukewarm, and neither hot nor cold, I WILL SPIT (VOMIT) YOU OUT OF MY MOUTH." Notice there comes a time when He will no longer deal with the rebellious dilatants of the visible Church. These people are the tasters or samplers who do not want to eat His flesh and drink His blood. They are like wine tasters who sip the wine, roll it around in their mouths and then spit it out. We see here, in the last of the seven churches, the great falling away - the apostasy - from God's sovereign view point and response. GOD spews out all the nauseous elements that will not lose their own identity and be digested or absorbed into His Body. In II Thess.2:11 we even see how God will, as He did with Saul (I Sam. 16:14),"send them a deluding influence (a lying evil spirit) so that they might believe what is false" and be confirmed in their own hatred of the truth. In the Scriptures dealing with apostasy in II Thess.2:3 we see a man closely connected with a concept. The concept is lawlessness and the man is a MAN OF LAWLESSNESS. The KJV says, "Man of sin", but virtually all modern translations use the term "man of lawlessness." Many have identified this individual as the Antichrist and this may be true. But for now, notice that his primary characteristic is LAW-LESS-NESS.

In the United States of America in the 21st century, we have seen a popular faction emerge in both the political realm and the cultural realm. In the political realm we now have a national party that is virtually in support of every value that attacks the Scriptures. This political party, the Democrat Party, has supported notions that are against virtually every law regarding sexual conduct that is in the Scriptures. This party is far more sympathetic with the perpetrators of crime or law breakers than it is with their victims. This party supports the suppression of LAW enforcement officers in their pursuit of criminals. Through the machinations of their own private anti-law organization, the American Civil Liberties Union, they have hamstrung LAW enforcement officers from arresting and incarcerating criminals. Most of the people in this party believe that criminals are victims of either the rich, Capitalism, or America itself. Our culture has likewise been changed. At one time LAW enforcement officers were considered to be the heroes of the people. Now, the news media often takes the side of the criminal in any conflicts between the police and law breakers. Movies and television shows often depict homosexuals, adulterers and rebellious children with sympathy. Record companies showcase the criminal activity of rappers and have made heroes of criminal gangs and gang leaders. If there is any spirit hovering over and in the midst of the culture and the political party that we have just discussed, it is the spirit of LAW-LESS-NESS. Please understand that in order to maintain or regain political control we are likely to eventually see the Republican Party come to embrace many or all of these anti-scriptural views that are held today by the Democrats.

Also notice that this man of lawlessness takes his seat IN THE TEMPLE OF GOD. Many are looking for the Antichrist to actually physically seat himself in the physical, rebuilt temple of the Jews in Jerusalem. This may be so, but there is certainly a more appropriate and immediate meaning for us to see. The temple of God is the Church of God, the visible Body of Christ. The temple of God is the people of God, those whom He dwells within. A more important application of this Scripture is that some day there will come forth a spiritual force or a man who will have great influence and authority with God's so-called people, in the so-called church that is called by His name.

These men of lawlessness, like the man of lawlessness, are closely associated with apostasy in the Church. Again see II Thess. 2:3, "Let no one in any way deceive you, for it will not come unless the apostasy comes first, and the man of lawlessness is revealed, the son of destruction." LAW-LESS-NESS is an interesting word. The word means absence of law as opposed to the concept of exaltation of sin. NO law. Not AGAINST holiness or FOR sin, just NO LAW. Certainly no minister in the Church would ever preach against holiness and would never preach for sin. But by avoiding the teaching of the law he will allow for more unholiness and more sin to dwell in his people. By classifying potential converts as "hurting people" and "victims", these false teachers inhibit their hearers from being taught by the law as a school master to expose their sin.

The last forty years have produced a remarkable shift in doctrinal emphasis among the so-called Evangelical and Charismatic churches. Currently we make sure that we preach the love of God and, of course, that is absolutely necessary. Charismatics make sure that they preach the power of God to heal and deliver. And most of all, Evangelical and Charismatic churches make sure that they preach the grace of God, for that is the cornerstone of our faith. Without grace NOTHING is available to ANYONE. Not even Faith! Eph. 2:8 says, "For by grace you have been saved, through faith: and that not of yourselves - it is the gift of God." All of these doctrines are consistent with much that has been preached since the Protestant Reformation which began almost 500 years ago. But we are missing an important element in our

Gospel preaching. We seldom use the law in our preaching. We seldom quote Scriptures that deal with sin and in the KJV, 1John 3:4 says, "…sin is the transgression of the law."

We must use the law to show people their utter hopelessness before a Holy and Righteous God. We must use the law to expose sin-ridden hearts. We no longer even teach that Christians are expected or commanded to obey the law of God. The Great Commission says in Matthew 28:19-20 "Go therefore and make disciples… teaching them to observe ALL THAT I COMMANDED you…"

Our Gospel has become a LAW-LESS Gospel. It is not at all the same Gospel preached by Jesus or Paul. Jesus used, among other teachings, the Sermon on the Mount to explain that the righteousness of man is totally repugnant to God. He explained the exceeding sinfulness of sin and the corruption of our hearts. He showed us that even looking at a woman to lust after her was breaking God's law and was tantamount to committing adultery in our hearts. In Romans, Paul uses the law to expose sin, and then teaches grace and faith to relieve the burden placed on us by the law. He then directs the Romans in later chapters to obey the law in all respects, NOT FOR THEIR SALVATION, but because it is their reasonable response to God's great grace. This obedience exists because they are new creatures in Christ who now possess the power to love and obey their Savior. The Scripture makes it clear that it is reasonable to honor God and demonstrate love for Him who gave His life for them. Paul, like the Lord Jesus, and the other apostles, gives much instruction in righteousness - he tells the people WHAT TO DO. He tells them not to associate with false brethren. He tells them to present their bodies as a living sacrifice. He tells them not to offer the members of their body to sin. He tells them to work, to give, to love each other, and to love God. He commands them to do many things. He explains God's law to them and strongly exhorts them to obey it completely.

INFORMATION AND INSTRUCTION IN RIGHTEOUSNESS

You can divide many of Paul's epistles into roughly two sections. First he gives us INFORMATION. He tells us who Jesus Christ is, what He thinks of us, what He has done for us, and what we can receive from

Him, both in this life and throughout eternity. This information is usually the FIRST section of many of his epistles. Romans and Ephesians are two good examples. After Paul has given us the information regarding God's plan and purposes for our salvation, he then proceeds to give us instructions in righteousness. He teaches us what we are to do. He, like Jesus in the Sermon on the Mount, gives us very personal and practical interpretations regarding the need to obey God's law. For example, Romans 12:1-2 says, "Present your bodies a living and holy sacrifice acceptable to God...do not be conformed to this world." Here Paul gives general instructions and then goes on in succeeding verses and chapters to give detailed instructions.

John reveals the relationship between our obedience to God's law and our love for God, when he says in I John 5:3, "For this is the love of God, that we keep His commandments: and His commandments are not burdensome." (His commandments are not burdensome to a person who has been truly born-again). In John 14:23, Jesus says that those who love God are the ones that obey God and are the ones that His Father loves. He also says that the one who does not love Him does not obey Him.

John 14:23-24, "Jesus answered and said to him, 'if anyone loves Me he will keep My word; and My Father will love him, and We will come to him and make Our abode with him. He who does not love Me, does not keep My word; and the word which you hear is not Mine but our Father's who sent Me.'"

When we read the New Testament carefully, we will see that the New Testament writers taught about God's law extensively. Jesus Himself says that instruction in righteousness is absolutely necessary. In the Great Commission Jesus says, in Matthew 28:19-20, "Go therefore and make disciples of all nations baptizing them in the name of the Father and the Son and the Holy Spirit, TEACHING THEM TO OBSERVE ALL THAT I COMMANDED YOU; and THEN, lo, I am with you always, even to the end of the age."

Unfortunately most churches do not instruct in righteousness (except for teaching the people to give tithes and offerings, submit to their spiritual leaders, and witness a lot). They present a virtually LAW-LESS New Testament. Some, if they do present the law, make sure to remind the people, "We are not under law but under grace" (as if THAT had anything to do with what Jesus, James, John, or Paul said).

A good test for determining whether you are hearing the Full Gospel is to listen for both information and instruction in righteousness. If you are continually being told only about witnessing, the antichrist, the mark of the beast, the gifts of the Spirit, the love of God, techniques of worship, and how to have faith, money, or healing, you are not hearing the whole Gospel. If that is all you are hearing then you are hearing a LAWLESS gospel and you are in spiritual danger. Even if you are hearing a word which tells you who Jesus is and who you are in Him, and yet you are not being instructed in righteousness, you are still in spiritual danger. Even doctrinally correct teachings must be accompanied by the appropriate instructions in righteousness. Only then will you not be hearing a lawless Gospel. On the other hand, if you are hearing only instruction in righteousness and never told who Jesus is, and of His great love for us, you are hearing a Graceless gospel and will fall into legalism, an equally corrupt misrepresentation of the Word of God. God's truth is always the truth, THE WHOLE TRUTH and nothing but the truth.

LAWLESSNESS AND GRACELESSNESS

It is important to notice that the man who is at the center of apostasy is not called a man of GRACE-LESS-NESS. He is called a man of LAW-LESS-NESS. This man puts no restraints on the people, and as a result of his LAW-LESS doctrine, LAW-LESS apostate people are birthed under his leadership. The focal point of the Reformation in the sixteenth century was law verses grace; salvation by faith or salvation by works plus faith. Even though the activities of the Pope and many of the church leaders were indeed lawless, their doctrine was legalistic and left the impossible burden of man's salvation resting on his own shoulders. Thus obedience to the law of God, the laws of the Roman Catholic Church, and the law of the Popes was presented as exceedingly important, if not necessary, for salvation. Today, in this time of unparalleled and ingenious deception, those who are falling into apostasy recognize the truth that we are saved by God's grace. Where the leaders are failing is in their NEGLECT of the rightful place of the law in our Christian walk and teaching. Their law-less doctrine of demons has caused many to not have the FEAR of God in their hearts or a proper understanding of the sin in their lives or a desire to be holy as our Father in heaven is Holy. When proper teaching of the law is neglected, holiness is trampled underfoot and men and women are not truly born again because they never understand how hopeless and sinful they are in God's eyes. Instead they come to God with a casual, "I accept You as my personal Savior." They come with an almost reluctant, "OK God, I'll do both you and me a favor - I'll get saved." Of course they are not saved. You cannot receive the grace of God to believe in Jesus, as your Lord and Savior, until you have received the grace of God to have His law expose your exceeding sinfulness and hopelessness. Thus the law-less gospel, in the end, is also a grace-less gospel.

"God loves you just the way you are", was the standard closing remark of a popular Christian TV show years ago. This was a terrible misleading statement since the hosts did not instruct their audience in righteousness. People were led into believing that it is not important to be a DOER of His Word and that God was not particularly concerned about their repentance.

THIS PHILOSOPHY (God loves you just the way you are) has been the ruling philosophy in the Saul Church, and as a result many of the people in our churches have no real love for our Lord Jesus Christ because they are not truly His. People must be convicted of their sin before they can be born-again. They also have no knowledge, or at best a perverted knowledge, of the meaning of our Lord's words from John 14:23-24, "Jesus answered and said unto him, "If anyone loves Me, he will keep My word; and My Father will love him, and We will come to him, and make Our abode with him. He who does not love Me does not keep My words; and the word which you hear is not Mine, but the Father's who sent Me."

The Saul Church is AFRAID to teach the above-mentioned Scripture without altering its straight-forward meaning, because they are concerned that if they teach the law they will drive many of their members away. They believe that most of the members of their church do not like the law. All apostates either hate the law or pick and choose only the parts they find agreeable. The Saul Church has NO concept of the Scripture that says in John, "My sheep HEAR My voice." They seem to have no problem enticing goats into the household of God. In fact, goats often become teachers, worship leaders and even pastors. They don't seem to understand that it is scripturally incorrect to cast pearls before swine. The problem is, that many of these "converts" are not really HIS sheep! They may be the pastor's sheep, or the teacher's sheep or even the evangelist's sheep, but they are not necessarily THE LORD'S SHEEP. His sheep want desperately to be HOLY and obedient and DESIRE the washing of the water of the Word of God. The goats may well want to be members of a local church, have their hurts healed and be thought of as good people, but because they were never challenged by the law of God and never truly knew Him, they will seek out a church where they are not challenged by the law or encouraged to be righteous and holy. They will ONLY respond to a Goat Gospel, and will only follow Goat Herders who let them eat whatever they want!

How different from the author (believed by many to be David) of Psalm 119. Listen to Psalm 119:1-6,21,34-35,53,113,118,158-9 which says, "How blessed are those whose way is blameless, who walk in the law of the Lord. How blessed are those who observe His testimonies, who seek Him with all their heart. They also do no unrighteousness; they walk in His ways. Thou hast ordained Thy precepts, that we should keep them diligently. Oh that my ways maybe established to keep Thy statutes! Then I shall not be ashamed when I look upon all Thy commandments. Thou does rebuke the arrogant, the cursed, who wander from Thy commandments. Give me understanding, that I may observe Thy law, and keep it with all my heart. Make me walk in the path of Thy commandments, for I delight in it. Burning indignation has seized me because of the wicked, who forsake Thy law. I hate those who are double-minded, because I love Thy law. Thou hast rejected all those who wander from Thy statutes, for their deceitfulness is useless. I behold the treacherous and loathe them, because they do not keep Thy word. Consider how I love Thy precepts; revive me, O Lord, according to Thy loving kindness." All true sons and daughters of the Living God desire greatly to know precisely what to do to serve and manifest their love for our Lord and Savior Jesus Christ. All others are ANATHEMA (accursed).

The man of lawlessness may not yet have taken his seat in the temple of God, BUT the spirit of lawlessness is already at work in the Saul Church. This lawless spirit rules and has already paved the road for a mass exodus from the Body of Christ. Even now this spirit has tempted many to apostatize IN THEIR HEARTS. The Great Falling Away is already happening IN THE HEARTS of millions of Saul

Christians. They have SEEN, and TOUCHED the Lord and been TOUCHED by Him; they have TASTED and SEEN THAT THE LORD IS GOOD." They have even "TASTED THE HEAVENLY GIFT AND EVEN HAVE BEEN MADE PARTAKERS OF THE HOLY SPIRIT AND HAVE TASTED THE GOOD WORD OF GOD AND THE POWERS OF THE AGE TO COME" (Heb 6:4-5). But they would not truly consume Him and His salvation on His terms. Therefore, like an undigested piece of food, they will be vomited out of His mouth. Like a hearer who does not obey, they do not have their foundation on the solid Rock. When the storms come and the winds blow, what they have built will fall away and be destroyed.

Today at the beginning of the 21st century the people of God have more tools and aids available for the study of Scriptures than we have ever had before. It is similar to what went on precedent to the Protestant Reformation. The printing press allowed for men's ideas to be exchanged and proclaimed more quickly than any time in history. We in the 21st century have no excuse for not understanding God's plan of salvation. God has given us every opportunity to study and understand His Word. With the computer, truth is literally at our fingertips. God will use this great opportunity to cleanse His Body in preparation for BOTH the judgment that will come first and the revival that will follow. In Scripture we see this same process occurring decades before God judged Judah. Immediately before the nation of Israel was revived under Josiah, God revealed the law to Josiah and Judah. In II Chronicles 34:1-3, 8, 15, 19-21, 26-27 we read, "Josiah was eight years old when he became king, and he reigned thirty-one years in Jerusalem. And he did right in the sight of the Lord, and walked in the ways of his father David and did not turn aside to the right or to the left. For in the eighth year of his reign while he was still a youth, he began to seek the God of his father David; and in the twelfth year he began to purge Judah and Jerusalem of the high places, the Asherim, the carved images, and the molten images. Now in the eighteenth year of his reign, when he had purged the land and the house, he sent Shaphan the son of Azaliah, and Masseiah an official of the city, and Joah the son of Joahaz the recorder, to repair the house of the Lord his God. And Hilkiah responded and said to Shaphan the scribe, "I have found the book of the law in the house of the Lord." And Hilkiah gave the book to Shaphan. AND IT CAME ABOUT WHEN THE KING HEARD THE WORDS OF THE LAW THAT HE

TORE HIS CLOTHES. Then the king commanded Hilkiah, Ahikam the son of Shaphan, Abdon the son of Micah, Shaphan the scribe, and Asaiah the king's servant saying, "Go, inquire of the Lord for me and for those who are left in Israel and in Judah, concerning the words of the book which has been found; for GREAT IS THE WRATH OF THE LORD WHICH IS POURED OUT ON US BECAUSE OUR FATHERS HAVE NOT OBSESRVED THE WORD OF THE LORD, TO DO ACCORDING TO ALL THAT IS WRITTEN IN THIS BOOK." But the king of Judah who sent you to inquire of the Lord, thus you will say to him, "Thus says the Lord God of Israel regarding the words which you have heard, "because your heart was tender and you humbled yourself before God, when you heard His words against this place and against its inhabitants, and because you have humbled yourself before Me, tore your clothes, and wept before Me, I truly have heard you," declares the Lord.""

Josiah was a man who, like David, sought the Lord even as a youth. Because he wanted God, the Lord revealed His law to him. Thus Josiah learned about the terrible judgments God brings to His unrepentant people.

In the Old Testament, even before God would judge His people by turning them over to worldly enemies, He would send His prophets. For over one hundred and fifty years, they proclaimed to the people the true meaning of the law and the judgment that would surely come because of their disobedience. Isaiah, Jeremiah, Ezekiel and others taught and warned the people that obedience was not some mechanical exercise of do's and don'ts but was the normal result of a heart that loved God. In the New Testament Jesus taught the same thing, particularly in the Sermon on the Mount. Of course Jesus did more than teach the truth. He, with His perfect love for the Father, obeyed His Father's commands without fail.

Today, once again, before God judges His unrepentant people and while he is purifying those who are after His own heart, we see Him showing us the importance of obedience to His law. We see the Lord showing us how mechanical and heartless and selfish most of our supposed obedience has been. Even as He is hardening the hearts of those who will not repent, He is also convicting His own of the need to cry out to Him for new, soft hearts that hate sin and love Him for Who He Is.

The Church of David is a Church that loves the law of the Lord. These people are not afraid of having their hearts exposed by proper instruction of the law. These people no longer want to be lulled to sleep by receiving only interesting information. We want to have our self-righteousness and pride exposed by instruction in His righteousness and we WANT Him to DEAL WITH US. We want to know precisely what God desires and demands. We want to have hearts that are sensitive to God's Holy Spirit and are quick to respond when we are shown our sin. We will in no way cooperate with the foul spirit of lawlessness that always leads to lovelessness for our Lord and Savior Jesus Christ and ultimately to apostasy in the Church.

In our desire to obey all that God has for us in His Word, we MUST be very careful not to go beyond the content or intention of Scripture. We MUST not give in to the CERTAIN temptation of the enemy to "make sure" that people don't become lukewarm by placing unscriptural and legalistic directives on them. Adding to God's Word in this way is just as harmful as taking away from God's Word.

We see a great amount of lawlessness in the Church today. We see that as lawlessness has increased, most people's love for the Lord has grown cold. We see a growing apostasy, but we also see God dealing with His people in judgment, because the law is no longer taught. After this judgment of God, we anticipate revival - a revival of love for His law, a love for holiness, a true love for one another, and a love for Himself for Who He Is.

CHAPTER 17

SECOND STORM WARNING

This chapter, "The Second Storm Warning," seems clearer today than it was over twenty years ago when the Lord first revealed it to me. This is often true regarding prophetic messages or visions from God. Often the words or images are not understood until the events actually take place or near the time that these events are about to take place. It is a grievous error to interpret something that the Lord does not interpret for you. Unfortunately, this practice is commonplace among people who attempt to prophesy for the Lord. At that time, as I related the vision to a group of churches at a denominational prayer meeting, there were parts of it that I did not understand. Since then, as events have unfolded, I have added some of my own interpretations. Judge for yourself and see if they seem correct.

In June of 1986 on a Friday morning, I was praying that God would move in a prayer meeting that we were to have with several other churches that night. At this time the Lord showed me a vision of a storm that He would send to His Church. Later that night at the meeting, the anointing of the Lord came upon me in a very sovereign and compelling way and I prophesied what the Lord had begun to reveal to me earlier. He showed me an army camp with thousands of tents pitched. It was night and most of the soldiers were asleep in their tents. There were men and women soldiers fully armed with guns, grenades, rocket launchers etcetera and fully clothed to do battle. They were sleeping very soundly and dreaming pleasant dreams. I could see their dreams: they dreamed of good times at the beach, beautiful homes, and fine luxury cars. They dreamed of getting money and spending money. They even dreamed of bigger and more successful ministries. In the far distance I could hear thunder rolling and see lightning flashing. A storm was brewing off to what was the east in my vision and the storm was being blown toward the camp of the Lord slowly but steadily and became progressively brighter and louder. Then with loud crashes of thunder and bright flashes of lightning the storm broke with full force over the camp of God. But VERY FEW of the soldiers woke up. The vast majority just kept on sleeping with satisfied smiles on their faces. I saw some stir and almost wake up but they just changed positions and went back to their sweet dreams. A few others woke up, grabbed their weapons and went to stand on the wall that surrounded the camp and look out on the horizon to see if anyone was coming. The wall surrounding the camp was not fully intact and had many places where the enemy had broken through in previous encounters. These places had never been repaired, but on top of the walls there were places to stand and watch for the enemy. The Lord said that this was the beginning of the second storm that He would bring to His Church but that the crashes of thunder and flashes of lightning would only wake a few of the fully equipped but peacefully slumbering soldiers. He said they were too busy dreaming about their churches, the success of their ministries and their material blessings. Because of this they would not wake up. This scene repeated a number of times. The thunder cracked, the lightning flashed, a few woke up and ran to the wall to watch and warn, but almost everyone went back to sleep.

After the last of the thunder and lightning passed over the camp of God, the Lord showed me many cannons that were similar in style to those used in the Civil War. These cannons came from the left as I viewed this scene. The Lord made it CLEAR that the storm came from the EAST and the cannons came from the LEFT. He did not refer to the East as the right and He did not refer to the left as the West. They were slowly but steadily rolling up to within close range of the camp, many within ten yards of the wall. The soldiers who had awakened earlier and were standing on the broken wall shouted a loud warning to the ones who were asleep, but few stirred and even fewer got up to see what was happening. Then the cannons all rolled even closer and cut loose a terrible volley that brought down the wall that faced them. The cannons were then aimed at the people who were beginning to wake up. So devastating was their attack that the majority had time only to stand up and cry, "O My God," and then were quickly cut down by the barrage. I saw that many were hit in the chest. Most of the people were then completely awakened by the horrifying sound of the attack but were not ready and were cut down. A few woke up and had time to properly ready themselves to fight, but the majority of the people inside the sparsely-guarded, weak, and broken-walled camp were either killed or terribly injured.

As I finished delivering this vision/prophecy to the Church, the Los Angeles skies lit up with what was the most awesome spectacle of thunder and lightning that I had ever seen. It was so unusual in our area that it made front-page headlines in the Los Angeles Times the next morning.

An unusual thing about this particular word was that it was the second storm that God had shown us. Earlier, in February of that year, God showed me a storm that was for the cleansing of His Church and the exposure of the sin of many men, particularly those in high places. When I received that message, I had asked that God would confirm the word with actual thunder and lightning. But He didn't. In just two or three weeks after the delivery of the FIRST STORM warning, however, we saw the spiritual storm that He brought to the Body of Christ with the revelation of the P.T.L. scandal.

This second storm prophecy WAS confirmed by a tremendous electrical storm. I felt that God confirmed this vision and not the first, because the first storm happened very shortly after He told us about it. This next storm however, was likely not to happen for a long time.

Shortly after I shared this vision, the people were exhorted about our ties with material wealth. The Lord was showing us that we were far too involved with our toys, our comfort, and our ministry successes, and God was trying to shake us loose from this mentality. He was showing us that our time spent, our attention given, our identification with the world's concept of what is important cripples us regarding the doing of His will. Our desire to seek men's approval and our need to identify with success was especially dangerous to Christians. If any of these attitudes were in our hearts, we would have to part with these attitudes in order to fully apprehend God and His will.

GOD RIPS OFF THE SKIN

In October of 1987 my wife and I took a trip to New York to witness the opening of David Wilkerson's new work in the city. It was called the Times Square Church. We had attended several meetings and were between meetings touring the city with our two sons: Jedidiah who was 14 and John who was 13. I distinctly remember that we were walking on the sidewalk just talking together. All of a sudden I was almost thrown to the ground by the impact of what God was showing me. I did not fall to the ground but my knees buckled and it was very hard to walk. I had never had an experience like that before and have never had one since. I saw a gigantic man standing before me that towered above the city. The man had no clothes on. All of a sudden a huge hand from the sky reached down and grabbed the scalp of the man and pulled straight up very quickly. Then I saw that all the skin of the man had been pulled off by this powerful yank. I saw sinews, muscles and nerve fibers. It looked just like the pictures that are in medical books that show a human without skin. The man yelled in pain as he stood completely vulnerable to all the elements around him. In my mind I cried to the Lord, "What is this Lord?" The Lord said quite clearly, "I am going to pull the skin off the city of New York."

Immediately after this, He showed me a huge thumb that was pressing down on the City of New York. He said, "This will put great pressure on the people of New York and what is inside each person will be forced out for all to see. If love is in the heart of the person, love will be forced out. If hate is inside the person, hate will be forced out. If fear is inside the person, that will be forced out. If faith is inside the person, that will be forced out. What the person truly felt and believed would be exposed by this terrible event."

After I recovered my senses and my composure (I was brought to tears by what I had seen), I haltingly tried to explain to my wife and sons what I had just seen. I didn't really know what it meant, but I had some ideas. After contemplating what I had seen and after praying about it, it become clear that what God was going to do was remove His protection from the city of New York, and the people would be open to attacks of the enemy in a way that they had never been before. He also made it quite clear that this dramatic experience of quickly removing His hand of protection would be duplicated throughout the whole country.

I didn't precisely know what New York or any other city, or the nation at large would experience. At first I thought that there would be a great stock market crash that would trigger another Great Depression.

I thought that perhaps the skin was money. In fact, several days later, we saw the stock market drop 700 points in one day. This crash ultimately did NOT affect the city of New York or the country at large in any significant way. But I knew that God would dramatically remove His hand of protection, and that New York City and our country would experience disasters and dealings like the heathen nations have experienced in other places.

God would leave us to fend for ourselves because we have rejected Him in so many ways. Heathen countries on a regular basis have experienced disaster after disaster where thousands of people have been killed by earthquakes, flash floods and hurricanes. They have suffered greatly from attacks of "nature" and attacks from armies. They have experienced devastating financial collapses. The United States compared to Russia, the European countries, China, Africa, India and the rest of the world has been relatively unscathed.

These days soon will be over for America. These events will happen to America because the federal government, the judicial system and many state governments have done everything they could to reject God and His Word. Most judges and many politicians seem to hate the Word of God and want nothing to do with God the Father, the Lord Jesus Christ or His Holy Spirit. It is obvious from their rulings regarding the Name of Jesus Christ, the Ten Commandments and the freedom of Christians to express their views, that they either hate God or do not believe in His existence. The greater tragedy is that a huge number of people in our country really don't care. If America will not listen to God and if its people choose to exclude Him from their lives, then God will no longer protect them as He has in the past.

More importantly and more disturbingly is that our country is in great danger because of the void that the Church has left. The Church fears and depends upon man more than the Church fears and depends upon God Himself. As has been mentioned earlier, most churches have not taught the law of God. They are all too aware that many would leave their churches if they did so. They are afraid of offending people who have not left their sin and even in the midst of their churches, are comfortable with their sins and have no intention of leaving them and obeying God. They know that if they preach the law and its consequences as Jesus, Paul, James and John did, they would be accused of being legalistic. We have forgotten that trusting in, appreciation of and obedience to God and His law through faith in Jesus Christ is what protects us.

In the year 2005 God made it abundantly real to me that there was something wrong in the way we Christians protest so strongly the removal of the images of the law and the Ten Commandments displayed in and around our court rooms. As I was praying about the court decisions that were made concerning the removal of the Ten Commandments from government property, He spoke very clearly to my heart: He said, "How can you expect Me to keep the images of the Ten Commandments in a secular setting while many leaders of My people have kept the Ten Commandments out of their churches?"

The Church in America MUST bear the greatest responsibility for the lawlessness and people pleasing attitude in our country. We have left a SPIRITUAL VOID in the land. At one time, the Puritans held a high standard of the law in America. In the last century or so the secular world has unmercifully mocked these holy men and women of the Reformation both in literature and movies. Even many modern Christians consider Puritans to be stodgy, sour faced and legalistic. This disrespectful and wrongheaded notion must be dispelled by correct teaching of church history.

We seem to have become much too sophisticated. In many churches it is common to see Christian parents turn a blind eye to the adulterous activities of children living in their home. Because teaching the law as Jesus taught the law is discouraged from the pulpit, we have provided a HUGE spiritual void that has been filled by the cults, eastern religion and secular philosophy. Even our Christian President who was anointed by God to be the President in a transparent effort to please everyone after the terrible attack on the Twin Towers on 911 said in his speech to the nation that Allah (the "god" of the Muslims) did not condone the attack on the Twin Towers. This blind blasphemy came from a man that seems to be genuinely born again. As a nation and as Christians we often give more respect to false religions and abominable sinners than we do to God's law.

I have a great concern that we will lose the protection of God from the domination of tyrannical leaders. My concern is that if God no longer protects us from these men that we will see not just the blood of millions of aborted children, but also the blood of those who love the

Lord Jesus Christ. I am concerned that if the liberals in our country are able to convince the majority of the people, we will see our country succumb to the ravages of Communism or even a nuclear attack or attacks, from any number of our enemies. Perhaps the worst judgment of all would be a bloodless takeover of our country where we lost the wonderful freedom to worship God that we have experienced for more than two hundred years.

The Church of Jesus Christ will most certainly suffer if and when the majority of the voters in our country choose to give the liberals and radicals control of the judicial, the executive and the legislative branches of government. The Christians especially and others in our nation will most certainly be susceptible to attacks from both outside the country and inside the country from the media and the government itself.

I don't know when this storm will occur, but the events that have occurred over the last decade have given great indication that things are much closer than they were twenty years ago. We certainly were jostled out of our sleep at least temporarily with the thunder claps of the September 11th attacks. These terrible attacks and murders of thousands of Americans were orchestrated and accomplished by men of the EAST. The Muslim terrorists have merely been the ungloved hand of the demon powers that rule Mohammedism. It is no coincidence that the greatest enemies of this false religion are Israel and the United States: Judaism and Christianity.

Some of God's people awoke to help those that were devastated by the 911 attacks and even more woke up to help the victims of Hurricane Katrina. They became aware of what could happen as the result of the attacks of men and the ravages of extreme weather. Many Christians were awakened to the needs of New York City and the Gulf Coast and gave generously, but the Church STILL must recognize its own measure of spiritual responsibility in these matters.

The civil war cannons that lined up against the walls that protected the people of God were always a mystery to me. At one time I suspected that these Civil War cannons might indicate a literal civil war that our country would need to experience once again. I knew that they were an important part of the vision. One of the reasons was that in 1987, when we were on a trip back east, and visiting the battlefields of Gettysburg,

I felt a strong anointing of God come on me that brought me to tears. This feeling stayed with me for some time and it made me think of the vision of the civil war cannons lining up against the walls that protected God's people.

I wondered if it meant that someday we might have another civil war in our country, but I dismissed it as being extremely unlikely. I thought perhaps it might even refer to in-fighting in the Church, but thought that unlikely. I never considered that the attack that came from the LEFT of my vision had any political implications.

However over the last few years, the left wing of the American political system has become progressively more aggressive and progressively less principled. The Democrat Party has been taken over by men and women who are sympathetic to Marxist ideology that wants a society without Jesus Christ or Biblical laws and principles. The ultimate goal of ANY Marxist organization is anarchy (lawlessness). It is no wonder that they mock the Lord, the Bible, the Ten Commandments and God's people.

They have become increasingly violent and cruel in their attacks on all that is good. The leaders and many of their followers have become completely blind to God and His purposes, and the political left, if given the opportunity could certainly cripple or destroy the Church of Jesus Christ in America. Michael Moore's so-called Documentary "Fahrenheit 911" was embraced by the media and received no criticism from liberal politicians. I believe we are seeing political events that are dangerously similar to the same political events that occurred in Nazi Germany in the 1920's and 1930's and in Russia in the early 20th century.

These leaders of the left will say or do anything to accomplish their goal of gaining more power in the American political system. If they were able to do so, they would use that power against all that is good and anyone who interferes with them. The same horrible demonic force that controlled both the Nazi Party and International Communism has inhabited them. They may well be the ones that will attack the sleeping Church with the civil war cannons in the vision of the Second Storm. Since Bill Clinton's presidency we have seen no one in the Democrat Party subtle enough or skilled enough to successfully attack their enemies. Michael Moore for example could convince no one who is not already with him of the rightness of his cause. Both Al Gore and John Kerry were inept. With the labor unions, the entertainment industry, the legal profession, academia, the newspaper media and most of television on their side, they still could not fool the majority of Americans. Only God's grace has kept us from the devastation of God's people that happens when the walls will crash down, but if the Church in America does not wake up EVEN GOD will not spare us from this attack.

This attack will be a judgment against the people of God because of our lethargy regarding the truth of His Word and the power of His Holy Spirit, and our love of the world, our love for the things of the world and more importantly, our love of the ways of the world. We have embraced doctrines of demons. We have become convinced of our need to balance the Scripture with secular psychology and devious ways of getting money to build the kingdom. We have added to the Word like no other movement since the Roman Catholic Church. We have softened the commandments of God and cheapened the grace of God. We have been more concerned about unity than we have about truth. We truly are rich and in need of nothing in our own eyes. But God has judged us poor, blind and naked.

We MUST take the lion's share of the responsibility concerning the judgment that is about to come to America. We have not fought the war with the Word, the whole Word and nothing but the Word. We have grown blind to the enemy that has weakened us in our own midst and caused us to be oblivious to our own failures and shortcomings. The Nazi's easily conquered a people that had been blinded by the false doctrines of Higher Criticism (a liberal theology of the 19th century that discounted the spiritual authority of the Scriptures). The communists easily conquered Eastern Europe because the people had been blinded by the legalism and deadness of Eastern Orthodox churches. If we don't wake up, and it seems almost inevitable that we will not, we will most certainly be vigorously attacked and the Church will suffer GREAT loss! The Church of Jesus Christ in America has become tolerant of evil conduct and doctrine, and has been unable and unwilling to judge what is of God and what is not of God. Because of this it is no wonder that God has not sent a country changing revival even though we have prayed for decades and asked God a million times for that revival.

The revival will come but not until our hearts have been purified by judgment and persecution. We will be judged by God because we have failed to recognize that WE, not the unsaved liberals in our country, not the whores of Hollywood or the abortionists, murderers, and other sinners; WE are the ones that need to repent so that the Church can have the strength and be the leaven of righteousness to change this country and this world for Jesus Christ.

My greatest concern is that when judgment comes to God's people as a whole, most will self-righteously proclaim that they are being persecuted for righteousness sake. We MUST realize that we have been asleep to God's will, asleep to God's battle, and asleep to God's call to speak out the truth of His Word. We have embraced the very church that God Himself separated us from in the 16th century – the Roman Catholic Church. We have been systematically dismantling the Protestant Reformation of 1517. We no longer recognize the necessity of Sola Fida (Only Faith), Sola Scriptura (Only Scripture) and Sola Gratia (Only Grace). Many Christians, especially Charismatics, comfortably co-exist with Rome. We Christians have made ourselves ripe for judgment, along with the unsaved masses who have certainly abused the freedom they have been given.

Referring back to the vision of the Second Storm, the storm that awakens some of God's people WILL precede the terrible attack from the left. These events have already begun to happen. We have heard the thunder claps of God's warning and been stirred to be aroused from our sleep for a few minutes. We are even seeing the Muslims fill the spiritual void we have left because of our disobedience to God's Word. Throughout the world and even in our own country they are gaining sympathy. The left wing media hates any person or party that keeps the "liberal progressives" from achieving their ends, but has become sympathetic to the terrorists. Some day we may well see an alliance between the Left and the Muslims that is hell bent to destroy all that is good in America.

In the Old Testament, God's people were judged because of their overt idolatry. Out-rightly they worshipped the gods of heathen nations. They made little statues that honored and represented Baal, Ashtera, Molech, and many others. They offered cakes to the queen of heaven. God expressly outlawed those practices and promised terrible judgment if His people continued to worship these idols and other gods. If the Children of Israel, who did not have the full revelation of Jesus Christ and the Gospel of peace, were judged for their idolatry, how much more will the Church of Jesus Christ today be judged for the subtle idolatry of worshipping ANOTHER JESUS? Many worship ANOTHER JESUS. This Jesus is manifested in many ways.

II Corinthians 11:4 says: "For if one comes and preaches ANOTHER JESUS whom we have not preached, or you receive a different spirit which you have not received, or a different gospel which you have not accepted you bear this beautifully."

This other Jesus that many worship is not concerned about holiness and would NEVER judge his people because he loves them so much. He will tolerate fornicators and adulterers in his church who claim to be Christians because he knows if they hang around Christians, they will be changed by the love of their brothers and sisters. He is not concerned at all that these adulterous so-called Christians could hurt or leaven the church with their sin. This Jesus is VERY tolerant. He is not judgmental about what a person wears, what entertainment he sees or exposes to his children, or even if members of his family fellowship with impure people. This Jesus makes sure that the leadership of his church would NEVER teach a message that would judge the sinful activities of the people because that is the job of the Holy Spirit. He never wants anyone to feel bad about themselves and if they are ever concerned about their sin, he assures them that Satan is putting them under condemnation.

ANOTHER Jesus is the one who is vitally concerned with the financial prosperity of his people. People who have faith in this Jesus believe that they are the children of the king and that they will be blessed financially and amass sufficient wealth to impress people in the world. Unfortunately this king is an IDOL. He has another name; that name is *Mammon*.

Yet ANOTHER Jesus is the totally positive Jesus. He never instructs his people regarding the consequence of sin. Any pain or chastening they may experience is an attack from Satan. This positive Jesus understands that the people of today are different from the people that lived during the time of the early Church when the Apostles walked the earth. They are also different from the Puritans of the 17th century and the people in England and America during the Revival times in the

18th and 19th centuries. The negative Scriptures were OK for those people, but modern 21st century Christians don't need any of these negative Scriptures. What's more important, the world in which they minister would be terribly offended by a negative message.

This positive Jesus that so many worship in the so-called Christian churches of the 21st century is perfectly content to have Scriptures omitted and words redefined and softened so as to not offend. People do not need to be told they are sinners or that they have a need to repent. This positive Jesus is very kind, loving and understands our hurts.

Unfortunately, this positive Jesus is ANOTHER Jesus that is really just an IDOL that we created because it fits our modern irresponsible way of thinking. Worshipping this Jesus will lead many people straight into the very bowels of Hell itself. The church and the people of that church will be judged TERRIBLY by God.

We can be spared from the judgment if we shun these OTHER JESUS'S who are really only false Messiahs and stir ourselves to be fully awake. We must then run to the walls that surround God's people and cry out warning to those who have been lulled to sleep by idolatry.

This major attack from the left could occur in forty weeks, forty months or forty years. I don't know when, but I DO KNOW God is warning us to wake up and get ready NOW! All of God's so-called people will not become more spiritual. Great trials generally serve the purpose of exposing a man's true heart, not creating a good heart. What a man truly loves he will try to preserve. The Word to us today is to get our hearts ready by letting God purge us of idols, seek Him diligently in the Scriptures, in the prayer closet, and in our loving obedience to Him as He directs us very specifically to deny ourselves, take up our cross and follow Him.

The years or months that come will either give us more time to repent and embrace God or it will be the beginning of a great and terrible judgment.

The issue is not political. It is not important that all evangelicals vote conservative so we can have a conservative Supreme Court or Congress or President; the issue is NOT fundamentally political. The issue is spiritual and we must recognize that the Church is in dire need of another Reformation.

We must pray that God would raise up men with prophetic insight concerning the Word of God and His will. We must pray that God would raise up our own Martin Luthers, John Calvins, George Whitfields and John and Charles Wesleys. We must pray that God would send us not merely a renewal or even a good revival, but that He would send us the Reformation that we so desperately need so we can turn from the world to the Word and establish His kingdom in our hearts and in our churches and have the power to effectively fight against the enemy of our souls. But most importantly, we must pray that WHATEVER IT TAKES, He will raise up a people that have repentant and God seeking hearts like David and are willing to speak and do ALL that He desires!

CHAPTER 18

PEARL HARBOR

In December of 1984, about a week after I purchased a 1940 Cadillac sedan, I was driving around thinking about times gone by, particularly the time before and during World War II. Suddenly I heard the Lord say to me, very softly, "It's 1940 and Pearl Harbor is coming up for the Church." I thought about betrayal, warfare, death and awakening! I prayed to the Lord about it and He began to reveal to me more about Pearl Harbor. He reminded me of a scene from the film <u>Tora Tora Tora</u> in which one of the Japanese military leaders remarked, after their attack on Pearl Harbor, "I fear all we have done is to awaken a sleeping giant and fill him with a terrible resolve." I thought about the Church finally waking up to her true condition. I thought about the terrible price our country paid, in the 1940's to wake up to the realities of the world political situation. The price was human life, suffering, and destruction. But we did wake up. I thought about December 8, 1941 when we declared war against the Axis powers. Before that time we were sending arms, supplies and money to our allies, but we were not sending men to help fight. We watched China, the Pacific Islands, France and much of Europe fall to Germany, Italy, and Japan, but we were not personally affected so we did not enter the warfare. It took a catastrophic event to wake us up.

I prayed about and meditated on what I had heard until May of 1985, when I again heard from God during a baptismal service in our Church. The person to be baptized was an older lady who was quite concerned, even a little frightening, about being fully immersed. But she, after fifty years of disobedience and rebellion against God, desired to be baptized for the first time. Right before I was going to enter the water with her, a message in tongues came forth from my wife. The Lord gave me the interpretation by means of the following vision. This vision describes a future time of great hardship and great blessing for the Body of Christ.

He showed me a deep harbor with blue-green water that was clear and calm. There was a Person in the water. This Person was not swimming or standing, but just floating in an upright position. He was motionless, like a sailing ship listing on a windless sea. Many Japanese Zero aircraft came in from the east and proceeded to dive-bomb and strafe the body in the water and the body began to slowly sink. Eventually the body was entirely under the water. As He went down, I could see that there were many little people on this Body. As this Body sank deeper into the water, many of these small people jumped off just before they were about to enter the water. There were thousands of people jumping off and swimming away from this slow but steadily sinking Body. Some of these people jumped onto beds, which the Lord made clear to me were beds of adultery, and floated away off to the left. Others jumped onto whiskey bottles and paddled away; still others jumped on books, while others swam off on their own strength. All of the people were floating, swimming or paddling in the same direction. I looked over in that direction, which was to my left, and I saw an extremely beautiful, gigantic woman, with skin and clothing of a deep reddish purple hue standing solidly on the harbor floor. She stretched out her arms toward the sinking Body and got the attention of many as she very sweetly, seductively, and sincerely called out, "Come unto me all ye that are weary and heavy laden, and I will give you WHAT YOU WANT!

The people who were jumping off were in a panic, like rats leaving a sinking ship. Some scurried to higher ground on the Body, going from the shoulders to the ears and finally jumping off the top of the head right before it went under. It was clear that THEY DID NOT WANT TO LEAVE THIS BODY, but it was equally clear that they were not going down under the water with it either. The Body now was completely under the water, sinking steadily toward the bottom. Some of the little people hung on as it sank, but after a few seconds of holding their breath, they gave up, swam for the top, gulped a mouth full of air, and swam off toward the woman.

The apparently lifeless Body sank deeper and deeper into the clear blue-green water. As it sank I could see at the bottom of the harbor a beautiful, large, perfect pearl - obviously of great value. It was supernaturally large and beautiful, lustrous, pure and round. As I watched, I could see the Body change shape from that of a single being, with little people desperately hanging on it, to many little individual people swimming deep enough to get to this beautiful Pearl. As they went deeper, many chose to quit and swim to the surface for air and life and then go over to the beautiful woman. All who quit diving eventually swam over to the beautiful woman.

Finally, I saw a number of these small people swim to the Pearl and touch it, and embrace it. But to do this, everyone who dove down reached a point when they realized that their own natural ability to hold their breath and dive deeper would not be enough. Those who dove down and touched this Pearl all came to understand that they would have to expend all of their natural strength before they touched and embraced the Pearl of Great Price. This did not keep them from diving down though, because the closer they got to the Pearl, the more of His beauty they saw.

I saw many touch and embrace the Pearl and then immediately shoot straight up. As each of these little people shot up from the floor of the Harbor, each had the Pearl. As this group of individuals rose higher and higher, they all became one Body again. By the time these Pearl-laden people reached the surface they burst forth from the waters as one Body, the Body of Christ. These people were manifestly His own possession and they in turn possessed the Pearl of Great Price, Jesus Christ Himself.

As the Lord was showing me this beautiful picture, He spoke to me and said, "Even as Jesus came out of the waters of baptism, so My Body will come out of Pearl Harbor with a new and powerful anointing of My Holy Spirit, and a new and deadly power to fight the enemy." He said that there indeed would come upon the Church of Jesus Christ a Pearl Harbor experience like the United States experienced on December 7, 1941. He said that when the Body of Christ begins to sink under the water, because of a soon-coming, devastating attack of the enemy, MANY will choose to desert our Lord Jesus Christ because they do not esteem the Pearl of Great Price (Jesus Himself) worth the price - death to their own selfish desires. They will not make the selfless effort of love to dive deeply enough to embrace Him because they do not love Him more than their own lives. Many will choose not to identify with what they assume is a defeated individual or group. They look upon themselves as winners and will not identify with a Jesus that is apparently being defeated. They will choose to identify with the beautiful woman of the harbor who gives them what they want. As the vision revealed, many who leapt off the sinking Body did so because the woman of the harbor promised them success. Because of this they went to her. Many others did not feel that it was necessary to pay such a high price to apprehend Jesus, and they felt that the beautiful woman would give them Jesus on their own terms.

As the Body of Christ came out of the waters of death, the Lord said that His Body was now fully alive and would fight the enemy with purpose and real anointing. Also His Body would now use only supernatural weaponry. He spoke so clearly to me about the weapons. He said, "Even as the United States entered the Second World War using conventional weapons to fight the enemy, and ended the war with the atomic bomb, a weapon beyond their comprehension; so My people will begin this spiritual war with conventional weapons in the Spirit, but by the end of this war to end all wars, they will be using atomic bombs of the Spirit." The Lord made it clear that we will come out of the water equipped with God-given anointing to REALLY heal the sick, work miracles, and deliver those in demonic bondage. He also made it clear that before the warfare ends, we will be moving in a dimension of spiritual warfare that is unimaginable to us now. We will do greater works than Jesus did and we will see the demon hordes routed like never before.

After this message in tongues and interpretation was given, my attention turned back to the woman who was to be baptized. Then the Lord said that the Pearl Harbor experience for His Church would be similar to this woman's baptism. I closely watched this baptism to see what the Lord meant. The woman was very nervous and quite afraid of going under the water. I assured her that she would be all right. After several moments of prayer and a short teaching on what baptism represented, she was plunged underneath the water. She came out of the water with her hands lifted up, praising God. I had not told anyone what the Lord told me about this woman's baptism, because I did not know exactly what was going to happen. When she recovered her composure, she began to testify about what had just happened to her. She said that she was extremely fearful at first, but that when she got under the water a Beautiful Peace swept through her, and all her fear was gone. This beautiful peace became joy as she came out of the water and she praised God for His great comfort, love and mercy.

I believe that God was showing us that we need not fear what He will put us through. His purpose is to bring us peace, joy, cleansing and power. He was also showing us that His Church will go through a baptism. It is a baptism of the Body of Christ. It is a death and a resurrection. We must trust Him to bring us out of this watery tomb of death and into the glorious resurrection power of His Son. We must understand that a harbor is a place of SAFETY and REFUGE. God's people who are involved in these events will need to be safe and protected. The Harbor of the Pearl of Great Price is the only harbor that will provide refuge and safety, and ALL who truly believe will be more than willing to pay the price of dying to their own desires.

Pearl Harbor is the death and resurrection of the Body of Christ, being prepared to do His work in His way, with His heart. It is the final separation of David from Saul - the David Church being purified and separated from the Saul Church. It is the final AWAKENING blast of the trumpet of God to rouse His people for battle. It is the judgment that begins with the house of the Lord. It is the refining fire that separates the gold from the dross. It will be preceded by the Lord dealing with His true people to both survive and desire this final preparation for battle. It is the promise of unmatched power and purity: power over sin, power over the enemy, power to live a much more virtuous life, and power to glorify our Heavenly Father through Jesus Christ by the power of the Holy Spirit. Even now, God is dealing with those in the David Church even as God dealt with David. Whenever David would start to fall asleep to God's purity and purpose, the Lord would abruptly DEAL with David to AWAKEN him. God did not waste this kind of effort on Saul because Saul CHOSE to be asleep to God and His desires.

Pearl Harbor is a warning of betrayal and disaster. The Church in the past has gone through many Pearl Harbors of betrayal and disaster. Jesus was betrayed and killed and rose again. English Puritans experienced Pearl Harbor in the early 17th century and survived because they could not obey the law that the Church of England tried to force them to obey. They fled England and eventually sailed to the New World, where they laid the spiritual foundation for what eventually became one of the greatest revivals in the history of the world. John Bunyan, wrote

Pilgrim's Progress at the bottom of the harbor as he was betrayed by his own country and thrown in jail for not attending the services of the Church of England and for preaching in a way that did not conform to this church's directive. Had he given in and done that which they asked he could have been a free man. But for conscience sake he chose not to do so. Because of this uncompromising obedience to the Scriptures and to God Himself, he was able to rise to the highest place in the history of Christian literature. Today he still blesses us with the fruit of that resurrection power.

To those who are not awake and prepared, Pearl Harbor will come suddenly and tragically, as thief in the night, and they will be swept away to Great Deception. To those who are more open to the will of God than they are to pleasing religious men, it will be an expected ordeal, a call to arms, and a prelude to great victory. The initial stages will be the harbinger of the greatest move of God in history: the greatest Revival and the greatest manifestation of Christian Unity that the world has ever known.

CHAPTER 19

DIVISION, UNITY & REVIVAL

Across the United States, from many churches and radio and television ministries, over the last twenty-five years, we have been hearing a cry for Revival! This cry has been the loudest from the Charismatics. They are realizing that much of the anointing of God is gone from their movement and the culture shaking revival that they have desired has not yet happened. The plea to pray for Revival has gone forth from the Assemblies of God and Foursquare Churches, Trinity Broadcasting Network, Promise Keepers and many others. Many Charismatics have periodically prophesied that just such a move of God was only a year or two away. Even though we have had several outbursts of revival in Toronto, Canada and Pensacola, Florida, we have yet to see a revival that caused more than a mild stir. The Toronto Revival had small repercussions in England and America and for the most part attracted men and women who wanted to experience "holy" laughter. The Pensacola or Brownsville Revival, which was deeper, still had no substantial impact on the culture of America.

These two moves of God, which certainly touched many in the Charismatic Movement, were essentially Saul revivals. During this time I visited Pensacola, Florida (home of the Brownsville Revival). I also visited a number of meetings in the Oregon area that were led by people from the revivals in Toronto and Brownsville. I could not help but notice that people usually got what they prayed for or desired, and no more. I saw dozens of people at a variety of meetings answer the preacher's call to "belly up to the bar of the Holy Spirit." They would come back with an experience of laughter that, upon reflection, seemed to change nothing in their lives. Some did not even experience the joy of the Lord; they just laughed. Even at Brownsville, some just seemed as if they would be satisfied with falling over, and that was all they got. Others however, during the baptismal services, expressed a deep regret for their lives spent in sin and an equally deep thankfulness for the forgiveness that God had worked in them. Most of these that were so affected were young people in their teenage years and early twenties. Many, I learned later, were markedly changed.

At other meetings across the country, however, I only saw the shallowest of experiences: many laughed, many walked very strangely and many talked in disrespectful terms about the power of the Holy Spirit that was around them. When they fell down, they would talk about doing "carpet time", and the phrase "belly up to the bar of the Holy Spirit" was uttered far too many times. The Lord spoke to me during those times, and He told me that this WAS a move of God, but that it was a Saul revival: shallow and for the purpose of giving the people what they wanted. He would give people what they wanted, and in most cases no more than they asked.

Many were united in their desire to have an experience with God. Many pastors were united in their desire to have a larger church by giving people an experience with God. I saw few that just wanted more of Jesus Christ. Most were satisfied to go to meetings and have experience after experience after experience. I saw some that said they wanted more of Jesus, but all they talked about was the experience of being filled with laughter and how much carpet time they had spent.

Along with the cries for revival has come an equally loud call for unity. The Charismatics are aware that the 120 in the Upper Room on the Day of Pentecost were in one accord when the Holy Spirit came upon them. The Saul Church has been striving for God's people to "be in one accord" and to "bring the Body of Christ together in unity." They have had many seminars, camp meetings, conferences and prayer sessions, all in an effort to bring about unity and then revival. They have filled football stadiums, auditoriums, city parks and downtown Washington D.C., but with little spiritual impact on America.

The truth of the matter is that they HAVE come to be in "one accord." They ALL believe that doctrine is not very important and they ALL believe that all you need to do is love one another and have lots of prayer. They are in one accord regarding the need for lots of prayer and unifying regardless of doctrinal positions. Church history, however, teaches us differently. The Roman Catholic monks were in one accord with the Roman Catholic Church and prayed for hours every day for more than a thousand years, and things only got worse!

The accord that they and everyone else needs to strive for is to be IN ONE ACCORD WITH GOD'S WORD! To accomplish this, individuals must seek for the Lord Himself with all their hearts both in their time with Him in prayer and in their time spent in the Scriptures. As men and women do just that, they can anticipate finding Him in all His glory and He will pour out His Holy Spirit of love and power so that He may be glorified by His people. This prayer must be couched in terms that make it clear that "whatever it takes Lord, bless us with the fullness of Yourself." The Scripture makes it clear that if we seek Him with ALL our heart, we WILL find Him and He will be glorified by our faith-filled love and obedience.

It almost seems that as the Saul Church's desire for unity has become stronger and stronger and has spread to more and different religions, doctrine has became progressively less important and the Church has become much weaker. The greater they have sought for unity the less powerful the Holy Spirit has been in their midst. This is not coincidence. When you essentially dismiss what Scripture says in order to achieve unity, you are dismissing the Holy Spirit also. The Charismatics have reached out to Methodists, Baptists, Possibility Thinkers, Christian psychologists, Roman Catholics and anti-Trinitarians to complete the unity that they believe will bring down the power of the Holy Spirit in Revival.

Many Reformed Christians and some Evangelicals have risen up and rejected this appeal to unity as being based on tolerance of error at the expense of truth. Neo-Calvinists have increased dramatically over the last twenty-five years and have rightly filled the internet with warnings against the systematic dismantling of Reformation truth.

Many of the sharp divisions that have occurred over the last twenty-five years seem to have come about after God's people began to pray for Revival. Because of this division and apparent confusion, the unity people have become even more committed to unity and have loudly rebuked "divisive" critics who criticize the Charismatics for compromising sound doctrine to achieve unity. These Charismatics claim and apparently sincerely believe that Satan is behind most if not all the division and divisive people in the visible Body of Christ today.

Unfortunately these people have neglected a prominent Scriptural principle and a prophetic truth. Jesus says in Matthew 10:34-35, "I did not come to bring peace but a sword. For I came to set a man against his father and a daughter against her mother." Jesus spoke these words several years before His disciples were in one accord in the Upper Room and experienced the mighty baptism of the Holy Spirit. The years preceding this tremendous revival were years of division and turmoil. The words of Jesus had indeed become a sword. The remnant of disciples who followed Jesus were divided from the Pharisees and the Sadducees. These two groups constituted the majority of religious life in the nation of Israel. It is a sad fact that the only display of unity during the time of Jesus' ministry was when the Conservative Pharisees and Liberal Sadducees were united in their goal to have Jesus crucified and His followers either destroyed or punished severely.

When we look at every revival since Pentecost, we see this principle operating. First the sword of the Word comes and a small group of people who have hungry hearts for God are divided from those who are satisfied with the status quo of their churches. Typically in all these culture shaking revivals, this small group of people or Remnant has been vilified or ignored by the powers that ruled the existing churches.

The Word of God divided Martin Luther, Zwingli, John Calvin and others from the Roman Catholics, then the Lord brought a measure of unity to the Protestants and His Church was revived and reformed. These men realized that "the just shall live by faith" and that salvation came by the power of God and not by doing penance, paying for indulgences, or any other work of man. They realized that the Roman Catholic Church was either dead or asleep and needed to be revived and reformed. The priests and most Catholics refused to go along with reformation and revival because they were basically satisfied with the way things were going.

The Early Methodists both Calvinist-Methodists and Wesleyan-Methodists, in England were desperately hungry for peace and a joyful relationship with God and were not receiving much life giving ministry from the Church of England in the 18th century. These men, led first by George Whitfield and then John Wesley, started the culture shaking revival that changed the British Isles in the 18th century. This hungry remnant was considered unbalanced and was vilified or ignored by most leaders and many members of the Church of England. Similarly in America, the Great Awakening under Jonathan Edwards and others re-established the strength of the dying Church in the 13 colonies. The mighty power of the Holy Spirit that literally knocked men and women over with deep conviction for their sins was dismissed by the Church of England as merely an attack of "emotionalism." Also, most ministers taught their congregations that they really didn't need to be "born again" as the preachers of The Great Awakening taught their listeners.

In the latter part of the 19th century, once again, men were concerned about the lack of spiritual life in the churches. Particularly in the United States small groups emerged that were very hungry for God and desired to see His power over Satan once again manifest in the supernatural gifts and ministries of the Holy Spirit that existed in the New Testament Church. Their prayers were answered by an outpouring on people who spoke in tongues and ministered the gifts of healing and prophesied. As in earlier revivals, these "holy rollers" were either vilified or ignored by most in the established churches. These churches did not believe that the supernatural power of God could flow through men after the establishment of the Canon of Scripture. Neither did they believe that ministries such as apostle or prophet could occur outside the New Testament Church time. These Pentecostal people became united in their desire to preach what they called "the Full Gospel" and went on to touch the world with their message, and in many cases, minister the fullness of the Holy Spirit to God's people.

Historically we have seen that even in the new unity that God created, there were divisions in this unity. Even people of revival have embraced wrong doctrine and have given men and their ideas more respect than God and His Word. There typically has been, however, a unifying desire to see God move more deeply and effectively in His people. Often there has been a unifying doctrinal thrust that characterized each revival movement.

Eventually, in any revival, men are driven out of and divided from the movement that needs revival, because at first it is always a small group of people that hear God's cry for His people to wake up to the truth.

Today we are seeing Division in the Body of Christ. We prayed for Revival and God is answering our prayers as He always has - by separating out for Himself a people whom He will bring back to true life (REVIVE). He will only revive people who realize their own lack of spiritual life. He will only revive a Church that knows it is spiritually near death or asleep. Revival is only for people who are DESPERATE for help. Most in the Saul Church who pray for revival are essentially satisfied with their own lives and the condition of the Church. All the Charismatics really want to do is see more people "saved" and more non-Charismatics "filled with the Spirit." They see no need for basic changes. They really are not DESPERATE for Revival because they do not think that they are spiritually asleep or near death. What they really want is for God to IMPROVE and expand what they already have. God will NEVER revive a people who are self-satisfied and no longer hunger and thirst deeply for righteousness, either as individuals or the Church as a whole. These people will not experience revival until they see that they need to be revived. Unfortunately the Saul Church is content to re-define the word "revival" to mean church growth, larger budgets, more recognition by the world, the election of a Christian president, or an exciting speaker for three or more consecutive days.

To be involved in God's mighty Holy Spirit outpouring we MUST REALIZE that we are in desperate need of Life and that we need to be separated from those who are satisfied with sleep or death. We must OPEN OUR EYES to see what God wants and is doing. We must identify with Jesus and His Word, which is the sword, as it comes down and divides God's people by challenging them to repent of error and embrace truth. WE MUST CHOOSE to line up with the One who is bearing the sword. Most importantly, we MUST REALIZE even before revival comes that IT IS GOD, NOT SATAN who is causing much of the division.

DIVISION BECAUSE OF THE DEALINGS OF GOD

Around twenty years ago as I was praying about an upcoming prayer meeting involving several churches, the Lord gave me a vision and then explained the vision. He said that He was going to send a storm to His Church. He said "Lightning will not awake the blind and thunder will not awake the deaf, but My sheep will hear My voice in the thunder and see My purpose in the lightning. I will awaken with My thunder and shatter with My lightning. In the midst of the lightning and thunder I will bring a driving rain, not to soften the earth for planting, but to CLEANSE the land. Those who thirst for ME will drink and be cleansed. Those who are satisfied with the way they are will not drink, and will be washed away. My lightning bolts will strike many who are called by My name and expose their lives of sin. My people are asleep. They have been lulled to sleep by preachers of profit and comfort who feed them drugged desserts and withhold the meat and EVEN the milk."

In the vision I saw dark storm clouds rolling in very fast and furiously. Elohim Himself was thrusting many lightning bolts earthward. He said, "Many will run for cover - because they fear the effect of My lightning and My thunder and the exposure of their sins. But those WHO ARE MINE will let the lightning strike them, and do its work of death. Then they will be raised up and do My works with power and with an electricity of life that results from being crucified to the world and alive to Me. Others will come out from their safe dwelling places to see the lightning, but will not like it, and will scurry back to their comfort. But the PEOPLE whose hearts are after Me will REJOICE in the storm that I bring. And some will even CALL for the lightning to fall and will PRAY for the floods to come to cleanse My land." The Lord made it very clear that the storm He would send would come FROM HIM and NOT THE ENEMY.

In March of 1987, several weeks after the Lord spoke, we saw a storm hit the visible Body of Christ. We saw God start to deal very personally. He dealt with a televangelist and his wife. We saw the lightning bolt of accusation hit this man and in the brightness of its flash, illuminate his heart and deeds for all to see. We saw this man scurry from those blasts to the convenient protection of his own self-righteous excuses and counter accusations. He could have been humbled by this experience immediately and during this time pour out his heart in complete confession and true repentance before the same people that he had failed: his television audience. But he chose not to. He could have asked forgiveness from others whom he had compromised or betrayed because of his sinful lust and greed, but he did not. He could have been like David and respond to the words of those who accused him with, "I have sinned against the Lord." This response could have been without rationalization or excuse. Instead, he responded like Saul. Initially he grudgingly admitted to the facts that were irrefutable, but made excuses and denials as long as that served his purposes. Then he took a vow of silence for the supposed purpose of peace and unity, but really for the preservation of his own righteousness. If he would have stood firm and let the lightning bolt strike deep into his heart by publicly repenting of his sins, God would have given him a NEW power in his life and ministry. He would have found that the same electricity that illuminated and electrocuted him would have also empowered him.

Eventually, after years in prison and eventual release, he acknowledged and repented of the fact that he had taught a gospel of prosperity that was not in Scripture. To the best of my knowledge, he did not publicly repent of many other sins that he was apparently involved with, but he did seem to have a better attitude towards God and ministry. It was not as complete a repentance as many wanted, but it has been a fairly good start. He has worked with homeless people and consistently spoken against the unscriptural "prosperity" gospel. It is up to God to judge the true intents of his heart.

Shortly after the exposure of this man and his wife, at a national meeting of a prominent Charismatic denomination, one of the leaders exhorted the hundreds of pastors present to pray against the devil and the newspapers and other media that exposed the activities of this televangelist. He believed this man and his ministry had been set up for destruction by Satan and the media, and that we should all stand shoulder to shoulder with our brother who was being attacked so viciously.

After this exhortation, I approached a district supervisor at the meeting and told him the word that God had shown us shortly before the exposure took place. When I mentioned the part that said that God was the one who would expose the sins of men in both high places and low places for the purpose of cleansing His Church, he was shocked. He verbally chastised me severely and made it clear that what I spoke was definitely not from God, and that he would not allow me to deliver that message.

In October of that same year, we witnessed the exposure of another popular televangelist. This fiery and sometimes anointed preacher of holiness was shown to be a hypocrite. This man was extremely critical of men who fell into adultery and was almost gleeful in his condemnation. Unfortunately for him, his own sexual relations with prostitutes came to light. He was asked to step down from his position of authority by his denomination's governing body. Even though he uttered publicly the words "I have sinned," he never felt that his years of sexual sin merited his temporary removal from leadership in his denomination. Instead of submitting to the men over him, he decided to leave the denomination and form his own work. His rationalization was that he was the one that God had called to supervise this ministry of evangelism and telecommunications and if he quit, the work would fail. Eventually the work was essentially destroyed and left without power because of his inability to recognize the depth of his sin and the dealings he was experiencing from God Himself.

God's lightning storm has sent bolts of lightning to many. He has dealt with and is dealing with His people in very personal and very shocking ways. The bolts He is thrusting at us are to test us concerning our desire to repent and become like Him. So many of us say that we want to be like Jesus, but when the Lord challenges us to forsake our sin by sending us a lightning bolt (often in the form of a crisis or a clear-cut but difficult decision that we need to make) we run from the lightning bolt and cling to our sin or our own will. Thus the true nature of our heart is exposed by His illuminating flash.

In the denomination that I ministered in for eight years, we experienced the lightning bolts of God. We lost both a divisional supervisor (an elder over five or six other churches) and a district supervisor (who shepherded the pastors of over 130 churches). We lost both of these men because of their adulterous relationships. One of these men who had slept with a number of women in his congregation refused to be corrected in any way and left the denomination along with the people of his church. The district supervisor, however, completely acknowledged his sin before all 130 pastors that he had shepherded. In no way did he blame his wife, or the woman he was involved with. Like David, he accepted the exposure of his sin. He accepted his punishment of being removed from authority as just and merciful dealings from God. I have heard that he has found success in other ministry and is considered to be a man of wisdom. I don't know what happened to the adulterous divisional supervisor.

With David the lightning bolt was the confrontation with the prophet Nathan. In Nathan's simple story of a poor man and his little sheep (see II Samuel chapter 12) David's treacherous, lustful heart was exposed. David could have done what many kings and religious leaders would have done. He could have called for the prophet to be thrown out or killed. Or he could have been religious and said, "I understand what you are saying; I receive that Nathan. It took a lot of courage for you to deliver that word to me. I will pray about it. By the way Nathan, don't call me, I'll call you." Then David could have continued to rationalize his sin and eventually he would have become another Saul and been judged by God for his rebellion. But David chose to immediately, humbly, and repentantly submit to this terrible lightning bolt from God. He chose to not only let the lightning expose His terrible sin, but he allowed the lightning bolt to smash right into his heart and deliver its excruciatingly painful sentence of death to his pride. He chose to be dealt with by God completely and immediately, without excuse. Why did David do this? Why was he different from Saul? It is because David measured the worth of the Lord's abiding presence and love against the desire to maintain his own pride and self righteousness. In the end, David wanted God's love more than he wanted to keep his own pride and self righteousness. David's pride was electrocuted but his heart was electrified and empowered to write one of the greatest songs of God's forgiveness, love and mercy - Psalm 51.

God is dividing the Davids from the Sauls. When lightning illuminated Saul's rebellious, materialistic, and people-pleasing spirit the best he could do was to make excuses. But in doing so he also excused himself out of the kingdom of God, away from the abiding presence of the Lord, and into a life of being ruled by the spirit of rebellion that God had attempted to put to death. He did not let the lightning into his heart to perform the required surgery. He ran from the lightning because he loved the darkness more than the light. But as he ran from the dealings of God, he ran away from God Himself. God then divided Saul from Himself and His kingdom by the lightning bolt He delivered through Samuel the prophet.

The storms from God are for the purpose of setting apart (dividing) those who truly are called by His name. The lightning bolts that hit prominent Christian figures will also fall with equal force on those of us who are not prominent. The purpose, as with our leaders, is to give us an opportunity to put to death our sins of rebellion, self-justification and pride.

All through the Body of Christ men and women are being challenged. The lightning bolts of God, either through prophets, circumstances or a direct word from the Lord, are exposing monument building, dependence on money to minister, fear of a spouse, the love of luxury and comfort that the world offers, lust, presumption, pride, rebellion, and double-mindedness. We must not run from His lightning bolts! We must let Him illuminate the sin in our hearts and electrocute our old man. We MUST be found among those who call for the lightning to come. And because we hate our sin and our divided hearts, we must not care who sees us as we really are, ALL BECAUSE WE WANT TO BE WITH HIM AND PLEASE HIM—WHATEVER IT TAKES!

DIVISION OF THE PURE FROM THE IMPURE

Years ago at a meeting of ministers, the Lord spoke to me about the need for Christians to judge righteous judgment. He showed me a fountain gushing out of the earth and a stream that came forth from that fountain. From a distance the fountain looked relatively clear. When I got closer to it, I could see debris in the fountain. The fountain contained clods of dirt, tin cans, refuse, and garbage – but the debris did not make the water undrinkable, you just had to be careful. Then I saw the fountain split and there were two fountains. One of the fountains was becoming clearer; there was less and less debris and refuse as it continued streaming forth. The other fountain was getting more and more filthy until eventually all that came out of it was a horrible smelling, sludge-like material. Eventually the smelly, sludge-like material just stopped and that fountain ran dry. The stream that was getting progressively clearer became perfectly clear and this stream flooded over everything and even the fountain of filth was swept away. Then the pure stream became an ocean and covered the whole earth.

I asked the Lord the meaning of the vision and He said that the single undivided fountain and the stream that came from it was the move of the Holy Spirit on the earth as it existed at the time of the vision. He said that the stream would split into two streams, because He was going to bring division. He said that there would then be two "apparent" moves of His Holy Spirit upon the earth. One stream, the stream that becomes progressively more pure, will be made up of people who HONESTLY look at the stream of the Holy Spirit in their own lives and in the life of His Church. He said that those who see the impurities (sins and unscriptural doctrines), acknowledge these sins and unscriptural doctrines, confess these sins and unscriptural doctrines and repent of these sins and unscriptural doctrines will be a part of the move of His Spirit and will become progressively more like Jesus. The stream that gets dirtier, until it is completely filthy, is made up of people who will NOT see the impurities (sins and unscriptural doctrines) in their own lives or in the life of the Church. These people will stubbornly choose NOT to let God's Word and God's men JUDGE their hearts and doctrine. They will take the position that they do not need cleansing and that it is not necessary to JUDGE the CHURCH with regards to matters of doctrine or the practices of its leaders and sheep. These people are SATISFIED to remain in their current condition and are confident that God will put this unacknowledged and unrepented sin and carnal ministry "under the Blood." They feel sure that His love will cover their multitude of sins and poor doctrines. These unrepentant, presumptuous people will become progressively more impure until they are totally defiled and the movement that they are involved with will also become totally defiled.

The Lord said that soon He will raise up men who will expose the filthiness in the Church, both doctrinally and personally. He said that it is NECESSARY that we listen to these men. Those who speak against and mock or IGNORE them are in danger of being part of the FILTHINESSS described above. But all who fall on their faces before God and repent of their terrible carnality, and cry out against the abominations that are being committed in His Holy Temple will be spared the filth and the judgment that follows. In our day it will be as prophesied by Ezekiel in chapter 9, ""And the Lord said to him, "Go through the midst of the city, even through the midst of Jerusalem, and put a mark on the foreheads of the men who sigh and groan over all the abominations which are being committed in its midst."" And only these men were spared from the sword of judgment.

A year or two after the Lord showed me the fountain vision He showed me a grassy plain with a huge fault line stretching off to the horizon. There were tens of thousands of people straddling this fault line when all of a sudden the earth began to violently shake. The earth split in two and I could see some of the people jumping to one side and others jumping to the other side But I could also see thousands who could not make up their minds. As the crack widened these fell into the apparently bottomless crevice between the divided parts of the plain. One plain was rising upward away from the other part as the split grew. As the one side was slowly rising I saw a man, who at the last minute, realized that he had made the wrong choice. He leaped from the lower side towards the higher side. He tried to grab hold of the higher side as it rose away from him, but all he could grab was a chunk of turf. This gave way and he fell with the turf in his hand, screaming out to God as he fell. Then I saw a Hand reach down and catch him in mid air, and place him on the rising side.

This vision is clear. We are in the first stages of a great division that God is performing. We are being FORCED by God to choose THIS DAY whom we will serve. We are being given an ever clearer view of the impurity of the visible Church and the great gulf that is beginning to form between two opposite viewpoints. One viewpoint, held by those who emphasize unity at the expense of truth, is that everything is basically okay and we should just love one another in spite of our differences, get together and pray and not be concerned about the unrighteousness that is so prevalent in the Church. The other viewpoint held by the "divisive people" is that there is a desperate need for radical surgery in the visible Body of Christ. We must recognize the need to mercifully expose sinful doctrines and stop trying to protect sinful, unrepentant men. We must choose, as the "split" widens, which way we will jump. We must leap to the side which is rising to a walk of holiness, a place of reigning, in purity and truth, with our Savior. And even if we have seen the split, have been on the wrong side, and are falling fast, we must CRY OUT TO GOD for FORGIVENESS and MERCY and TRUST HIM to catch us in His hand and plant us on the solid ground. From now on our spiritual lives depend how well we discern God's truth and choose to live according to God's Word.

SECTION III

THE DAVID CHURCH

CHAPTER 20

APPOINTED AND ANOINTED FOR GOD HIMSELF

This chapter deals with the heart of the Scriptures. For those in the Saul Church the concept that we will discuss here is particularly difficult to grasp. We have come to believe either directly or indirectly that the Scriptures are there essentially for man's sake. They are about the creation of man and his earth, man's fall, man's sin, man's forgiveness, man's redemption and man's ultimate state of glory with God. This totally counters the intent of Scripture. The holy Scriptures from Genesis to Revelation are about: 1) God's sovereign rule over His creation, particularly man. 2) God's love for man. 3) God's character, 4) God's power, 5) God's purpose, 6) God's glory. The Westminster Confession put it so well: "The chief end of man is to glorify God and enjoy Him forever." Another thought is, "The chief end of man is know God and to glorify Him forever."

The Scriptures are clear, we are not the primary issue, God is the primary issue. It is not what man is, what man thinks, what man says or what man does for God. Rather it is who God IS, what He thinks, what He says and what He does. Jesus is the perfect example of the perfect Man, and we are to emulate Him. Everything that Jesus was, everything He thought, everything He said, everything He did emanated from what He knew about His Father. He only did what He knew His Father would do. John 5:30 says of Jesus, "I can do nothing on My own initiative. As I hear I judge; and MY judgment is just, because I do not seek My own will, but the will of Him who sent Me." He only did what He saw His Father do. John 5:19 says, "Therefore Jesus answered and was saying to them, truly truly, I say to you, the Son can do nothing of Himself, unless it is something He sees the Father doing; for whatever the Father does, these things the Son also does in like manner." His life was and is the perfect expression of the Father's will and ways and thought. Everything that Jesus did and said was first and foremost FOR the Father. He was anointed and filled with the Holy Spirit principally to glorify the Father.

It is not the powerful prayers of men that change the world. It is the great God who answers these prayers. It is the grace of God that makes the difference. The more we truly know Him, His ways and His will, the more we can trust Him and lay hold of that grace. Even in our warfare against the enemy, our armor according to Ephesians 6 is the Word and Words of God, the thoughts, ways and expression of His being, His character, His desires and His will. We will never defeat the enemy by using formula prayers that seem to fit a moment or the circumstance. We can only defeat the enemy with an intimate knowledge of God and trust in His character, His power and His desire. The issue is always to trust in His intimate personal love and His desire, power and will for each situation.

Psalms 103:7 says, "He (God) made known His WAYS to Moses, His ACTS to the sons of Israel." We are more like the Children of Israel whom the Psalms say knew His acts or deeds; we are not nearly enough like Moses who knew the ways of God. Our needs, our desires, our power, our abilities are not the essential issues. HE is the issue and our focus must always be on Him. Everything we do must be for His sake, whether it is prophesying, evangelizing, pastoring or teaching. When our hearts are set on pleasing Him and only Him, THEN we are much more likely to see hearts changed to love Him and to see many people being filled with the Holy Spirit. We are more likely to see many move in all that God has for them and more likely to see the enemy being driven back and conquered completely.

Saul's reign as king seemed destined from the very beginning to be only temporary. The whole foundation of the house of his reign was faulty. The first crack in the foundation was that he was chosen against God's best desire. God wanted Israel to want only Himself as King. The second crack was that the desire for a king emerged as an effort to imitate the Gentiles. The third crack was that God did not choose Saul for Himself but the people chose him for themselves and God allowed this apparent override of His will because the heart of the people had to be revealed for what it was. Not once did Saul show any evidence of truly loving God. In fact when Saul spoke to Samuel or David he continuously referred to Jehovah as "the Lord your God." Saul was basically not God's choice; he, like the people who chose him, was shallow in his relationship with God. He did not have a heart after God and he certainly did not love God enough to obey Him when he did not want to obey Him. Saul was the rebel king of a rebellious people, and eventually this rebellion caused Saul to not receive the conditional promise that his house would rule over Israel forever. Rebellion cost him the power to rule and eventually cost him his life. And it cost Israel their king.

The People's Choice was not able to endure. Eventually he fell on his own sword and the nation was defeated by the enemy and was left in a shambles. The ignoble experiment failed and the Theocracy was renewed with God's own choice on the throne. We see God's anointed man waiting patiently and faithfully for God to raise him up and place him on the throne. David, who was God's anointed choice, NEVER strove to be king. David was a man after God's own heart.

This man was not chosen to satisfy any of the people's shallow, carnal desires to be like the nations, prosper materially, or be a strong military presence in the Middle East. This man was appointed by God for God Himself with God's powerful anointing to do all of God's will. This man was chosen because of his loyalty to, his trust in, his desire for, and his relationship with Jehovah Himself. This was a divinely appointed and deeply anointed man chosen to do His will using His power for His glory.

I Samuel 13:14, 16:1, & 15:13 say, "But now your (speaking of Saul) kingdom shall not endure. The Lord has sought out for Himself a man after His own heart, and the Lord has appointed him as ruler over His people, because you (Saul) have not kept what the Lord commanded you. Now the Lord said to Samuel, 'How long will you grieve over Saul, since I have rejected Him from being king over Israel? Fill your horn with oil and go; I will send you to Jesse the Bethlehemite, for I have selected a *KING FOR MYSELF* among his sons'. Then Samuel took the horn of oil and anointed him in the midst of his brothers; and the Spirit of the Lord came mightily upon David from that day forward. And Samuel arose and went to Ramah."

This man was sought out by God to be the ruler of Israel. God searched the hearts of hundreds of thousands of men in Israel but

David's heart was the heart that He saw that would do all His will and glorify Him. He knew that David would not take lightly God's instructions. David was not a double minded religious man who was only interested in appearing spiritual. David's desire for God was not skin deep or reserved only for special occasions. His desire for God came from the depths of his being, from the heart of his heart; his love was for God and his desire was for His glory. David knew that it was God's love and grace that had given him this heart after Himself and he knew that he would have to trust that God's awesome wisdom and power would be given to him to guide the Lord's people. David totally depended upon God's power to deliver and God's wisdom to guide. David completely trusted in the character, the holiness and the love of this Majestic Jehovah, and David wanted to do nothing else but to carry out His plan for His glory. David wanted to be Israel's ruler for God's glory. David wanted to seek God's favor and please His heart alone. David, the appointed one of God, was truly anointed FOR God, to bring Him glory through His people.

Even as God sought out for Himself a man after His own heart, during the time that Saul was showing himself to be a rebel, so today God is seeking out for Himself a people who are after His own heart whom He will use to rule for Him on this planet. He has allowed the people pleasing Saul Church to almost fully reveal their rebellion and shallowness. Their cup is almost full. He is now removing the precious Holy Spirit from their midst and is searching for a people who do not love the world nor cater to the flesh. He is seeking a people who are not concerned about their own self-image, but are concerned about God's glory, and will not seek to please men because they fear losing money, love, or respect. He is looking for a people who are concerned about God's honor and pleasing Him, a people who only fear losing God's Holy Spirit, His love and His approval. He is looking for a people who will spend as much or more time on their faces before Him as the Saul Church does indulging its senses at concerts, ski lodges, beach retreats, and "Christian Night" at Disneyland. He is looking for a people who will love His law and devour His Word, letting the Word break them into little pieces and reform them into His image. He is looking for a people who will ingest His Word with the same fervor that the Saul Church eats up books on self-help, instant answers, material success and church growth.

While millions of Charismatics in the Saul Church seek signs, wonders and money to build a strong movement, God is looking for a remnant that will seek God Himself as the only and complete answer. He is looking for a people who will not presume upon His grace and His power but still trust completely in the totality of His Word and the magnificent power of His Holy Spirit. He is looking for a people that are so filled with the Holy Spirit of God that they only minister as God directs their hearts. They will only do as they see the Father do, and only speak the words that He gives them to speak. No more shot gun approaches to the ministries of healing and miracles. He is looking for a people that know Him intimately and know His voice! People will lay hands on the sick because God tells them to, and because they really hear God, the people WILL BE HEALED. He is looking for a people that have been purified from their many Saulish errors and have deeply repented of speaking in the flesh with no REAL results because God did not speak to them. He is looking for a Church that prays for the sick and listens intently to God's voice, not so they can build the church larger, but so they can please the heart of God. No more using the power of God to build the kingdoms, churches or denominations of men. He is looking for a Church with a heart like David's. He is looking for and will find the David Church, even in the midst of Saul.

Who and what is the David Church? The answer is fairly obvious from our earlier study of Saul and David. Certainly we can make relevant comparisons between Saul's ministry and the visible Church as it exists today with the superficial anointing, the worldliness, the shallowness, the religiosity, the reliance on the material and the involvement with the demonic. It is very easy to call today's visible church the Saul Church.

But what about the David Church? Can we really expect God to raise up a Church comprised of people who (single-mindedly) love Him, depend upon Him completely, and move in such undeniable spiritual power as David did?

When we stop and think with our hearts and our minds about this issue, the real question becomes, "Could we expect God to do anything less, knowing His character, His ways and His Word?" How could God close this present age while allowing His name to be so thoroughly besmirched by such a shallow representation of Himself? He has always been concerned for His Holy Name. The Lord declares in Ezekiel 36:21-23, "'But I had concern for My holy name, which the house of Israel had profaned among the nations where they went. Therefore, say to the house of Israel, "Thus says the Lord God, *"It is not for your sake, O house of Israel,* that I am about to act, *but for My holy name*, which you have profaned among the nations where you went. And I will vindicate the holiness of My great name which has been profaned among the nations, which you have profaned in their midst. Then the nations (non-Christians) will know that I am the Lord," declares the Lord God, "when I prove Myself holy AMONG YOU IN THEIR SIGHT."'" God will always manifest Himself as holy and powerful, through His people to the world.

It is important to understand that the basic difference between the Saul Church and the David Church is their attitude about man and God. The Saul Church believes that man was damaged greatly at the Fall but still possesses great powers to build the kingdom of God. They believe in man's free will and his ability to choose God by exercising that free will. They believe in the nobility of man and evangelize because they love men and do not want to see men go to hell. It is good to love men, even as God loves the world, however, the David Church first and foremost evangelizes because it knows that this activity will please God. The Saul Church wants to see America return to the glory years of 100 years ago when most people in the country believed in being law abiding, chaste citizens. They want to see conservative, God fearing political parties that choose morally upright men to make scriptural decisions concerning abortion, homosexuality, immigration laws, drug laws and proper treatment of God's people. The David Church is not concerned about the glory days of America but is concerned about the glory of God, and the days when men in America will glorify God.

The Scriptures give example after example of God's people failing Him completely and God manifesting His glory through His new appointed leadership. Moses, David, and Josiah are three good examples. The centuries-long bondage to Egypt and idolatry was broken through Moses' leadership. David led the Israelites to victory after victory, following the embarrassing reign and defeat of Saul. Josiah became Judah's most righteous ruler and led the people temporarily out of idolatry after the depraved reigns of Manasseh and his son Amon. Even church history shows us that the Dark Ages, with its salvation by works, rampant idolatry, greed and lust was followed by The Reformation in Europe that started in the sixteenth century.

Today's shallowness is not unlike those other periods of shallowness both in the Scripture and in the history of the Church. God, now as then, will not leave His name to be a joke upon the lips of the heathen. He will raise up a holy people who love Him and trust Him enough to obey Him. God will build a Church which will bring honor to his name.

Years ago the Lord showed me that the shallow man-pleasing ministry that has been prominent in the visible Church was, in many cases, actually anointed by Him. He also told me that He was in the process of withdrawing that anointing from those Saul Church ministries. God revealed that He was looking through the small churches and the large churches. He was looking at the flashy ministries and the apparently humble ministries. He was searching the pews and the classrooms. He was allowing each man to be tested so that his heart would be exposed. He was dealing with many individuals and trying them as a smelter of metals would try gold in the crucible. He heard the cries from the hearts of His people and TESTED the legitimacy of their words. He was and STILL IS searching for men and women who are single-mindedly after His own heart. He will raise up prophets to challenge the false theologies and sins of His people and their leadership. He will not stop until He has found a people after His own heart and He will appoint and anoint that people to love Him even more, live for Him without regard to their own well-being, and bear His life and His glory with the fear of the Lord and with the greatest concern for His Name.

He showed me that some in the Saul Church would be desperately convicted of their double-minded living and their people-pleasing ministries which so misrepresented Him, and that they would break away from these ministries. He showed me that from some of the most self-advertising, gimmicky, cool, and hip rock-and-roll bands would come forth men who would become worship leaders in His great Church. Their music would still be loud and have the same beat in some cases, but not one note would be played to please the people. Not one word would be spoken to attract attention to SELF. All would be done for God's glory. He let me hear with my mind men who still played heavy-metal style music warning the people of the coming judgment of the lukewarm Church and the world. There were no special effects, no attention-getting hair cuts or dress, no fleshly hand-clapping and remarks of how cool the music was; only a sense of AWE generated by the anointing of God through electric guitars and synthesizers that pounded out the message of a coming sentence of God's judgment on an unrepentant Church and the who-the-hell-cares world. The words of the singers were clear and easily understood. The crowds were learning the fear of the Lord. Some were weeping under the conviction of the Holy Spirit. Others walked out unable to stand in God's presence. No one thought of who was playing and the musicians and singers were glad because of this. God and only God was presented to the hearers and God and only God was being glorified. The music changed to soft music and even the style changed to fit what God was doing. No one was bound by style. The style had become servant to the glory of God. Young people throughout the audience were on their faces seeking God's forgiveness. Men and women stayed all night to pray to God and to praise Him from their hearts. The service, for it was not fit to call this ministry a concert, lasted until morning and many met the Real Jesus for the first time. Many had been self-conscious attention-getting rockers from the Saul Church, but they had finally come to know the Real Jesus Christ through the awesome anointing of God. They were becoming men and women with hearts like David's heart. The admission was free but the people left understanding the cost. For the first time they realized the cost was their hearts and minds and souls. The cost was their own lives. But they were joyfully willing to wholly and completely give their lives to this awesome God of judgment and forgiveness; this magnificently Holy Hater of Sin and Lover of all who would come to Him on His terms only.

The David Church will be filled with many such men and women, musicians, preachers, ex-Christian television personalities, ex-stars, and ex-athletes; all manner of people whose identities are not defined by who they WERE but by whose they ARE. The David Church, like the Saul Church before it, is not a denomination or movement but really a shared attitude of the heart manifested both individually and corporately. It is comprised of people who would gladly rather lose their physical life, possessions or earthly loved ones than lose His precious Holy Spirit. It is a people who sin and stumble into error but know that the way out is through an honest, excuse-free recognition of the fact that sin is sin and that sin is what caused the stumbling or the bondage. They are willing to acknowledge every sin and turn repentantly away from each one, cutting off all avenues which would allow a return to that sin, regardless of what anyone else may think. They understand that complete forgiveness is in the Blood of Jesus Christ. The David Church trusts God like the Church of the Book of Acts. The David Church knows that it is not only unnecessary but evil to manipulate or bait people into following Jesus Christ. The David Church cares little for either success or failure. This Church neither values The Big or the Little but only desires to do His will for His glory. The David Church covets the best gifts but only in obedience to Him, in His time, for the purpose of showing people the Real Jesus Christ and bringing glory to God. The David Church is quick to defend God's honor and trusts that when God is involved in an undertaking, He will take care of it without having His people resort to begging or bribing. The people in the David Church are uncompromising but merciful, persistent, and patient. Like David in the Old Testament, they are utterly and absolutely dependent upon God to save them from their sin, walk a holy life and minister in the power of the Holy Spirit. The God of the David Church is a totally sovereign God who is in complete control of the destiny of His Church and this planet. The people in this Church, like David, when judgment comes, are quick to recognize their own responsibility and in no way blame the devil, men or God. They are quick to see the other side of judgment as they repent and ask for God's forgiveness.

The David Church is utterly and absolutely dependent upon God. This Church trusts that it is the Father, the Son and the Holy Spirit working through God's people that will defeat the enemy and establish the kingdom. This Church understands that our part in this is to listen carefully and heed quickly, both from the Holy Scriptures and in our prayer life.

The David Church is God's CHURCH for the last days!

CHAPTER 21

JUST A SLING AND FIVE SMOOTH STONES

Samuel 17:32-50 says, ""And David said to Saul, "Let no man's heart fail on account of him; your servant will go and fight with this Philistine." Then Saul said to David, "You are not able to go against this Philistine to fight with him; for you are but a youth while he has been a warrior from his youth." But David said to Saul, "Your servant was tending his father's sheep. When a lion and a bear came and took a lamb from the flock, I went out after him and attacked him, and rescued it from his mouth; and when he rose up against me, I seized him by his beard and struck him and killed him. Your servant has killed both the lion and the bear; and this uncircumcised Philistine will be like one of them, since he has taunted the armies of the living God." And David said, "The Lord who delivered me from the paw of the lion and from the paw of the bear, He will deliver me from the hand of this Philistine." And Saul said to David, "Go and may the Lord be with you." Then Saul clothed David with his garments and put a bronze helmet on his head, and he clothed him with armor. And David girded his sword over his armor and tried to walk, for he had not tested them. So David said to Saul, "I cannot go with these, for I have not tested them." And David took them off. And he took his stick in his hand and chose for himself five smooth stones from the brook, and put them in the shepherd's bag which he had, even in his pouch, and his sling was in his hand; and he approached the Philistine. Then the Philistine came on and approached David, with the shield bearer in front of him. When the Philistine looked and saw David, he disdained him; for he was but a youth, and ruddy, with a handsome appearance. And the Philistine said to David, "Am I a dog that you come to me with sticks?" And the Philistine cursed David by his gods. The Philistine also said to David,

"Come to me and I will give your flesh to the birds of the sky and the beasts of the field." Then David said to the Philistine, "<u>You come to me with a sword, a spear, and a javelin, but I come to you in the name of the Lord of hosts, the God of the armies of Israel, whom you have taunted. This day the Lord will deliver you up into my hands,</u> and I will strike down and remove your head from you. And I will give the dead bodies of the army of the Philistines this day to the birds of the sky and the wild beasts of the earth, <u>that all the earth may know there is a God in Israel, and that all this assembly may know that the Lord does not deliver by the sword or by the spear; for the battle is the Lord's and He will give you into our hands.</u>" Then it happened when the Philistine rose and came and drew near to meet David, that David ran quickly toward the battle line to meet the Philistine. And David put his hand into his bag and took from it a stone and slung it, and struck the Philistine on his forehead. And the stone sank into his forehead so that he fell on his face to the ground. Thus David prevailed over the Philistine with a sling and a stone, and he struck the Philistine and killed him; but there was no sword in David's hand."

When we look carefully at this familiar portion of Scripture we can see how God and His chosen people will fight the enemy. At this point in Israel's history Saul is still the visible ruler but he has lost the anointing and an evil spirit has been sent from the Lord to torment him. The Philistines have challenged God's people to a battle, pitting their champion Goliath of Gath against Israel's champion to decide which nation will serve the other. Goliath, their nine foot warrior, is taunting the Jews. Saul, even though he is older, is the logical choice to fight Goliath. Saul is also a very large man, standing a full head taller than the other Jews. He is a warrior of great experience, but he has lost the anointing of God. As this challenge is hurled at him, he realizes perhaps for the first time, how fearful it is to meet a monstrous enemy with only his own natural strength and without God's help. He knows that he is hopelessly over matched and thus he is "dismayed and greatly afraid." The only volunteer to fight the giant is a young man who by natural appearances has no possible chance of success. David is apparently too young, too small and too inexperienced; but he is the only one who will try, so he is allowed to attempt to do battle against Goliath. David explains to Saul that he does have experience in fighting enemies who have had an overwhelming advantage; he has fought and single-handedly destroyed both a lion and a bear. This experience proved to him that God would protect him and enable him to slay any enemy that would threaten him or his charges. He cites the fact that Goliath has taunted and dishonored the armies of the living God. David's main reason for fighting Goliath was because God's honor was besmirched by the Philistine. The main issue for David was the honor and the glory of God. Regarding his chances of success, David reasoned that if God has protected him from wild beasts because he was protecting his father's sheep, it makes perfect spiritual sense that God will also protect him against this one who so brazenly makes fools of the Israelites and their God.

After Saul agrees to let David fight he tries to outfit David in his own armor and offers his sword, but David is not comfortable with it and decides not to use it because he has not tested it. David is not at all concerned that he is going to battle Goliath without armor or a sword because HE KNOWS that armor and a sword is not the issue. He is confident that the Lord God Jehovah will be his protection and his strength. The weapon that the Lord tells David to use is a very simple weapon. It is a sling. The ammunition is similarly simple: five smooth stones.

The angry reaction of Goliath to young David and his sling is predictable; he disdains, mocks, curses, and threatens him. He even calls forth the terms of his own judgment, as he tells David what he will do to him. In actuality what Goliath predicted was exactly what happened to him and his people. He is judged and condemned according to the words of his own mouth. David's response is righteous anger and confidence in God without any hint of fear. He tells Goliath that he himself will be used by God to kill and humiliate him and his men for the purpose of showing "all the earth that there is a God in Israel", and that "the Lord DOES NOT deliver by sword or by spear; for THE BATTLE IS THE LORD'S and HE will give you into our hands." David has complete confidence and faith that God will bring the victory to him for His glory. David proves this by stepping out in FAITH PLUS virtually NOTHING. He has no sword, no helmet, and no armor. All he has is a sling and five smooth stones. But the weapon that David wielded was the Word of God which the Lord had spoken in his heart regarding the demise of Goliath. The Bible emphasizes the lack of David's weaponry by repeating in verse 50 the fact that "there was no sword in his hand."

We see this much smaller, younger, less experienced, virtually weaponless but faith-filled David defeat Goliath so quickly that Goliath has no time to even put up a fight. We see how God alone is glorified since the arm of flesh is not bared. We see God using the natural weakness of man as a launching pad for a great victory that brings to Him and His people much glory and causes the Philistines to run in fear and have a new respect for the Jews and especially for their God.

If the Church of Jesus Christ is ever going to regain the fear and the respect of the Philistine world, not to mention the approval of God, we are going to have to emulate David. We must return to the simplicity of David and the simplicity of the Early Church. We must become inexperienced in the ways of the world but experienced in moving in real faith. We must get close enough to Him so we can KNOW beyond a shadow of a doubt His ways and how to bring Him glory. If we are to be the David Church we must allow God to prepare us even as He prepared David. Before we can go out and fight Goliaths we must know, as a principle in our own lives, God's protection and power. We must WALK in the knowledge of the fact that He wants to and is able to take care of every part of our life. We must, as we truly walk in love and obedience, trust God to be our Rock, our Fortress and our Deliverer. David LIVED the principle in Matt 6:24: "seek ye first the kingdom of God and His righteousness and all these things shall be added unto you", and we must do so too. Instead, we typically have arranged our lives to protect ourselves. We make decisions based on money, "benefits" and comfort. We Christians in the Saul Church always see to it that we are well taken care of materially before we "move out in faith spiritually." Often we will "put out a fleece." A typical fleece is "if we can make a certain amount of money, then that would be God confirming our desire to move." As Saul Church Christians we often make our major decisions based on how much money or comfort we will get. The kingdom of God is not our priority; it is secondary to our material priorities. Most relocation moves are made not on the basis of spiritual opportunity, but for material opportunity. We make sure that our material needs (Mammon) are well taken care of, and then we "trust God for a good church." We seek first a good job with good benefits (life insurance, health insurance, retirement plan and financial security) and only then do we expect God to meet our spiritual needs by providing a good church for us. We DO NOT seek for spiritual food and opportunities to bless others. We do not seek first for God's will concerning our spiritual well-being; instead we seek FIRST for earthly security and then expect God to give us spiritual security. David placed spiritual matters first and then was able to trust God for his material needs, just as Matthew 6:24 dictates. He sought to obey the desires of the King and the King took care of him. We need to seek first the Kingdom of God and His righteousness and THEN we can expect Him to take care of our material needs. Before we can trust God to slay our Goliaths, we must learn to seek and obey His will, and trust Him in everyday practical things such as health and material provision. This is NOT meant to be an argument that says we must not go to doctors. Remember, one of Paul's good friends and ministry partners was Luke, the blessed PHYSICIAN.

Scripture says that Goliath disdained David when he came to battle him without armor, sword or spear. The world will certainly disdain the Church when the Church comes without the world's weapons and the protection those weapons provide, but we must realize that before Goliath disdained David, he had already mocked Saul and all the Israelites. We must realize that WHATEVER and HOWEVER we minister the world is going to mock and disdain us. If we minister using their methods they will mock us for trying to copy them. If we minister in the simplicity of the Holy Spirit they will accuse us of being old-fashioned or merely stupid. We cannot win the approval of the enemy and his people and when we try to do so, we WILL lose God's approval.

Unlike Saul, David did not care if anyone was impressed with him. All he wanted was to silence this mocker of God and His people. The only approval David wanted was to be a man approved by God. As we walk in integrity and concern for God's honor, we'll see His protection, deliverance, victory and approval.

The armor of Saul, for various reasons, proved to be a hindrance to David. The fact that David didn't use any armor or sword brought great glory to God. If the Church of Jesus Christ is ever to function with the world-shattering, Goliath-slaying power of David WE MUST TAKE OFF AND PUT DOWN SAUL'S ARMOR. We must understand that IT IS THE LORD'S BATTLE. He will wage battle miraculously in the Spirit when we stop waging it in the flesh. We don't need the trappings of Saul. The early Church did not rely upon philosophies of men, entertainment personalities, education, or EVEN (I know it's hard to believe Church, but it is true), the New Testament Church did not rely upon MONEY!

The David Church will function in the mighty delivering power of God because it will take off Saul's armor. It will realize that it is not only unnecessary, but that this armor actually gets in the way of doing battle by the Spirit of God. Also, when we wear this armor, God does not get the glory and, as we are sadly finding out, God will no longer provide His anointing for power to people who depend upon Saul's armor. In the last days the David Church, whether it comes into being in a year, a decade, or a century, will defeat the enemies of God without the armor of money, fashion, personality and without the sword of religious psychology, or higher education. It will not even need the world-pleasing testimony of an athlete or entertainer. The David Church will not be involved in television ministry as the Saul Church is today. Ministries will not be dominated by men who depend upon their business acumen or worldly means to build the kingdom of God. The leadership of the REAL Church will no longer strive to raise money and build large churches with extravagant facilities. The youth will need places to pray more than they will need gymnasiums. Quite possibly true Christians will not even be allowed to minister on television or the radio. But they WILL have the Holy Scriptures, the fullness of the Holy Spirit, a sling and five smooth stones.

What is the sling that will be used and what are the five smooth stones? The sling will be the local church lifted to its highest point in history wielded by our David, the Lord Jesus Christ. The five smooth stones that He will use in these last days to slay the monstrous enemy we face will be Living Stones, which will include the teacher, the pastor, the evangelist, the prophet and the apostle.

The days of the Saul Church fighting our battles are drawing to a close. Even as the Children of Israel asked for a king to "go out before us and fight our battles" (I Samuel 8:20), so the Saul Church has prayed for and received leaders who have stood head and shoulders above everyone else. These attractive and clever men have gone out before us and raised up powerful ministries to fight for us. They did not really even require us to put our bodies on the line. They did not expect or make much of an appeal for us to join the battle ourselves. All they asked from us was to keep sending them our money, help them enlarge their kingdoms, and they would do the fighting for us. They were a small but apparently effective mercenary army that God has used for a season. But they were exactly what we wanted. We did not really want to fight anyway. We wanted to pay others to do our fighting for us. Much of the fighting that we have done has been mere tokenism. Because we gave these men and their ministries so much power, the influence of the local church has waned. It has became so weak that we literally can not function without these Saul ministries. We began to depend upon the rock bands and the summer camps to take care of our children. We need and depend upon the headline speakers to revitalize us. We lost our ability to help people with "problems" so we sent them to "experts" with training in religious and secular psychology. But those days are passing away. God will begin to strengthen the local church so it will once again be an autonomous entity in the sense that is not DEPENDENT, in a lazy way, on outside help but is still an integral part of the Body of Christ which will both RECEIVE and GIVE ministry when called to do so.

God will soon dispense with the battle plan devised by the people of the Saul Church. Their plan is to buy big guns and pay big men big bucks to fight for us. God will dismantle this Saul army and, when all looks totally hopeless, we will see our David, Jesus Christ, stride onto the battle field and, as was mentioned earlier, He will use the sling of the local church. In the early days of Christianity the local church was the sling that hurled the living stones—Paul, John, Phillip, Peter and Stephen - in the face of the Roman Empire. In these last days God's people will again meet an enemy that more television stations, bigger rock and roll concerts, the cleverest of programs and greater sums of money cannot defeat. But the local church will be resurrected and used as God has intended. Many large and cumbersome ministries will fall as the money runs out. Then, just when things look very dark for God's people, we will see the local church, the sling of God, begin to raise up true teachers, pastors, evangelists, prophets and apostles--men and women to enter any battle and be thrown anywhere their David, Jesus Christ, throws them one stone at a time, choosing each ministry as is needed. These living stones will find His mark because they will trust Him completely and not resist His guiding hand. The local church may be "the church that meets at Fred's house" or it may meet in a warehouse or even in a church building. It may be large or small. It may periodically join with other churches, but it will be a church where the Word, the whole Word and nothing but the Word is taught. It will be a Spirit-filled church that bears the anointing of God and loves the Lord purely and passionately.

God has always hurled only men and women who completely love Him directly into the face of the enemy, guided on the narrow path of the true Gospel. In the face of religious slavery in Germany, God hurled Martin Luther. In the face of spiritual deadness and possible anarchy in England, God hurled George Whitefield and the Wesleys and others. And in these last days, in the midst of the Laodicean deception, He will hurl men and women with hearts of David, men and women who represent a kingdom that is FOR HIMSELF and for His Glory.

Our loins will be girded with truth. We will wear the breastplate of righteousness. Our feet will be shod with the preparation of the Gospel of peace. We will take up the shield of faith. Our minds and our heads will be protected by the helmet of salvation. Then, we will take up the sword of the Spirit which is the Word of God, and then, after we have done this, we will, with all prayer and petition, pray at all times IN THE SPIRIT with perseverance and petition for all the saints!

We will depend upon God because we truly know Him, and He will be able to use us as He wills because we will be a people after His own heart. We will trust His Word to be the truth, the whole truth and nothing but the truth.

CHAPTER 22

REVIVAL IS FOR THE REMNANT

The story of David continues in I Samuel 22:1-2, "So David departed from there and escaped to the cave of Adullam; and when his brothers and all his father's household heard of it, they went down there too. And everyone who was in distress, and everyone who was in debt, and everyone who was discontented gathered to him; and he became captain over them. Now there were about 400 men with them."

After the Spirit of God left Saul and the Lord sent him an evil spirit, the king grew increasingly unsure of his power base and increasingly paranoid. On two separate occasions he tried to kill David with a spear. Finally he devised a plot to have David murdered in his sleep but this plot was foiled by the Lord and David fled. David moved from place to place and for a time was living in the Cave of Adullam. While there, four hundred distressed, debt ridden, dissatisfied men, along with his brothers and his father's household met with him and he became their leader. In these Scriptures we see God causing a division in His people as He separates the dis-anointed Saul and his supporters, numbering in the hundreds of thousands, from the anointed but as yet uncrowned king David with his band of four hundred men.

The band of four hundred was a small portion of the nation of Israel, but it was the beginning of a kingdom that would spread to the whole tribe of Judah and eventually the entire nation of Israel. This kingdom would have the most authority, respect and power that the Jews would ever have. This remnant would lay the foundation for the most prestigious kingdom that ever existed: the kingdom ruled by the Son of David. This government in exile was really the seed that would blossom and bring forth much fruit decades and millennia later. This group, which did grow somewhat, but still remained extremely small, remained powerless for a time while waiting for the Lord Himself to set up the circumstances that would allow their leader David to assume his rightful place as the appointed and anointed ruler of God's people. To the vast majority of Israelites, however, this group was merely an annoyance, if it was even that. The dis-anointed and paranoid Saul was their leader, the people were satisfied, and there was no move to make David king. That would come later, after God had finished making his anointed ready to assume rulership and after He had allowed the cup of Saul's iniquity to become full so that Saul would be fully judged.

Today, we see a very small group of men and women, who in the Spirit are brothers and sisters with David. They are men and women who love God and desire Him for Himself alone. We see men and women who are members of David's Father's household. These people hunger and thirst for a return to the type of Christianity they see documented in the Book of Acts. Some have seen glimpses from the pages of Church history of mighty moves of God that have brought forth leaders who have manifested an anointing of God and have spoken a word from heaven. This word and this anointing caused men and women to serve Him in the war against Satan and his formidable army.

These people desire to move only with the simple spiritual armor and the same trust that enabled David to glorify God when he defeated Goliath. They have an honest concern for God's honor and God's people. They are like those who left Saul. They are distressed, in debt and discontented. They are distressed by what they continue to see happening in the Saul Church. They are distressed with the bait approach to ministry. They are distressed with the rationalizations they have seen others make concerning everything from raising money to justifying sin and selfishness to even the alteration of the Word of God to accommodate flesh. Worst of all they are distressed with what they have seen happen in their own lives. They are distressed with the fact that they have become double-minded. They are even ashamed of the fact that they love God so slightly and walk in such shallowness, disobedience, and compromise. They realize that they have half-swallowed the Laodicean lie and are afraid for their souls. They see others, by the score, lose the precious anointing of God, and they are even now abandoning all that they have invested in the Saul Church to retain or reflame His Holy Spirit in their lives. They are distressed with the ever-increasing blindness of the Saul brothers who defend the dis-anointed and call sin another name and side openly with the unrepentant who are now moving in realms of evil never before thought possible. They are no longer content to let Saul clothe them luxuriously in purple and gold. They have discovered that they have given far too much of their heart in exchange for accumulating toys and pursuing materialistic diversions. They are in great debt to the Lord for their folly and are coming together with others who share their heart's desire. There is an emptiness in their hearts that entertainment, greed, and shallow ministry can no longer fill. And they are no longer concerned about what the vast majority does or thinks. They are no longer even concerned about one of the greatest and last idols of all to go: the idol of church growth. They want to move in true love and absolute truth, regardless of whether there are 400 or 4,000,000 who are with them. They are definitely a Remnant when compared to the rest of the various movements that exist in the Evangelical and Charismatic churches today.

In the 1980's when several churches in southern California were seeking the Lord at a Friday night prayer meeting, the Lord showed me how He was going to build His Church. He showed me a huge, hard rock made of marble or a granite-like substance. I saw lightning bolts thrust by Him that struck the rock. There was a flurry of these lightning bolts and chips flew in every direction. After this, I commented to the Lord that I could see that He was shaping His Church like a sculptor would shape a huge block of marble by chipping off the excess pieces with his chisel. He replied to me that I was missing the point. He said that He was making His Church from the original piece of marble, but His program was to use only THE CHIPS. He was not shaping the large piece of rock to become His Church, He was gathering the chips, the smaller pieces of stone, and He was going to make His dwelling place out of those chips. He was going to throw away the main part and save the small pieces for Himself to be His Church. He said these small pieces would be the Living Stones that would be the Remnant Church that He was building. This division of the Remnant from the main body (the chips from the marble rock) would be a sovereign work of God.

Scripture deals with the concept of God's ultimate people, His bondservants, His bride, His Revival Church coming forth as a Remnant from the larger number of people who are seemingly Christian. Micah 4:1, 6-7 says, ""'And it will come about in the last days that the mountain of the house of the Lord will be established as the chief of the mountains. It will be raised above the hills, and the people will stream to it. "In that day," declares the Lord, "I will assemble the lame, and gather the outcasts, even those whom I have afflicted. I will make the lame a Remnant and the outcasts a strong nation. And the Lord will reign over them in Mt. Zion from now on and forever.""

In our day the Remnant consists of the lame, the outcasts, and the afflicted of the Lord. They are the distressed, the indebted and the discontented of our time. They have been brought to the point where they have no strength of their own and some have no standing in the Saul Church or the world. They have been dealt with severely by the Lord. David's Remnant also had no strength, little standing with Saul's people and was also being dealt with severely by the Lord. In our day, even now, God is blasting the chips off of the rock with laser-like precision and gathering together these chips to form His David Church. It is a very painful process to be separated from the rock from which they have been chipped. Many now have been chipped off the main rock but are lying alone and have not yet been united with the other chips. This is a major part of the dealings of God with the David Church. Before many of these people will be united with the other chips, they must develop an intimate love and an absolute dependence on the Lord Himself. In this way they are starting to pay the debt of love and intimacy with God that is their reasonable response to such a magnificent Savior. These people must trust that God has not left them, but in fact, is drawing them closer to Him. Still, many of these people will wonder if they are out of God's will because they have been separated from the Saul Church. They must understand that this is part of the process. These chips may lie alone for some time. In God's time He will either bring them home to Himself and the Heavenly Church or He will bring them together with other brothers and sisters.

This Remnant will be the men and women, who like Jacob, have been dealt with by God and had their natural strength crippled. This Remnant, like David's Remnant, is even now in the process of being overwhelmed and cast aside by the Saul Church. Even as we saw the Methodist Remnant of the eighteenth century and the Pentecostal Remnant of the earlier twentieth century, so we will see the distressed, debt ridden, discontented, and disillusioned David Remnant of the 21st century routed by Saul from the mainline Evangelical and Charismatic churches. For now we must wait for God to put these living stones together again and build a Church that is strong enough to withstand everything that enemy throws against it.

CHAPTER 23

REFORMATION NOT RENEWAL: THE GREAT SHAKING!

In the previous chapter we looked at I Samuel 22:1-2. In the Cave of Adullam we saw a remnant of 400 men who were distressed, discontented and in debt. These men, with David as their leader, were the beginning of God's greatest work in the time of the kings. Those 400 men, who were once part of the Saul kingdom, were now a separated remnant. God was literally RE-FORMING His Davidic kingdom, using the remnant (chips) from the Saul kingdom. In I Samuel chapter 20:1-2 in the Cave of Adullam we see a RE-FORMATION of God's people by God for the purpose of bringing a purer and more powerful people forth from the masses in Saul's kingdom. God was looking for a leader that would be after His own heart and not the people's heart. God was looking for a people, taught by this leader, who would also love Him for His heart's sake and not merely to satisfy their fleshly desires. We see in these Scriptures the principle of Reformation as God prepares a people for the great task of cleansing the land of the enemy and establishing His kingdom. The reformation started with Saul trying to kill David and driving him away from himself. It did not end until years after Saul's suicide. The Reformation of God's people did not really end until David defeated the last of Saul's supporters and established a unified kingdom of all the tribes under the anointing and authority that he received from God years earlier.

At the present time we are in the early stages of God's current and probably last Reformation. Other Reformations have occurred, but God will do it again. God's re-formed people of the future will be a small Remnant who will wait and watch as God continues to search for more people after His own heart. All Reformation times are difficult times for the Church and only come about because spiritual darkness has blinded the existing churches. At such times the "ruling" spiritual body, whether it is the Catholic Church of the sixteenth century or the Saul Church of the twenty first century, always finds it virtually impossible to recognize the NEED for Reformation. Their desire is always to RENEW what already exists. They are always promoting renewal and branding any idea of Reformation as coming from the devil. The sixteenth and seventeenth century Catholics attempted to renew their church, in reaction to God's Reformation, but all they did was make it more appealing for people to remain in idolatry. The modern day Evangelicals and Charismatics, particularly the Charismatics, are responding to the first stages of today's Reformation with the same spirit as the Catholics of the sixteenth century. They are trying to renew the Church as it exists and thus are resisting the Reformation that God is doing and will most certainly bring to completion. Some refer to I Samuel 11:14 which says, ""Then Samuel said to the people, "Come and let us go to Gilgal and renew the kingdom there."" They are trying to renew the Saul Church, which God has already rejected as being un-renewable. The Pentecostals did have a renewal in the 1960's-1970's (in fact, they even gave themselves a new name - Charismatics) and that renewal very likely WAS ordained by God. The Saul Church will NOT be renewed again.

Reformation is totally different than renewal. Renewal, even in its most radical form, is a restoration and refining of the existing Church. As was just mentioned, this is exactly what happened in the so-called Catholic Reformation of hundreds of years ago. Re-formation occurs when the basic structure MUST BE CHANGED! The Saul Church, the visible, Evangelical, Charismatic Church of today, is quite literally in no condition to be renewed or restored.

The Church must and will be re-formed into a new structure by God Himself. Just as He took a Remnant from Saul's kingdom and reformed them into a kingdom under a man who was after His own heart, and just as He took a Remnant from the Roman Catholic Church of the sixteenth century and re-formed them, using divisive protestors such as Luther, Calvin, Knox and others, into the Protestant Reformation, so in these last days, in the twenty-first century, God is taking a Remnant from the Saul Church and will reform them into the David Church which will be a Church for His own glory. There will be no more Gilgals. There will only be Adullam's caves, the mighty that fall slain on Mt. Gibron, separation, and spiritual battles between Saul's followers and David's followers until God brings His victory to the ones whose hearts are after Himself.

Those who continue in their campaign to renew the existing Evangelical and Charismatic Churches will be placed in the same category as were the Catholics of the sixteenth and seventeenth centuries. The Catholic priests and leaders who fought anti-renewal proponents such as Martin Luther and John Calvin were found to be fools who were only fighting God. Many of the Saul Church leaders of our day will also choose to resist God's Reformation. These leaders may continue to receive the praises of men, as many popes did, but they will NOT receive the approval of God.

The Reason for the Shaking: When the Tall Buildings Fall

In the spring of 1993 there was a man who had prophesied a physical earthquake to occur in the Portland area and many Christians heard that prophecy or read about it in the newspapers. Some churches also received letters articulating that prophecy. This prophecy was very specific and mentioned a particular day that the earthquake would destroy Portland. The day came and went, and no earthquake occurred.

Shortly after this time, God gave me a vision of a great shaking where I saw many tall buildings come crashing to the ground. He made it clear to me that this was not a physical earthquake but a spiritual earthquake and He would be the one who would orchestrate the event. God showed me a surrealistic view of the downtown skyline from a bridge passing over the Willamette River. The buildings stood tall, straight and imposing. The scene was very similar to what we saw in New York several years earlier in the financial district. I saw many people walking in the shade of these buildings. The sun shined brightly and with great strength behind the buildings, but the people were shaded from the hot, penetrating rays. I asked the Lord what that meant and He said, "These tall buildings are blocking the light of the sun and the warmth of the sun from touching My people." He said that the sun was in fact the Sun of Righteousness, Jesus Christ. He told me that it was important that I pray that these tall buildings would fall down, even though these buildings represent THE VERY STRENGTH

OF OUR COUNTRY--WHAT PROTECTS and ELEVATES THE PEOPLE. There must be nothing between His Son and His people. He must be seen in all His Awesome Glory. He said that His people had been shaded from the Son of Righteousness for decades by these imposing structures and that it was important that this blocking of the sun be removed. He said that there were people that would never pray for the buildings to come down because they enjoyed their cool shade and did not really care to look upon His Son directly. He said there were others who would desire deeply to look upon His Son directly and that these people would pray for the buildings to collapse. They would be blinded to the things of the world by the brightness of the light but they would see Him more clearly than they had ever seen Him before. The others who did not want the buildings to fall would be blinded to the presence of the Son of God when the buildings fell, but they would see even more clearly the world in all its glory, fascination, pain and confusion.

These buildings have provided comfort from the harsher elements of the light of Jesus Christ, but still enabled His people to bask in the cool shadows and experience the comfort that this shade brings. The height of these buildings may indicate how impressive they are to many people in the Church.

At one time I thought that it was the wealth that we Christians in America have experienced and the temptations that come from holding and seeking this wealth. I thought that perhaps the falling down of the buildings represented a collapse of the financial system in America. In my vision, the buildings certainly did remind me of the gigantic financial buildings in the Wall Street district of New York City.

As we have watched events unfold in America over the last two years, it seems that the fall of these tall buildings COULD represent the collapse of CAPITALISM. This financial system as used in America has been a great gift from God, but both the secular world and the Church of Jesus Christ have abused this system. Basically both the secular and the spiritual worlds have used this system NOT for the glory of God, but to selfishly bless themselves. The Church has built thousands of very costly edifices that in some ways have become monuments to the success of the builders. This has been especially true in the last forty years. God seems to be in the process of bringing this system down. If He is doing so, it is because not only the Church has used this system to

REFORMATION NOT RENEWAL: THE GREAT SHAKING! 245

bless itself, but mainly because the comforts they have derived from this system have blocked out the pure and perfect light of the presence of Jesus Christ Himself. We have used the blessings of this system to block out the Sun of Righteousness.

I believe, however, that millions of Christians would gladly trade their comforts and even their provisions for the abiding and illuminating presence of the Lord Jesus Christ. They desire to experience the warmth of His love and the brightness of His Being even if they will lose the comforts of this present life.

I KNOW the vision was from God. I know that the tall buildings will collapse. I know that these buildings have blocked the people of God from the light and the warmth of the Son of Righteousness. What that represents will be made clear in the future. What I have given you is my opinion as to what these things mean.

Often in both the Old and the New Testament, no such interpretation is given by the prophet who delivers the Word of God to God's people. In the New Testament in the Book of Revelation, John does not specifically interpret most of his prophecy. In the Letters to the Seven Churches this is especially true.

The prophet often does not know when and in some cases how these events will unfold. Often he does not know exactly what the images represent that he sees depicted. It is a grievous error for one who delivers prophetic utterances to *always* interpret the images that God speaks through him. SOMETIMES God does give the one who prophecies the interpretation of the image, vision or word, but often He does NOT give the interpretation of the vision. It is important that the prophet NOT give his own interpretation of the Word of God except that the interpretation has been revealed to him by God. Many prophecies that I have read, by men who see visions, seem correct until these men start to interpret these visions. Often it is my sense that they were not given the interpretation by God, but they were given the vision by God. The hardest thing for God's visionaries to do is to know when to stop. Some prophets are good SEE-ers of visions but have not been given the interpretation by God but feel that it is necessary to explain what the vision means, and then do so out of the flesh and NOT by the Spirit.

People today are still arguing and discussing and contemplating and surmising and speculating on whether or not God will come before the

Tribulation, in the middle of the Tribulation or after the Tribulation. Often their interpretation of these events is given as gospel truth. Their human investigation has confirmed in their own hearts that they have received divine guidance regarding the exactitude of interpretation of many Bible events. Whether one is an interpreter of visions and prophecies that God gives to him or whether he is an interpreter of prophetic Scripture regarding what will happen in the future he MUST clarify that, a) he has received a direct revelation from God confirming that his interpretation is correct, b) he feels strongly from the evidence of Scripture that this is the correct interpretation, or c) his observation is an educated speculation. When the interpreter of prophecy presents his material in such a way as to virtually guarantee its accuracy, IF HE IS WRONG, he is functioning in the same way that a false prophet functions. He is essentially saying "thus saith the Lord: this interpretation is the gospel truth." A TRUE prophet or interpreter of prophecy will always separate revelation from speculation and identify speculation for what it is.

The Result of the Shaking: God's Hand on His Church

In the 1980's the Lord showed me a vision of what He is doing in His Church. He showed me how He is RE-FORMING His Church. He showed me a medieval-style cylindrical castle made of stones. It looked like a huge, stone, grain silo. This cylindrical castle reached ten stories high into the sky and could be seen clearly at a great distance. The Lord identified this castle as the Saul Church as it exists today. Then there was a terrible earthquake and shaking. Not only did the ground shake but the Lord laid His own hands on the ten story castle and shook it. The castle shook from bottom to top until all of the stones tumbled down and there remained only a large pile of stones. Then the Lord picked up the stones and started to separate them. He threw most of them away; however, He began to build with those that remained. By the time He was through, I could see a stone castle (with the same cylindrical shape) that was one story in height. All of the other stones were on the garbage heap. The one story castle was much shorter and less conspicuous than the original castle, but it looked much more solid and was much wider than it was tall. It appeared to be unshakable. This building was God's Church that was after His own heart that He had re-formed for HIS own use, using the stones of the Saul Church.

The TRUE unity of His people will be accomplished by a great shaking, a division of the stones and a consequent RE-FORMATION. The true Church or Remnant will be only a small percentage but it will be virtually unconquerable and unable to be compromised. This is the David Church, built on the unshakable foundation of having a heart wholly after God for Himself alone, a heart that is correctable and will do all of His will.

CHAPTER 24

THE AGE OF JOHN - LOVE AND THUNDER

Those in the Church of Jesus Christ who apprehend the Pearl of Great Price and burst forth out of the waters of Pearl Harbor will be a magnificent, deeply anointed Church. As stated earlier, this anointing will be a deep anointing, similar to the one that David experienced, because this Church is chosen by God and is after His own heart. This Church, will obviously need to have a much deeper anointing than the shallow, self-seeking Saul Church. However, the depth and the magnitude of the anointing that this Church will experience is determined by yet another factor. Pearl Harbor will usher in the last Church Age. New and deeper anointing, understanding, and vision will accompany this last days overcoming Church. In order for us to fully comprehend this new factor we must digress for awhile and look at some pertinent church history.

In Galatians 2:9 Paul tells us that Peter, James and John were reported to be PILLARS of the Early Church. These were the three apostles that were closest to our Lord. They were with Him both on the Mount of Transfiguration and in the Garden of Gethsemane. James was martyred early yet the Lord still decided to have three pillar apostles during the Apostolic Age. Paul, who was an apostle "untimely born", replaced him. The three names, Peter, Paul and John stand far above the others as the three pillar apostles of the New Testament Church.

Peter was the foundation apostle, the Rock apostle, upon whose confession the Church was built. The Lord said to him, "upon this rock I will build My church." Peter's name means rock. He was the PASTOR-APOSTLE to whom the Lord said, "Tend my lambs...shepherd My sheep...tend My sheep" (John 21:15-17). He was the leader of the apostles in the Upper Room. He was their spokesman on the Day of Pentecost. So great was his anointing that when his shadow passed over the sick they were healed. He was the apostle of the circumcision. His influence eventually was felt even in the capitol city of the Roman Empire.

Paul was the second apostle to gain great influence in the Early Church. He was the apostle to the Gentiles; the great EVANGELIST/TEACHER-APOSTLE who spread the Gospel throughout the known Gentile world and received and formulated the life-bringing doctrines concerning the Gospel of Jesus Christ. He taught that the just are saved by faith alone. He was a Rabbi-scholar with a fine, well-trained intellect. His teaching demanded more from the mind than did Peter's teaching. Peter recommended Paul's letters but, concerning them, cautioned that there were "....some things hard to understand, which the untaught and unstable distort".... (II Peter 3:16).

Mark 3:17 says "... to them (the brothers James and John) He gave the name ...Sons of Thunder... John, one of the Sons of Thunder, did not become preeminent until after the martyrdom of both Peter and Paul. During the foundation time of Peter and the expansion time of Paul, John is virtually unheard of in Scripture. However, this PROPHET-APOSTLE eventually emerged as the overseer of the seven churches in Asia Minor and his writings proved to be even deeper than those of his pillar predecessors. Philip Schaff, an historian of church history in the nineteenth century wrote of John,

> "He was waiting in mysterious silence, with a reserved force, for his proper time, which did not come till Peter and Paul had finished their mission. Then, after their departure, he revealed the hidden depths of his genius in his marvelous writings, which represent the last and crowning work of the Apostolic Church.
>
> John has never been fully fathomed, but it has been felt throughout all the periods of church history that he has best understood and portrayed the Master, and may yet speak the last word in the conflict of ages and usher in an era of harmony and peace. Paul is the heroic captain

of the Church militant, John the mystic prophet of the Church triumphant."[1]

Peter was the man of action, Paul was the man of the mind, but John was the mystic seer of the Spirit. Peter established the Church. Paul preached the Gospel of the kingdom. But John prophesied, experienced and knew the revelation of Jesus Christ Himself. Peter did not speak to us at all in Scripture of the third heaven and the glories of God. Paul spoke of being lifted into the third heaven and experiencing these glories, but he could not reveal to us what they were. John, however, was commissioned to relate to us, with the eyes of a seer, activities in the third heaven that Paul was not allowed to share. John is given the liberty to describe the descending city of God, His throne room, and even the glorified Lord Jesus Christ Himself.

John's influence in the Early Church lasted for several decades after his death. Then, from the early post-apostolic days to the Protestant Reformation starting in 1517, we see that one apostle stands out above the others. That man is Peter. He is the apostle to whom the Early Church paid greatest homage. Even the apostate Roman Catholic Church considered him their first Pope. They even named their greatest cathedral in his honor. His simple, energetic spirit typified the best of the early period in church history. The shepherd-apostle Peter and his confession became the rock on which centuries of holy and unholy men built the Church. For several hundred years this early Church strengthened God's people but then for over one thousand years the apostate Catholic Church deeply weakened men and women who sought God.

In 1517 God poured through the heart of one man, Martin Luther, a church shattering revelation. That revelation was "the just shall live by FAITH." The Church was no longer the issue to the Reformers. The Reformation of the sixteenth century was built not on the Church but on the Gospel of Jesus Christ. No longer was Peter the preeminent pillar apostle of God's people. Paul, because of pen, parchment and the Holy Spirit of God, was able to explode the Gospel of Jesus Christ in millions of minds during those Reformation times. Paul, the evangelist/teacher apostle would now instruct Christians for the next four or five hundred

---

[1] Schaff, Phillip, The History of the Christian Church, Vol. I (Wm. B. Erdman's Publishing Company 1979) p. 205

years. Paul's Gospel had been all but dead for century after century after century, but in 1517 God breathed His Word to and through a man who would be the first of many men through whom God would speak the message of salvation by faith in the shed blood of Jesus Christ alone. Many men of mighty mind and insight would be raised up by our Lord to explain and plumb the depths of the Gospel of Jesus Christ. Along with Luther, God used John Calvin, John Owen, John Bunyan, and others to teach us this once lost truth. God also raised up evangelists to preach this Gospel of freedom. George Whitfield, John Wesley, Jonathan Edwards, Charles Spurgeon, D. L. Moody, and many others preached the Gospel with great spirited force. Not since the days of Paul the apostle had the world heard the Gospel preached with such purity, power, and perseverance. Men and women were taking this "new" Gospel to the ends of the earth. Paul's Gospel literally transformed and reformed the Church of Jesus Christ into a new and dynamic spiritual force. Reformed scholars who had been touched by this gospel-reformation spirit began to study the Scriptures and expound on the Bible in ways not seen since apostolic times. The Pauline spirit had captivated the Church, and Paul, the apostle of the Gospel, was without a doubt the apostle who typified the Protestant Reformation. Those who were revived by this Gospel message have been called "Evangelicals" in honor of the Gospel or Good News of Jesus Christ. Even as Peter typified the First Church Age, so Paul typified the Second Church Age.

Today we are on the verge of a Reformation which will bring about the new and final Church Age. God's people are about to experience a new and deep anointing and sense of God's presence never before experienced. Even as Paul's anointing was deeper than Peters, and the Protestant anointing was deeper than the Early Petrine anointing, so the anointing of the last days Church, the Church that John typifies, will be deeper than the preceding two. This third and final Church Age will not be dominated by the concept of either the Church of Jesus Christ or the Gospel of Jesus Christ, but by the Revelation of Jesus Christ. Neither His flock nor His message will be preeminent, but HE, HIMSELF, will be preeminent. The Person of Jesus Christ, the ever expanding revelation of Jesus Christ, will be exploded in our hearts by the Holy Spirit. Even as Paul's message was incomprehensible to the Catholic Church for hundreds of years until the first Reformation, so John's message, the Revelation of Jesus Christ, has been incomprehensible to many of us in the Age of the Gospel. But it is the time of the end, and God is even now beginning to unveil His Word to us. Eventually we will be anointed to have eyes, like John, to see the kingdom of heaven in all His glory. We will be anointed by God to experience His love and to love Him like John, with our heads resting on His bosom, close to His heart. The anointing of the shepherd apostle Peter was on the Church for a short season and then left and the Church fell into apostasy for over one thousand years. The anointing of the apostle Paul (the teacher & evangelist) was on God's people for four hundred years, and is now leaving, and the people once again are heading towards apostasy. The anointing of the prophet apostle John, however, will rest on God's people until the Bridegroom returns.

Pearl Harbor will be more than a revival. It will be a Revival/Reformation. It will be the last Revival/Reformation. Those in this Revival/Reformation who endure to the end will have the anointing of David and the anointing of John. They will have the anointing of the prophet/king, the anointing of the prophet/apostle. They will have the anointing of the SEER who SEES the spiritual realm as David partly and passionately saw. They will have the anointing of John who saw even more than David as he stood with the glorified Jesus Christ both on the Island of Patmos and in the heavenly throne room.

The anointing that is on this last days Church or last age Church will certainly be the anointing of John. But this anointing of John is twofold. Most certainly John was the apostle of love. Of the three pillar apostles, John was the one who was closest to the heart of our Lord. He was the disciple whom Jesus loved. He was the disciple to whom Jesus entrusted His mother. Two images of love that come immediately to our mind are first, John laying his head on the bosom of our Lord, and second, John speaking these words, "Little children, love one another." But there is another aspect of John's anointing that is summed up in the surname given to him by our Lord, in the Gospel of Mark. Jesus calls him and names him: "Son of Thunder." Undoubtedly this was, as Philip Schaff says,

> "....an epithet of honor and foreshadowed his future mission, like the name Peter given to Simon. Thunder to the Hebrews was the voice of God. It conveys the idea of ardent temper, great strength and vehemence of

> character...The same thunder which terrifies does also purify the air and fructify the earth with its accompanying showers of rain. Fiery temper under the control of reason and in the service of truth is as great a power of construction as the same temper, uncontrolled and misdirected, is a power of destruction."[2]

John was both the apostle of love and the thundering prophet. No other apostle or disciple carried the mantel of prophet so graciously and so dynamically as John. As a Seer his vision spanned from before the beginning of time to after the end of time. He saw back to before the creation when he tells us that, "In the beginning was the Word, and the Word was with God, and the Word was God." He also saw beyond the end of time to the beginning of eternity as he describes "a new heaven and a new earth... (Where) the Lord God, the Almighty, and the Lamb are its temple. And the city has no need of the sun or of the moon to shine upon it, for the glory of God has illuminated it, and its lamp is the Lamb."

As a prophet John rebukes, exhorts, warns, and comforts throughout his writings but especially in The Revelation. We too, the Church of the last age, will carry the mantel of prophet and have the heart of love. We too will have this two fold anointing.

As we look back on the differences between the Catholic Church of the fifteenth century and the Reformation Church of the sixteenth through twentieth centuries, we see that the light of the Reformation Church was almost unbelievably brighter than that of its predecessor, even at the high point of the Early Church. We can expect that the light of the Church of the new Reformation, the last reformation, the David-John Reformation, will be even greater in difference than that of the Protestant Reformation's light. Unfortunately, to the unadapted or unadaptable eye great light produces great blindness. Even as the Catholics of the sixteenth through the twenty-first centuries have been blinded by the light of the Reformation and even now still remain blind, so the majority of the first Reformation Church will be blinded by the great light of the New Revival/Reformation that God will bring to His Body except they desire with all their hearts to fully apprehend God regardless of WHATEVER IT TAKES! With the compassion and

---

[2] Ibid., p. 417

severity of John we must understand that this blindness will occur. We must have compassion and not be condemnatory, but we must also severely and uncompromisingly cling to the Word as He is being revealed to our hearts through the Scriptures. Even as John was uncompromising and severe in his gospel, his letters, and the Revelation of Jesus Christ, so we too must steadfastly practice, preach, and prophesy what the Lord reveals to us. Philip Schaff discusses this temperament of John,

> "(John) had no doubt a sweet and lovely disposition, but at the same times a delicate sensibility, ardent feelings, and strong convictions. These traits are by no means incompatible. He knew no compromise, no division of loyalty. A holy fire burned within him, though he was moved in the deep rather than on the surface. In the Apocalypse, the thunder rolls loud and mighty against the enemies of Christ and His kingdom, while on the other hand there are in the same book episodes of rest and anthems of peace and joy and a description of the heavenly Jerusalem, which could have proceeded only from the beloved disciple. In the Gospel and the Epistles of John, we feel the same power, only subdued and restrained. He reports the severest as well as the sweetest discourses of the Savior, according as he speaks to the enemies of the truth, or in the circle of the disciples. No other evangelist gives us such a profound inside-view of the antagonism between Christ and the Jewish hierarchy, and of the growing intensity of that hatred which culminated in the bloody counsel; no apostle draws a sharper line of demarcation between light and darkness, truth and falsehood, Christ and Anti-Christ, than John. His Gospel and Epistles move in these irreconcilable antagonisms. He knows no compromise between God and Baal. With what holy horror does he speak of the traitor, and the rising rage of the Pharisees against their Messiah! How severely does he in the words of the Lord attack the unbelieving Jews with their murderous designs, as children of the devil! And, in his Epistles, he terms everyone who dishonors his Christian

> profession a liar; everyone who willfully sins a child of the devil; and he earnestly warns against teachers who deny the mystery of the incarnation, as Anti-Christs, and he forbids even to salute them. The measure of his love of Christ was the measure of his hatred of Anti-Christ. For hatred is inverted love. Love and hatred are one and the same passion, only revealed in opposite directions. The same sun gives light and heat to the living, and hastens the decay of the dead."[3]

Even John's ministry as the Apostle of Love is different than the Church of today understands. Again I quote Philip Schaff,

> "John's Christianity centers in the idea of love and life, which in their last root are identical. His dogmatics are summed up in the word: God first loved us; his ethics in the exhortation: therefore let us love Him and the brethren. He is justly called the Apostle of Love. Only we must not understand this word in a sentimental way, but in the highest and purest moral sense. God's love is His self-communication to man; man's love is a holy self-consecration to God. We may recognize, in rising stages of transformation, the same fiery spirit in the Son of Thunder who called vengeance from heaven; in the apocalyptic seer who poured out the viles of wrath against the enemies of Christ; and the beloved disciple who knew no middle ground, but demanded undivided loyalty and whole-souled devotion to his Master. In him the highest knowledge and the highest love coincide: knowledge is the eye of love, love the heart of knowledge; both constitute eternal life, and eternal life is the fullness of happiness. The central truth of John and the central fact in Christianity itself is the incarnation of the eternal Logos as the highest manifestation of God's love to the world. The denial of this truth is the criterion of Anti-Christ."[4]

---

[3] Ibid., p. 418-419
[4] Ibid., p. 551

John's message of love is summed up in yet another way in John 14:23, "....if anyone loves Me, he will keep My word; and My Father will love him, and We will come to him, and make Our abode with him. He who does not love Me does not keep My words; and the word which you hear is not Mine, but the Father's who sent Me." The love that John speaks of, as manifested by believers and by God, Himself, is absolutely manifested in terms of obedience. As was written in an earlier chapter, the great division will be made clear by one fact: those who believe in the Lord Jesus Christ enough to obey Him from their heart, because of their love for Him, will be on one side, His side. Those who do not believe in Him enough to obey Him will be on the other side, the side of Anti-Christ.

Another division will take place between those who will not let go of this world. John spoke of the relationship of the believer and this world more than any other Biblical writer. John was aware that we are not of this world. And those who would EXPERIENCE to the utmost the other realm, the spiritual realm, the unveiled kingdom of God, will have to force their attention away from the attractions of the world. The realm of the kingdom of God will become more and more clear, more and more real, to those who will let go of the worldly realm and focus their attention, their energies, their devotion and love on the unveiled heavenly realm. Even as John was the most familiar of all the apostles with the heavenly realm, so the Pearl Harbor Church of the last days will be the most familiar with the heavenly realm. But it is imperative that we tear ourselves away from this disintegrating mist of a world. John dwelt in the mystic realm of the kingdom of God and related those experiences and that knowledge more compellingly than any other man. As we tear ourselves away and as we let God show us just how shallow and deadly this world is, we will SEE as John SAW.

The Pearl Harbor Church will have to be patient, even as John was patient. Philip Schaff says,

> "(John) had to wait til the church was ripe for his sublime teaching. This is intimated by the mysterious word of our Lord to Peter with reference to John: If I will that he tarry til I come what is that to thee? John out lived it personally and his type of doctrine and character will outlive the earlier stages of church history (anticipated and typified by Peter and Paul) til

> the final coming of the Lord. In that wider sense, he tarries even til now and his writings with their unexplored depths and heights still wait for the proper interpreter. THE BEST COMES LAST!"[5]

Without a doubt the progressive unveiling of our Lord and Savior Jesus Christ will be the BEST. It must have been wonderful to be a part of the Church during the early days. It surely was even more magnificent to comprehend the Gospel of the crucified and risen Jesus Christ with the first Reformers. But to be a part of the generation to whom The Revelation of the *GLORIFIED* Jesus Christ in all His majestic, holy and awesome glory comes, is surely the crowning and appropriate consummation. Even as Peter separated her from the world and Paul clothed her with the righteousness of Christ, so John sets the crown upon the bride's head by opening her eyes to SEE the Lord in all His glory, and opening her heart to KNOW Him and LOVE Him completely.

But for now, we must wait. John waited until his time, which was after the departure of Peter and Paul. David waited in the Cave of Adullam, figuratively, until the departure of Saul. So too must we wait until God brings our second storm [AUTHOR'S NOTE--When I first wrote this book back 1988-1989 the second storm seemed to be far in the future. However, as dark events in America rapidly progress, I have come to believe that the second storm is here NOW, and that the next phase will be the vicious attack of the civil war cannons from the left which will do terrible damage to the sleeping soldiers that would not go to the wall and warn others. (PLEASE SEE Chapter 16 Second Storm Warning)].

Until God simultaneously finishes the pre-eminence of the Age of Paul and the Church of Saul with Pearl Harbor, we must be patient. But we must also understand that as we wait for the refining fires that God will bring upon the people who are called by His name, EVEN NOW, God is beginning to plunge His true Body deep into the waters of His Word. Even, as in some future day, when the Church sinks and dives deeply into the waters of great tribulation to apprehend the Pearl of Great Price, so now we are being called to plunge into the Word of God to apprehend the full Revelation of Jesus Christ, the Pearl of Great Price. As we unconditionally plunge into those unfathomed depths, the Lord will begin and even now is beginning to open our John-eyes and our John-

---

[5] Ibid., p. 413

hearts, and even thunder through our John-mouths to see, and love, and speak as the thundering prophet/apostle of love.

When we individually and collectively apprehend with our dying breaths the Pearl of Great Price, fully seeing and knowing The Revelation of Jesus Christ, THEN this great Body will explode from the waters of her Pearl Harbor baptism with the anointing of John. THIS will be the Church that fully abides in the Revelation and this is the Reformed Body of Jesus Christ. THIS will be the Church to whom the Scripture in the Gospel of John truly applies, "Truly, truly I say to you, he who believes in Me, the works that I do shall he do also; and GREATER works than these shall he do; because I go to the Father. And whatever you ask in My name, that will I do, that the Father may be glorified in the Son. If you ask Me anything in My name, I will do it. If you abide in Me and My words abide in you, ask whatever you wish and it shall be done for you. TRULY, TRULY, I SAY TO YOU HE WHO BELIEVES IN ME, THE WORKS THAT I DO SHALL HE DO ALSO; AND GREATER WORKS THAN THESE SHALL HE DO." This faith-filled, abiding, resurrected/reformed Body of Christ will go forth in the mighty manifested power of Peter, the understanding of Paul, and the eyes and heart of John, ultimately ushering in the kingdom of David that will reign forever, the kingdom of our Lord Jesus Christ.

It is important to note that each Church Age had a different emphasis on the Person of Jesus Christ. The first Church Age that was dominated by the Roman Catholics and Eastern Orthodoxy often depicted Jesus Christ as an infant. The second Church Age dominated by the Reformers, Evangelicals and Pentecostals emphasized the earthly ministry of Jesus Christ, particularly His death on the cross and the tremendous benefits His death and resurrection made available to God's people. The coming Church Age, the Age of John, will emphasize the glorified Jesus Christ that stands among the seven churches, is at the right hand of God and will come as a Conqueror. This is not the meek and mild babe that lays in a manger fresh from Eternity, nor is it the gentle Shepherd who lays down His life in love to please the Father and redeem a people for Himself. This glorified Jesus Christ is a Being that engenders both great FEAR and great LOVE and is a terror to His enemies. We have much to learn about this Jesus Christ the Word of God and we will learn about Him before the culmination of this last age for God's people on this earth.

I have wondered when the Age of John or the David Church will emerge, and I have prayed and thought on this subject often. I still have no answers but I have noticed two things. First of all, events in this world seem to indicate that the world doesn't have much time left. On the other hand from history, I see that when the Church fell into the apostasy of Eastern Orthodoxy and Roman Catholicism, a Dark Age took over the Church and most of the western world. That Dark Age lasted for about 1,000 years.

I pray that the world and the Church will not fall into a nuclear Dark Age that lasts for hundreds of years. I don't think that this will happen, but I don't know what it will take to wake up God's people.

I've thought a lot about what I have seen in the visions that the Lord has given me and the revelations that He has poured into my heart in the last 25 years. I believe that I have come up with a few things that are of paramount importance as I end this book.

Everything is moving much more quickly than I ever imagined. I always assumed that the events of warning, judgment, and great power to the church would take scores and scores of years. I felt that the process might even take as long as three or four hundred years. I felt that the time of warning could last for as long as 100 or 200 years.

In the Scriptures, Judah was warned for more than 150 years that great judgment would come if the nation did not repent.

However, as I watch things unfold so rapidly, I am filled with a great sense of urgency. I fear that I have been too late in publishing this book. In the last few years I have heard and read numerous other warnings of the storm but I believe the storm has now already broken over the Body of Christ. I see that the civil war cannons from the Left in this country are already poised to unleash terrible damage, death, and judgment on the sleeping soldiers in the Church. This devastating attack seems imminent.

I am terribly concerned about those Christians who believe that God will come and bail his people out of great tribulation. I am concerned that there is not a desire in the people of the Lord to be counted worthy to suffer for His namesake. I am also concerned that so many Christians are completely oblivious to the fact that God would even judge His people.

God has always used nations and men to judge his people. I believe that He has raised up men and women that have embraced Marxism, Communism and radical socialism to lead our country. I believe He will use these people to execute judgment on the Church of Jesus Christ in particular and the nation as a whole. I believe that someday even politicians that are now conservative will gladly join in condemning God's people in America.

I am MOST concerned that the Church as a whole seems completely oblivious to the fact that we are the ones most responsible for the demise of our nation and the coming judgment that we will surely experience. All these concerns are legitimate. However, I do realize that only a small percentage of people who call themselves Christians will survive spiritually to be a part of the great Body of Believers in Christ that emerge from the waters of Pearl Harbor.

I exhort you with this last final urgent exhortation: prepare your hearts, your lives, your minds and your souls so that you will be contributors to the greatest Revival and Reformation that the world has ever seen!

CPSIA information can be obtained at www.ICGtesting.com
235343LV00005B/2/P